MW01251595

Regional Integration in South Asia

Essays in Honour of Dr. M. Rahmatullah

Prabir De and Mustafizur Rahman

Editors

KW Publishers Pvt Ltd
New Delhi

ISBN 978-93-86288-14-1
e-book ISBN 978-93-86288-15-8

Published in India by Kalpana Shukla

KW Publishers Pvt Ltd
4676/21, First Floor, Ansari Road, Daryaganj, New Delhi 110002
Phone: +91 11 23263498/43528107
Email: knowledgeworld@kwpub.com • www.kwpub.com

Printed and Bound by Bhavish Graphics.

CONTENTS

FOREWORD

Prof. Rehman Sobhan
Chairman, Centre for Policy Dialogue (CPD)

Rahmatullah's Role in Promoting Connectivity across South Asia

It is most appropriate and deeply gratifying to all those who loved and admired the late Mohammed Rahmatullah that this volume on *South Asia Regional Integration: Essays in Honour of Rahmatullah* is being published under the joint editorship of Prabir De and Mustafizur Rahman. Few individuals within the South Asia region did more to promote the process of regional integration than Rahmatullah who invested the final part of his life and professional work in committing himself to this agenda.

I had the privilege of knowing Rahmatullah since 1973 when he was invited by me to join the recently established Bangladesh Planning Commission. In my capacity as the Member in charge of Industry, Energy, Transport and Communication and Physical Infrastructure, I inducted Rahmatullah into the position of Section Chief and put him in charge of coordinating an ongoing survey of the prospective transport needs of an independent Bangladesh, which was being carried out in the Planning Commission. Rahmatullah did excellent work on the survey, which was extremely valuable in the drafting of the transport section of Bangladesh's First Five Year Plan.

When I was requested by the Chief of the Transport Division, at the United Nations Economic and Social Commission for Asia and the Pacific (UNESCAP) in Bangkok, to suggest an experienced specialist to work in the Division I had no hesitation in suggesting the name of Rahmatullah. He was invested with the responsibility of leading UNESCAP's landmark project the *Asian Land Transport* and *Infrastructure Development* (ALTID) programme designed to ensure seamless connectivity across the Asian region through the implementation of the Asian Highway (AH) and Trans-Asian Railway (TAR) projects. Rahmatullah eventually took over as the Chief of the Transport Division at UNESCAP in the early 1990s, which he led with great distinction and dedication till his retirement in 2000. As the Division Chief, he made the ALTID programme one of the flagship projects for UNESCAP, which served to design the architecture for integrating the transport networks of East and Southeast Asia.

Rahmatullah's attempts to extend the ALTID programme into South Asia ran up against various political challenges, which have historically constrained the process of South Asian economic cooperation. Ever since the inception of South Asian Association for Regional Cooperation (SAARC) in Dhaka in 1986, its attempts to promote the integration of what was once a fully unified transport infrastructure inherited from British India, proved one of the most intractable problems facing the newly established organization. Thus, whilst the ALTID programme proved a most valuable resource for East and Southeast Asia, South Asia lagged far behind in signing the protocols of the agreement to construct the AH and TAR and facilitate movements across the region. Progress in this area was held up because each country raised political concerns in providing transit to their neighbours.

Transit rights were essential to the construction of a serviceable, seamless, transport infrastructure across South Asia. The absence of a more integrated regional transport network emerged as a serious drawback for the SAARC mission of building a South Asian free trade area. It was unimaginable that a region, which historically had one of the most integrated economies across the developing world, was now one of its most fractured parts of the world. This thought deeply pained Rahmatullah, who had, himself from his vantage point in Bangkok, been witnessed to the enormous benefits, which had spread across East and Southeast Asia through strengthening economic cooperation.

Rahmatullah drew on his Asian exposure to move transport cooperation ahead in South Asia through sub-regional cooperation. He had noticed the benefits being realized through sub-regional cooperation through the Greater Mekong Sub-region (GMS) project, where China's Yunnan Province collaborated with its immediate neighbours in Vietnam, Lao PDR, Thailand and Myanmar to construct a sub-regional growth zone. In that time, I had published a slim volume, *Transforming Eastern South Asia: Building Growth Zones for Economic Cooperation*. So, Rahmatullah invited me to draw on this work to undertake a study on the economic benefits of establishing a sub-regional transport network drawing on the ALTID programme, which connected Yunnan Province of China with Myanmar, North East India and Bangladesh. The outcome of my work was later published as a book, *Rediscovering the Southern Silk Route:*

Integrating Asia's Transport Infrastructure. Rahmatullah drew upon this work to carry forward UNESCAP's ALTID programme in the sub-region.

The more conspicuous gaps in the AH and TAR networks related to the road and rail links into and across South Asia. Within South Asia there were pre-existing road, rail and riverine connections, connecting North East India, through Bangladesh with West Bengal state of India. Similarly, the Grand Trunk Road, connected Bengal, with Delhi, Lahore, Peshawar and extended upto Kabul. Rail links from North East India across Bangladesh extended to Delhi, Lahore and Peshawar. River routes connected North East India, through the waterways of Bangladesh, with Kolkata and were in regular use by IWT carriers upto 1965. Rahmatullah believed that the ALTID programme could, with much greater facility, be operationalized across South Asia, where the once integrated but now fractured, infrastructure was in place but needed to be reconnected and upgraded.

At an early stage of his endeavours to bring the South Asian countries into the ALTID programme, Rahmatullah was obliged to take cognizance of the difficulties, originating largely in the divisive politics of the region, which had for so long frustrated efforts at reconstructing economic links, which had been progressively dismantled over the years. His own country Bangladesh, during the 1980s and 1990s, remained reluctant to sign on to both the AH and TAR projects because of its largely politically motivated objection to permitting any form of transit for India across Bangladesh territory. Successive regimes in office in Bangladesh from 1979 to 1995 had emphasized that the AH was only acceptable, if it passed from Northern Myanmar into the Chittagong district and then connected with the road network in Bangladesh to tie up with India's road network in West Bengal. Such a route would have avoided, providing transit facilities across Bangladesh connecting West Bengal with North East India. Rahmatullah had personally discussed the possibilities of such a routing with the military regime in Myanmar and confirmed that they were not at all inclined to support let alone invest in tracking the AH originating in Thailand and Yunnan through the Arakan region into Southeast Bangladesh. The reluctance of Myanmar to accept the route preferred by Bangladesh was in turn pointed out by him to successive regimes in Bangladesh.

The reluctance of Bangladesh to accept a routing for the AH had opened up the possibility of the AH bypassing Bangladesh. In a meeting of the governments of India, Myanmar and Thailand, it was proposed to take the

AH route originating in Thailand, traversing through Myanmar into North East India to then extend it through the *chicken-neck* north of Bangladesh into mainland India. To pre-empt Bangladesh's exclusion from the AH, Rahmatullah intensified his efforts to persuade the government to agree to accept a routing across Bangladesh. Rahmatullah's persistence finally prevailed in the early 1990s, during the tenure of the BNP government under Prime Minister Khaleda Zia, who finally agreed to sign on to the AH routing from North East India into Bangladesh and across to West Bengal. The then Transport Minister, however, opted for a cumbersome and more lengthy routing of the AH taking it through Arunachal Pradesh into Bangladesh. It took all of Rahmatullah's negotiating skills with governments in both India and Bangladesh during a subsequent regime to get them to revisit the original route proposed for the AH and for both countries to sign on to the more sensible route originally proposed by UNESCAP for the AH, which connects Assam with West Bengal through Bangladesh.

Rahmatullah's task in obtaining a route revision and improving the prospects for support for ALTID was facilitated by the more constructive attitude of the Awami League-led regime, with Sheikh Hasina as Prime Minister, elected to office in 1996, towards strengthening Indo-Bangladesh relations. However, even with an Awami League regime in office the inheritance of hostility bequeathed by earlier regimes to extend transit rights to India inhibited the Awami League regime's approach to the problem. Rather than discussing the issue of transit up front either in parliament or with the Indian government, the Awami League regime preferred to discuss the issue within the framework of the ALTID programme. The regime accordingly encouraged the Centre for Policy Dialogue (CPD), which at that time had been a lone institutional voice for promoting discussion on issues of connectivity, to cooperate with UNESCAP to organize discussions within civil society, which could bring in the government and political opposition to discuss the advantages of the AH and TAR, and their routing through Bangladesh.

CPD organized two such dialogues in Dhaka in partnership with the Transport Division of UNESCAP, which was led by Rahmatullah, to spell out the features and advantages to Bangladesh of tying into these two pan-Asian projects. The dialogues opened up space for constructive conversation on an important subject. Rahmatullah was encouraged by his experience at the initial CPD-UNESCAP dialogue to subsequently convene a meeting of railway officials in Dhaka to identify the specifics of the TAR's routing across Asia. The official meeting was preceded by a CPD-UNESCAP dialogue on the same subject.

The UNESCAP-organized official consultations on the TAR were attended by senior railway officials from Bangladesh, Bhutan, India, Nepal and Pakistan. At this meeting, Rahmatullah almost brought to fruition what would have been an historic agreement for establishing rail connectivity across mainland South Asia. This agreement was frustrated at the last moment over the decision by the Indian delegation to seek a change in the routing connecting Nepal to Bangladesh to which they had originally agreed. This reversal of positions by India led to a cascade of withdrawals of offers of transit by the other delegations, which put closure to any possibility of an agreement.

It was eventually decided at the end of meeting that India would seek instructions from their superiors, following which another such meeting could be convened by UNESCAP to sign the TAR agreement. These instructions never materialized, and therefore no meeting could be held. Such small issues frustrated Rahmatullah's vision of an integrated rail network across South Asia. He periodically referred to the last minute frustration of an historic agreement as one of the saddest moments of this life.

On his retirement from ESCAP in 2000, I invited Rahmatullah to join us at CPD and take the lead through research and advocacy in pursing his dream of establishing greater connectivity across Asia and particularly South Asia. He took on this challenge with the same dedication that informed his leadership of the ALTID programme. By the time Rahmatullah returned to Dhaka, CPD had been invested with the responsibility of hosting the South Asia Centre for Policy Studies (SACEPS), where I had been designated as the Executive Director. Rahmatullah took on the added responsibility of working with me to operationalize this fledging think-tank which brought together with CPD, some of the leading think-tanks of the region as partners. During Rahmatullah's work with me at SACEPS, a number of landmark studies were completed, which provided the basis for a series of dialogues across the region on promoting South Asian cooperation in various areas.

Whilst working with me to build up SACEPS, Rahmatullah continued to pursue his goal of promoting transport connectivity in Asia. In his tenure with CPD-SACEPs, he took up several projects designed to operationalize the AH and TAR across the region. He also worked on a subset of this project to study the scope for integrating the sub-regional transport systems of Bangladesh, Bhutan, India and Nepal (BBIN).

In recognition of Rahmatullah's significant contribution to South Asian connectivity, the SAARC Secretariat invited him to lead an Expert Group to prepare a report for the heads of states of SAARC, which identified the specifics of the investment and policy decisions needed to be taken in order to integrate the transport network of the region. This work not only spelt out the transport gaps, which needed to be reconnected, but the actions needed to address the no less complex constraints involved in harmonizing cross-border protocols to facilitate movement. In his last days Rahmatullah had begun work on a project identifying the main reasons why such slow progress was being registered in operationalizing the report of the Expert Group led by him, which had been endorsed by most of the SAARC heads of state. CPD and SACEPS had planned to organize a series of dialogues around the region to discuss Rahmatullah's report on SAARC to draw political and public attention to the need to operationalize the recommendations of his report.

Whilst Rahmatullah's main engagement remained with the issue of linking up South Asia, he retained his commitment to the broader issue of Asian connectivity, which had been part of his mission at UNESCAP. He established himself as one of the premier contributors to the programme of what came to be known as the *Kunming Initiative*. This was a civil society network involving the Chinese Academy of Social Science in Yunnan Province, CPD in Dhaka, a number of think-tanks in India and the government of Myanmar. The objective was to promote sub-regional cooperation through linking up the economies of Bangladesh, Yunnan Province of China, North East India and Myanmar (BCIM). Over a period of 14 years, meetings were convened in Kunming, Yangon, Nya Pyi Taw, Dhaka, Delhi and Kolkata to identify agendas for cooperation in the areas of trade, tourism, transport and culture.

Over the life of the *Kunming Initiative*, Rahmatullah took the lead in identifying the main features of the programme for transport connectivity in the sub-region and presented papers on this issue in virtually every BCIM meeting. His final professional work on spelling out the specifics of transport connectivity in the region was presented at a meeting of the 9th BCIM group at Kunming in January 2011. It was during this meeting that the first signs of Rahmatullah's fatal illness, which eventually took his life, manifested itself. It was again symbolic that it was at this same meeting in Kunming that the BCIM grouping moved from Track-2 to Track-1 and was formally established as an inter-governmental grouping.

Inspite of his poor health, Rahmatullah made his final contribution to the Kunming Initiative at the 11th BCIM meeting, hosted by CPD in Dhaka in February 2013, where he played a catalytic role in organizing the passage of a BCIM car rally, originating in Kunming passed through Bangladesh on way to Kolkata and also presented a paper at the BCIM meeting on the state of play in the construction of a BCIM corridor.

Rahmatullah's efforts towards building a seamless BCIM corridor was formally recognized at the official level when experts were invited to present a series of country reports on operationalizing of the BCIM corridors identified by Rahmatullah. These reports were presented at an inter-governmental meeting convened in Cox's Bazar in December 2015 and served as inputs for preparing a programme for action by the BCIM governments. The reports indeed served as a fitting epitaph on Rahmatullah's vision for a more integrated Asia.

Throughout his career Rahmatullah demonstrated professionalism, commitment to his work, and exceptional integrity in expressing his views and beliefs. For all his region wide recognition as one of the main drivers of the vision to reconnect South Asia and integrate it into the wider Asian landmass he remained a person of great humility and exceptional decency in his dealings with all those around him. He was a deeply religious person but never ostensibly projected his beliefs to which he adhered not just ritually but through the way he lived his life. He was a devoted husband, father and friend. His premature departure remains a personal source of bereavement for me but is shared by a much larger community, which includes those who have contributed to this volume dedicated to Rahmatullah.

Prabir De and my colleague Mustafizur Rahman are to be commended on bringing together such distinguished scholars to produce this memorial volume which takes forward the vision of Rahmatullah to reconstruct a South Asian community built on peace and friendship amongst its people.

October 2016   **Rehman Sobhan** ·
Dhaka

PREFACE

South Asia is passing through another difficult time. There is a need to review the past and undertake new strategies to help us achieving a new paradigm of South Asian integration. This book makes an attempt to fulfill this objective through its economic integration narratives. It has 11 chapters and each chapter tries to capture essential features of the cross-cutting issues and attempts to draw some policy implications.

The subject of this book will be of special interests to regional cooperation and integration specialists, government officials, researchers and the students. The volume would certainly help them in formulating strategies and advancing knowledge in this field.

We would like to thank all the contributors, authors and partners for the enthusiasm, hard work and support that made this volume possible. In particular, we are grateful to Ambassador Shyam Saran and Prof. Rehman Sobhan for their guidance and encouragement. We also acknowledge the comments from experts, policymakers, research scholars, and government officials. We have benefitted from discussions with several scholars at Colombo, Delhi, Dhaka, Islamabad, Kathmandu and Kolkata. In particular, we are grateful to Saman Kelegama, Mia Mikic, Ajitava Raychaudhuri and Patricia Uberoi for inspiration and support. We are grateful to Opinder Kaur for her sincere editorial assistance. Mr. Jose Mathew of KW Publishers Pvt. Ltd. helped in the production of the book.

Views expressed in this publication are those of the authors and not the views of the Research and Information System for Developing Countries (RIS) or the Centre for Policy Dialogue (CPD). Usual disclaimers apply.

New Delhi and Dhaka   **Prabir De** and **Mustafizur Rahman**
October 2016

LIST OF TABLES, FIGURES, MAPS, BOXES

CONTRIBUTORS

DEBAPRIYA BHATTACHARYA, Distinguished Fellow, Centre for Policy Dialogue (CPD), Dhaka

INDRA NATH MUKHERJI, Former Professor of South Asian Studies, School of International Studies, Jawaharlal Nehru University (JNU), New Delhi

KAVITA IYENGAR, Economist, Asian Development Bank (ADB) India Resident Mission, New Delhi

KHONDAKER GOLAM MOAZZEM, Additional Research Director, Centre for Policy Dialogue (CPD), Dhaka

MADAN BANDHU REGMI, Economic Affairs Officer, Transport Policy and Development Section, Transport Division, United Nations Economic and Social Commission for Asia and the Pacific (ESCAP), Bangkok

MOHAMMAD ZAFAR SADIQUE, Senior Research Associate, Centre for Policy Dialogue (CPD), Dhaka

MOHAMMAD YUNUS, Senior Research Fellow, Bangladesh Institute of Development Studies (BIDS), Dhaka

MUSTAFIZUR RAHMAN, Executive Director, Centre for Policy Dialogue (CPD), Dhaka

NIRMAN SAHA, former Research Associate, Centre for Policy Dialogue (CPD), Dhaka

PRABIR DE, Professor, Research and Information System for Developing Countries (RIS) and Coordinator, ASEAN-India Centre (AIC), New Delhi

PUSHPA RAJ RAJKARNIKAR, Chairman, Institute for Policy Research and Development (IPRAD), Kathmandu

SAAD SHABBIR, Research Associate, Sustainable Development and Policy Institute (SDPI), Islamabad

SANJAY KATHURIA, Lead Economist, and Coordinator, Regional Integration, Trade and Competitiveness Global Practice, South Asia, The World Bank Group, Washington, D.C.

SOHAIB SHAHID, Economist, Trade and Competitiveness Global Practice, The World Bank Group, Washington, D.C.

SUBRATA KUMAR BEHERA, Senior Research Analyst, Dewry Maritime Services, Gurgaon

UMME SHEFA REZBANA, Senior Research Associate, Centre for Policy Dialogue (CPD), Dhaka

VAQAR AHMED, Deputy Executive Director, Sustainable Development and Policy Institute (SDPI), Islamabad

ONE

INTRODUCTION

Prabir De and Mustafizur Rahman

South Asia has achieved slow, but moderate progress in regional integration. Trade has grown amidst dense barriers at the border in South Asia. The region has undertaken five major trade liberalisation initiatives since formation of the trade bloc in 1985, which partially fuelled the rise of intra-regional trade volume from about US$ 10 billion in 2006, when the SAFTA was signed, to about US$ 26 billion in 2015, registered about 12 percent CAGR. Over time, importance of tariffs as barriers to trade has gradually come down, but there is a strong presence of Non-Tariff measures (NTMs) including high border transaction costs in the region.

Trade has always been at the forefront of South Asia's economic policies. However, the progress has always been undermined by the excessive costs and lengthy time associated with export and import of goods and services in the region. South Asia is a case in point where country-specific constraints impeded trade between countries. As a result, goods often lose competitiveness at home before being sold overseas.

South Asia has significant untapped trade potential. It is seen that large gains in welfare and growth could be realised from closer regional cooperation in South Asia. However, there are many obstacles that stand in the way of the region reaching its true potential. These obstacles include: (i) lack of integrated connectivity, both physical and digital, (ii) high costs of trading within the region; (iii) complicated and non-transparent NTMs that hold back intra-regional trade; (iv) lack of supportive policies for intra-regional FDI flow; (v) regulatory and other constraints to intra-regional trade in services; (vi) political differences among some of the South Asian Association for Regional Cooperation (SAARC) member countries.

The conventional wisdom based on the new trade theory holds that there is little room for fostering intra-regional trade in the region through collective action given the large trade barriers among these countries. There is a general consensus among policymakers, academicians and development practitioners that transport connectivity lies at the heart of deepening regional cooperation and integration in South Asia. It is being increasingly recognised now that development of production networks and value chains and promotion of trade and investment hinge critically on the efficacy of transport linkages within and across countries. In absence of good transport connectivity, exporters lose competitiveness, domestic producers face cost-hike and delay and consumers' interests get undermined. Throughout all his active life, Dr. M. Rahmatullah had relentlessly championed the cause of multimodal connectivity in South Asia, and also seamless movement of goods across all of Asia.

Dr. Rahmatullah's dream was to build an integrated South Asia through corridors and gateways, which will be well connected with pan-Asian transport networks. His seminal contributions had put connectivity as central to economic prosperity and regional economic integration in the region. One recalls that member countries of the SAARC had pledged to achieve the South Asia Economic Union (SAEU) by turn of the ongoing decade, where an efficient, secure and integrated transport network was identified to play a catalytic role. One of the key tasks before South Asian countries is, therefore, to build gateways and multimodal corridors, which are the building blocks for creating an integrated spatial economic region in South Asia.

In this backdrop, this collection of essays in honour of Dr. M. Rahmatullah deals with a diverse range of issues concerning trade and integration in South Asia, and assesses policy priorities, implementation imperatives and emerging challenges in view of this. This book also presents trade and transport facilitation measures for South Asian countries. It discusses the trade facilitation challenges and reforms agenda in order to establish a larger market in the region. The volume reviews the progress made in terms of trade and connectivity in South Asia, and suggests ways towards further strengthening of regional integration in the region.

This book is a tribute to the leadership of Dr. Rahmatullah, who was the Director of the Transport, Communications, Tourism and Infrastructure Development Division of UNESCAP from 1994 to 2000. He was instrumental in implementing the ALTID project. Later these regional initiatives were formalised through respective inter-governmental agreements. Dr. Rahmatullah joined ESCAP on 17 May 1978 and retired from ESCAP on 31 May 2000.

This book deals with the South Asia economic integration from the perspective of trade and connectivity. Each chapter in this book tries to capture essential features of the cross-cutting issues and attempts to draw some policy implications. Following introduction, it has 11 chapters; each is unique in dealing with important cross-cutting issues relating to South Asian integration process.

Chapter 2, written by *Sanjay Kathuria and Sohaib Shahid*, proposes several interventions in the context of dealing obstacles to regional integration. The chapter has proposed several proposals including forming a customs union, incorporating steps like an elimination of tariffs and sensitive lists, reduction of NTBs through the creation of a mechanism for reporting, monitoring and eliminating NTBs, and moving towards a CET, including the harmonisation of rules and standards under an MRA. The paper also proposes the formation of value chains by focusing on the textile and clothing sector as a pilot; promotion of intra-regional investment by pro-actively seeking flagship investors; improved connectivity through an experimental transit regime along a specific corridor on a mutual basis and exploring the idea of joint border posts with single clearances; promotion of services trade by focusing on a more liberal visa regime for specific categories of professionals as well as work visas.

The development of regional transport networks and connectivity is gaining prominence in Asia. Chapter 3, written by *Madan Bandhu Regmi*, presents scope and potentials of development of regional transport network in Asia. The chapter outlines historical perspective of regional transport, reviewed emerging trends and efforts of Asian countries to improve regional transport connectivity and put forward some policy proposals to improve physical transport infrastructure and their cross-border operation. Based on the review of the progresses achieved and the challenges and opportunities to develop regional transport infrastructure in Asia, this chapter also presents a set of policy recommendations to improve regional transport connectivity in Asia.

South Asian countries have undertaken various projects to develop cross-border connectivity. Chapter 4, written by *Khondaker Golam Moazzem*, presents a synoptic view of cross-border connectivity initiatives in South Asia and argues for a broader region-wide connectivity. It also tells us why it is important to review the progress of various cross-border projects under broader regional connectivity framework in South Asia.

As a corollary, Chapter 5, written by *Mustafizur Rahman, Md. Zafar Sadique, and Nirman Saha,* talks about the importance of regional motor vehicle agreements in South Asia and identifies the pathways to strengthen regional connectivity. The chapter recommends that all the three MVAs in the region will need to be seen and dealt with in a coordinated and comprehensive manner. Proactive engagement of all concerned parties will be necessary to move the process forward with the urgency.

The signing of BBIN MVA is historic. Chapter 6, written by *Prabir De,* reviews the progress in BBIN MVA, discusses the challenges and presents the way forward. However, to maximize the regional welfare, a region-wide MVA is necessary. The success of BBIN MVA would depend how quickly BBIN countries build the physical connectivity in the sub-region.

Chapter 7, written by *Vaqar Ahmed and Saad Shabbir,* deals with Afghanistan's trade and transit cooperation with Pakistan. This chapter discusses various trade and transit issues that require negotiation between Afghan and Pakistani trade officials. One of the recommendations of this chapter is to expedite the work on ongoing road and railways projects linking the various cities across the Afghanistan-Pakistan border. Both Afghanistan and Pakistan require technical and financial assistance in expediting reforms towards bilateral economic cooperation. This chapter also presents a list of future research agenda.

Nepal has entered into some landmark agreements with India and China. These agreements once implemented will have long-term impact on strengthening trade logistics required to support Nepal's trade. Chapter 8, written by *Pushpa Raj Rajkarnikar,* discusses the recent developments in Nepal's trade logistics, and the implications for South Asia regional cooperation.

Chapter 9, written by *Mohammad Yunus,* analyses the transit issues through Bangladesh, and discusses the prospects and challenges. This chapter reveals that in order to carry a large volume of transit and international traffic, considerable investment would be needed for improvement of infrastructure in Bangladesh. The chapter recommends that Bangladesh should negotiate regional and subregional agreements in order to take forward the regional connectivity agenda in South Asia.

Pakistan is losing by not being able to access cheaper intermediate and capital goods from India, while importing the same at much higher cost from third countries. The delay in normalisation of trade between

India and Pakistan has been prolonged for quite some time. Chapter 10, written by *Indra Nath Mukherji and Subrata Kumar Behera*, analyses the implications of Pakistan's trade normalisation with India. This chapter highlights that Pakistan has already opened a large part of its market to India under its positive list approach, whereas freeing its products out of its negative list may not cause a wide expansion in India's market access. Rather, accessing more competitive intermediate goods from the Indian market will only aid Pakistan's industrialisation. However, in order to facilitate bilateral and regional trade, Pakistan has to extend WTO compatible MFN status to India.

Multimodal transport is crucial for South Asia – Southeast Asia connectivity. Myanmar is the country which connects South Asia with Southeast and East Asia and vice versa. Northeast India, Bangladesh, and Myanmar are surrounded by the fastest growing areas in the world, namely, ASEAN, India, and China. Building more physical infrastructure to establish connectivity will boost trade and growth. At the same time, the economic changes taking place in Myanmar present an unprecedented opportunity. Chapter 11, written by *Kavita Iyengar*, discusses prospects and challenges of India and Bangladesh connectivity with Myanmar.

Chapter 12, written by *Debapriya Bhattacharya and Umme Shefa Rezbana*, discusses the Sustainable Development Goals (SDGs), outlines the need to strengthen regional efforts for implementing the SDGs and the new role for SAARC. The chapter analyses the prospects of strengthening regional cooperation and integration for successful implementation of the 2030 Agenda of SDGs, with special attention to governance, peace and security, in South Asia.

SAARC is passing through another difficult time. This was not the situation a few years back when member countries of the SAARC had pledged to achieve the South Asia Economic Union by turn of the ongoing decade, where an efficient, secure and integrated transport network was identified to play a critical role in realisation of the South Asia Economic Union. Economic corridors are the next phase of the SAARC transport corridors in South Asia, visualized by Dr. Rahmatullah.

Economic corridor integrates the markets by fostering trade. Economic corridor can have huge payoffs in South Asia at a time the region is looking for higher investments in industrial sector, and planning to deepen regional trade through global and regional value chains. Not having economic corridors can stultify regional integration process and also delinks with other regions such as ASEAN, which has undertaken measures to implement the Master Plan of ASEAN Connectivity (MPAC) 2025. Finally, making South Asia seamless would require complementary policy initiatives by countries, regional organizations, and multilateral development institutions to strengthen the capacity of countries for development of economic corridor.

TWO

BOOSTING TRADE AND PROSPERITY IN SOUTH ASIA

Sanjay Kathuria and Sohaib Shahid

Introduction

It is natural for neighbouring countries to trade more with each other. Yet South Asia has defied this natural relationship. Today, intra-regional trade in the region accounts for less than 5 per cent of total trade in the region and intra-regional foreign direct investment (FDI) inflows (very largely from India) are 4 per cent of total FDI inflows (see Figures 1 and 2). However, very significant untapped potential exists for regional cooperation. Artificial trade barriers have kept the countries distant and the resultant trade relations have not helped to ease the political tension and differences within the region.

Figure 1: Intra-regional Trade Share in South Asia

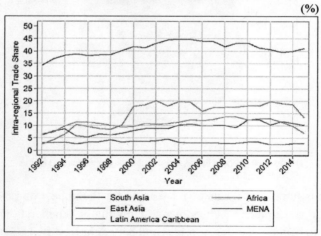

Source: Authors' computations based on WITS.

*   Views expressed are those of the authors and not necessarily those of The World Bank Group. The authors would like to thank, without implicating, Indrajit Coomaraswamy, Ishrat Husain, Swarnim Wagle, Prabir De and Nisha Taneja, as well as Mauro Boffa for research support. Usual disclaimers apply

Despite an increase in trade over the past few years, the untapped potential is large. A target of 30 per cent annual growth in intra-regional trade would boost trade to over US$100 billion in five years, from the current level of US$28 billion, as part of moving towards East Asian levels of intra-regional trade, and would increase intra-regional trade from 5 per cent to around 10 per cent of total trade.[1] This goal is admittedly ambitious, but it is not unachievable seeing the low base, several artificial barriers to trade, and the large amount of informal trade that occurs. Studies unanimously agree about the region falling short of its potential in terms of trade and investment, but emphasize that the gains from a more integrated South Asia (addressing tariffs, non-tariff barriers, and trade costs) are substantial.[2]

Figure 2: Sources of FDI inflows in South Asia

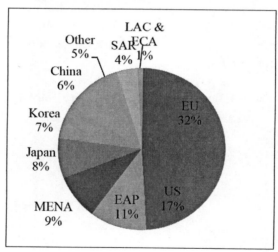

Note: EAP refers to East Asia other than Japan, China and Korea.
Source: Gould *et al.* (2013).

Trade is important for its own sake and for the impact on poverty and trust. Trade takes place when exchange is mutually beneficial, and allows consumer to benefit from lower prices and better choices. It also builds trust and interdependencies, and constituencies for peace. While all consumers

---

1. Assuming that total trade will increase around 12 per cent annually.

2   These studies include Ahmed and Ghani (2007), Ahmed, Kelegama, andGhani (2010), and Raihan (2014).

gain, regional integration particularly benefits landlocked, border sub-regions, which are relatively cut off from their 'mainland' and do not have access to the sea. Thus, in South Asia, Bhutan, Nepal and Northeastern India, as well as Afghanistan and Northwestern Pakistan will gain from enhanced cross-border economic cooperation.

Opportunity costs of low levels of trade and related forms of economic cooperation include reduced overall consumer welfare, higher input costs for producers, smaller markets for exporters and foregone customs revenue for the government. By the same token, a well-functioning South Asian Free Trade Agreement (SAFTA) can lead to large economic and welfare gains, arising from countries having access to larger markets, newer products, and a diverse trade structure.[3]

The time is opportune for some bolder thinking to galvanise trade and investment linkages within South Asia. This note proposes a way forward. The proposals include taking steps to moving towards SAARC's goal of an eventual customs union, such as harmonisation of standards to reduce and eventually minimise non-tariff barriers (NTBs), and moving towards a common external tariff (CET). The paper also proposes encouraging the formation of value chains by focussing on the textiles and clothing (T&C) sector as a pilot; promotion of intra-regional investment by seeking flagship investors; improved connectivity through an experimental transit regime along a specific corridor; promotion of services trade by focusing on a more liberal visa regime for specific visa categories. To normalise trade between India and Pakistan, the paper suggests increasing the list of items traded through the Wagah border; and the simultaneous granting of Most Favoured Nation (MFN) or Non Discriminatory Market Access (NDMA) status to India by Pakistan, and India reducing significantly the items on its sensitive list for Pakistan. Lastly, we propose the formation of safety nets during the transition process.

What are the Obstacles?
Overall trade regimes in South Asian countries are very restrictive. They are even more restrictive when it comes to trading with each other. Obstacles include:

---

3. These studies include De, Rosa and Govindan (1996); Govindan(1994); Hirantha(2004); Pigato *et al.* (1997); RIS (2004); Shakur and Rae (2005), among others. See also Kathuria and Shahid(2015).

- **High costs of trading within the region.** A key obstacle to regional trade is the high cost (it currently costs more to trade within South Asia than with countries in Latin America). Studies suggest that poor trade and transport infrastructure and restrictive rules and regulations for border trade are key reasons for high trading costs and resultant low levels of trade in South Asia.[4]

- **Absence of a Regional Value Chain (RVC).** A major reason why the region has not kept up with the rest of the world in terms of regional and global trade is the lack of a RVC network. The absence of value chains has prevented the region from generating stronger gains in terms of exports and employment generation.

- **Complicated and non-transparent NTBs.** A recent study shows that the presence of NTBs in South Asia decreases trade by nearly 8 per cent and if NTBs and tariffs were to be removed altogether, intra-regional trade may increase by 12 per cent (Kee, 2012).

- **Lack of intra-regional Foreign Direct Investment (FDI).** Trade and investment go hand in hand. While there are general constraints to investment in South Asia, there are also non-economic undertones that restrict intra-regional investment, which have held back major as well as small and medium size companies from investing in the region.

- **Regulatory and other constraints to intra-regional trade in services.** These constraints include licensing requirements, visa procedures and other regulations.

- **Political differences between the two largest economies in the region.** Relations between India and Pakistan have had a negative impact on intra-regional trade, as seen in the long sensitive lists and the NTBs that sometimes are specific to each other. Several steps could be taken to normalise trade between India. Pakistan is also yet to reciprocate the Most Favoured Nation (MFN) status (or Non-Discriminatory Market Access) to India.

What Can Be Done?

How can trade and investment linkages be intensified, so that the region is able to reap the benefits of proximity? A few priority measures are highlighted below (see Figure 3 for a graphical depiction).

---

4.   These studies include Subramanian and Arnold (2001) and Arnold (2007).

Figure 3: Steps towards Achieving US$100 Billion in Intra-regional Trade

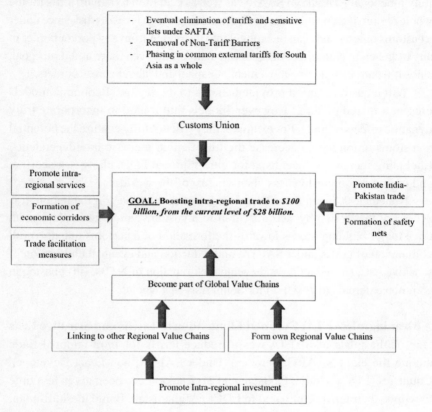

Move Towards an Eventual Customs Union

South Asia Preferential Trade Arrangement (SAPTA) was envisaged as a first step towards the transition to a South Asian Free Trade Area (SAFTA), leading subsequently towards a customs union and eventually towards a common market (economic union). A customs union can also play an important role in trade promotion. The Southern Africa Customs Union (SACU), Mercosur and the Andean Community, and the European Union Customs Union (EUCU) are all examples of customs union that have brought substantial gains for the countries.

A customs union has been articulated as a future goal for SAARC countries[5] and to achieve that, several intermediate steps have to be taken, including a

5.   See, for example, the declaration at the 18th SAARC Summit in Kathmandu in 2014 (all declarations can be found here: http://saarc-sec.org/SAARC-Summit/7/).

fully functional FTA within SAARC as well as Common External Tariffs for the whole region. It is an ambitious goal, demanding a high level of trust, since under a customs union goods can be brought into the region from any port or border in any of the eight countries. An economic union is an even more ambitious goal, since it would include free movement of capital and labour across borders.[6]

Will a customs union provide benefits to the region? Economic models present a mixed picture.[7] However, models find it hard to incorporate truly dynamic effects of trade. For example, they will not fully capture the potential a customs union has to decrease the trust deficit, increase interdependency (including increasing incentives for intra-regional FDI), allow risk sharing, and improve competitiveness vis-a-vis rest of the world.

Nonetheless, given the different stages of development in the region, it is necessary that a step-by-step transition to a customs union takes place, with three major building blocks towards the formation of a customs union: (i) full elimination of tariffs under SAFTA, and reduction and eventual elimination of sensitive lists; (ii) reduction and eventual elimination of NTBs; (iii) phasing in common external tariffs (CET) for South Asia as a whole.

A Meaningful SAFTA: Eventual Elimination of Tariffs and Sensitive Lists
One of the goals of SAFTA was to reduce tariffs for intra-regional trade among the eight SAARC members. Under SAFTA, non-Least Developed Countries (LDCs) (India, Pakistan and Sri Lanka) have been given less time to reduce their tariffs compared to LDCs (Afghanistan, Bangladesh, Bhutan, Maldives, and Nepal). It had also been agreed that India and Pakistan would bring down tariffs to 0-5 per cent on all items other than those on their sensitive lists by 2012, Sri Lanka by 2013 and Bangladesh, Bhutan, Maldives and Nepal by 2016.

Sensitive lists in SAFTA are an important barrier to regional trade.[8] Approximately 53 per cent of the total imports between SAFTA members

6. Given the current stage of the SAARC process, this paper does not further discuss an economic union.

7. There is a paucity of literature that looks at the potential impact of a customs union on the region, but Raihan (2014) has shown that a fully working SAFTA would bring positive welfare gains for each country in the region, whereas a customs union would generate mixed results. His research indicates that Bangladesh, India and Sri Lanka would experience positive welfare gains from a customs union, whereas Nepal, Pakistan and the rest of South Asia would incur a welfare loss. These results hold regardless of whether countries maintain a sensitive list or not.

8. Taneja and Sawhney (2007) and Weerakon and Tehnnakoon (2006), among others, found the sensitive list provisions in SAFTA too stringent, as the sensitive list could cover 20 per cent of tariff lines compared to 10 per cent which was initially proposed.

are on sensitive lists (see Table 1 for the number of products under the list). One of the major flaws of SAFTA has been that it does not provide a clear guideline for the phasing out of the sensitive list. Despite reductions over time, the lists are still very restrictive. For example, 53 per cent of Bangladesh's imports from Pakistan are under its revised sensitive list (see Table 2 for the share of imports of sensitive products in total imports in South Asia). With all these restrictions, there is clearly some distance between the avowed objective of SAFTA to promote intra-regional trade, and the reality.

Table 1: Number of Products Under the Sensitive Lists for SAARC Countries

Member State	Number of Products in the earlier Sensitive Lists	Number of Products in the Revised Sensitive Lists (Phase-II)
Afghanistan	1072	858
Bangladesh	1233 (LDCs) 1241 (NLDCs)	987 (LDCs) 993 (NLDCs)
Bhutan	150	156
India	480 (LDCs) 868 (NLDCs)	25 (LDCs) 614 (NLDCs)
Maldives	681	154
Nepal	1257 (LDCs) 1295 (NLDCs)	998 (LDCs) 1036 (NLDCs)
Pakistan	1169	936
Sri Lanka	1042	837 (LDCs) 963 (NLDCs)

Source: Authors

Table 2: Share of Imports of Sensitive Products in Total Imports

(%)

	Import from					
	Bangladesh	India	Nepal	Pakistan	Sri Lanka	Rest of SA
Bangladesh	-	47.72	97.56	52.93	40.18	52.38
India	0.01	-	0.00	17.13	11.25	0.06
Nepal	-	45.40	-	9.67	45.95	-
Pakistan	5.16	9.54	20.81	-	46.81	8.89
Sri Lanka	18.35	31.56	0.00	12.82	-	72.39
Rest of SA	63.48	52.63	71.88	80.34	54.23	-

Source: Raihan (2014)

Over and above this, South Asia has one of the most restrictive trade regimes of any region, with relatively high and dispersed tariff rates, and this keeps overall trade volumes lower than they would have been otherwise. Table 3 shows simple average tariffs and weighted average tariffs within the region, with the simple average tariff varying from Bhutan's 22 per cent to Afghanistan's 6 per cent; for weighted average tariffs, it varies from Maldives' and Bhutan's 21-22 per cent to Sri Lanka's and India's 6 per cent. Of particular concern is the high dispersion of tariffs as measured by the standard deviation, which means that there could be high tariffs in sectors that are of potential interest to trading partners. One indicator of high tariffs across many sectors is the very large number of tariff lines that have tariffs in excess of 15 per cent (Table 3)—and these do not even include the extensively used para-tariffs.

There is large trade potential in products included in the sensitive lists of South Asian countries—this is the reason why they have been protected. Hence, to be meaningful, the sensitive lists would need to be reduced as a priority, in a phased and time-bound manner; for those items that remain on the sensitive list (for a time-bound period). As a result tariffs, which currently range from 5-50 per cent, could be significantly reduced.[9] India could take the lead in virtually eliminating its sensitive lists, given that the impact of this relative to its overall imports is likely to be small, and given that its overall trade balances with countries in the region are strongly positive.

Table 3: Aggregate Simple Average Tariff and Weighted Average Tariff in SAARC Countries

Reporter Name	Tariff Year	Simple Average (%)	Weighted Average (%)	Standard Deviation	Number of International Peaks
Maldives	2011	20.37	20.75	13.73	5227
Afghanistan	2013	5.89	7.09	4.14	276
Bangladesh	2013	13.96	12.33	9.75	2870
Bhutan	2015	22.29	21.7	14.71	3551

9.. Raihan (2014) suggested sensitive list liberalisation based on trade potential, wherein 29 priority sectors have been identified to be common in the sensitive lists of India, Pakistan, Bangladesh and Sri Lanka. Most of the tariff lines protected under sensitive lists relate to textiles, electronic equipment, iron and steel, plastic and rubber products.

Sri Lanka	2014	8.36	5.91	10.91	3050
India	2013	13.28	6.3	17.04	1564
Nepal	2015	12	12.71	8.53	2086
Pakistan	2015	12.38	9.76	10.69	3224

Note: Table does not include para-tariffs; effective tariff levels may therefore be higher, because several countries in South Asia make extensive use of para-tariffs.
Source: WITS (The World Bank). Number of international peaks refers to all tariff lines greater than 15 per cent.

To take the first step towards an eventual customs union, an initial goal for South Asia is the implementation of a genuine FTA, with very few exceptions.

Eliminate NTBs

Non-tariff barriers include all measures other than tariffs, which protect domestic industries or affect the free flow of trade. There are primarily three types of NTMs; first, export barriers which include export subsidies, prohibitions, and quotas; second, import barriers which include import licensing, import bans and customs procedures; third, rules and regulations, like restrictive product standards, quality specifications, and labor and environmental standards, etc. In South Asia, most of the concerns center around the last category.

All countries can legitimately impose NTMs to protect consumers and ensure technical standards are complied with. It is only when NTMs become unduly restrictive that they become NTBs — for example, if border clearances are inordinately delayed, or customs valuation of imports is arbitrary, then a legitimate NTM becomes an NTB. According to an Asian Development Bank (ADB) study, NTMs related to technical barriers to trade (TBTs) and sanitary and phyto-sanitary measures (SPS) account for more than 85 per cent of all NTBs in South Asia.

There are several steps that can be considered to reduce NTBs and promote trade. These include:

• Fast-track harmonisation of standards through mutual recognition agreements (MRAs) and other means, and keeping international standards in mind, whenever practical. Can this process utilise the South Asia Regional Standards Organisation (SARSO), the South Asian body under SAARC?

- Accelerate technical assistance for conformity assessment of standards from India to LDCs. Development partner assistance can also be very useful.
- Set up a center for monitoring of trade complaints by the private sector, and follow up with a credible and effective dispute resolution body.[10]
- Address trade facilitation issues, such as code mismatches, inadequate transport infrastructure, limited trade through some border posts (such as Wagah), limited warehousing facilities, and a fragmented laboratory set up at borders.
- Address the information deficit that often restricts trade, as shown by recent studies. When surveyed, many business people in various countries in the region were unaware about the standards, procedural requirements, and opportunities in the country they wished to export their products to.

Bringing down NTBs would bring about substantial dividends for the region. A study conducted by the Consumer Unity and Trust Society International (CUTS) suggests that complete elimination of tariffs (as well as NTBs) under the South Asian Free Trade Agreement (SAFTA) may increase intra-regional trade by 1.6 times; and if the existing border infrastructure between India and Bangladesh is improved, trade can increase by six times over its current levels.

Moving Towards a Common External Tariff (CET)

This note recommends a Common External Tariff (CET) as a bold step in trade integration in South Asia. It is not recommended by some studies, nor is it a part of ASEAN integration. For South Asia, a critical benefit of CET would be a significant reduction in transactions cost of border trading, which is the most important hurdle in increasing regional trade. A CET implies that countries jointly set up external tariffs for the region as a whole and it is an essential step towards the formation of a customs union.

Though a CET would bring the region closer together, the transition towards a CET would bring its own challenges. In the South Asian context, special attention should be given to LDCs, as the tariff rates they currently apply are set higher than the likely common external tariff that would be set

---

10. Three economic communities in Africa have a common mechanism, called the Mechanism for Reporting, Monitoring and Eliminating NTBs (www.tradebarriers.org). These economic communities include the Common Market for Eastern and Southern Africa (COMESA), East African Community (EAC), and the Southern African Development Community (SADC).

up. This would mean possible losses in revenue in the short run for these countries. This is because larger countries in the region like India and Pakistan (that have lower tariff rates) would be given more weight when a CET is established, due to the size of their trade basket. A transparent mechanism should also be put in place for revenue sharing from tariff collection. Revenue sharing and compensation agreements require formula(s) that are agreed upon by all countries. This again would have implications for LDCs in the region, which is why it is important to keep them deeply involved in the decision making process. Another aspect when implementing a CET is that of sequencing. It would not be optimal for regional welfare to move straight towards a CET. There should be a gradual sequencing approach, in which more time is given to sectors that some countries consider sensitive. Such a transition would not only be optimal from a political economy perspective, but would also allow a 'soft landing' to many producers in the region. It is also important to set up time limits (sunset clauses) for the transition, so that that the market, and therefore, traders and investors can adjust their expectations. Lastly, setting up a CET is not enough, as enforcement can be quite challenging as seen from examples of other agreements having a common external tariff, including Mercosur.

A CET would only be truly effective if it proceeds in tandem with domestic efforts in all countries in the region to address obstacles related to regional cooperation. The countries should also continue to implement harmonised policies (policies in the areas of standards harmonisation, trade remedies, competition and export promotion) and strategies that facilitate the flow of goods within the region once imported from abroad.

Encourage Value Chains
International trade today is very different compared to a couple of decades ago. As the global economy reshapes itself, international trade is also going through a transition with the rise in South-South trade and investment linkages, demand from developed countries being replaced by demand in developing nations, and most importantly in a trade context, the rise of global value chains (GVCs). GVCs have been an important catalyst behind East Asia's sustainable growth, as they have allowed the region to improve its trade competitiveness and diversify its production chains.

Focussing on value chains brings benefits that go beyond a traditional trade policy perspective that focusses on final goods (IMF, 2015). Empirical evidence (such as Baldwin and Yan, 2014) shows that joining GVCs brings positive and significant gains in productivity. This is because GVCs reflect a more granular division of production and task specialisation, which allows each participating country to exploit small comparative advantage niches and raises the benefits from economies of scale and scope.

South Asia has so far not tapped deeply into value chains, even though regional value chains (RVCs) can play an important step towards fulfilling the untapped intra-regional trade potential of South Asia. Figures 4 and 5 show the low level of GVC participation by South Asian countries, especially with respect to buying foreign inputs and exporting them, after processing, into a value chain. The region should first target the formation of an RVC and then aim for linking up to a GVC, by: (i) initiating its own RVCs; (ii) linking to other RVCs; and (iii) eventually becoming a part of GVCs. This strategy would provide countries in the region with time to develop their capacities and capabilities before they join GVCs.

Figure 4: GVC Participation Index, South Asia and East Asia

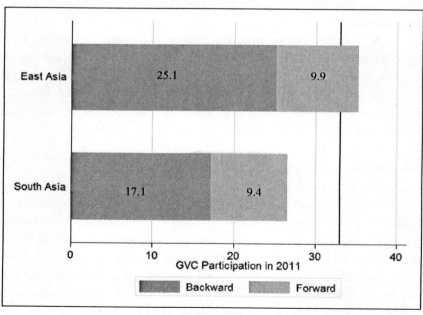

Note: Backward participation is the share of foreign value added in gross exports. Forward participation is the share of domestic value added in third countries' exports.
Source: Authors' calculations based on UNCTAD - UNIDO.

Figure 5: GVC Participation Index, South Asia

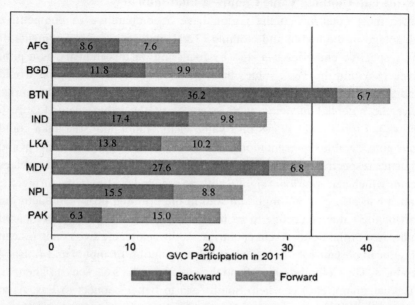

Note: Backward participation is the share of foreign value added in gross exports. Forward participation is the share of domestic value added in third countries' exports.
Source: Authors' calculations based on UNCTAD - UNIDO.

Policymakers could help form RVCs. Listing some of the policies and strategies that are needed to help the formation of a RVC, Banga (2014) proposed the formation of industry-specific regional industry associations, promotion of common regional labels, encouraging setting up of a joint-South Asian research and development body, and improving telecommunications and physical infrastructure. It would also be necessary to reshape the industrial and FDI policies of each member within the region to encourage FDI that would also facilitate RVC linkages among member countries. Encouraging foreign firms (not through fiscal incentives but general measures to boost the investment climate) to invest in South Asia could induce positive spillovers such as improved technology, improvement in labor skills, increased efficiency and productivity etc. This would in turn encourage other foreign firms to follow suit and invest in South Asia and consider it a value chain hub, both for services and manufacturing.[11]

---

11.   As part of encouraging foreign firms to invest it is most likely that the firms that will initiate investment will be large (in terms of capital and revenue) companies. Once small and medium sized companies see this, they would also follow the bigger firms and invest due to a 'demonstration effect.'

Textile and Clothing Value Chain – a Pilot Industry

Since most countries in the region have a comparative or competitive advantage in the textile and clothing (T&C) industry, the governments of the respective countries can start by focussing on this industry as a pilot project. Within the T&C value chain, most countries in the region would find themselves at one stage or the other. Together, South Asian countries have the potential of being at most stages of the value chain. Figure 6 shows the three main stages of a value chain. India and Sri Lanka could have considerable representation in the first and third stage, i.e., concept and logistics respectively. This is because of India's already established services sector which can contribute significantly to pre- and post-manufacturing. Sri Lanka can also play an important role in the pre- and post-manufacturing part of the value chain due to its relatively high skilled labour, compared to the rest of the South Asian countries. Additionally, the two countries can play an important role in logistics and distribution of inputs and finished products. The Colombo seaport and the ports on India's east coast (Chennai, Visakhapatnam, etc.) can help South Asia to better connect to East Asia. Countries like Pakistan and Bangladesh can play an important role in the low to middle-end manufacturing stage of the value chain. Since manufacturing usually brings more jobs than services, this would help Pakistan and Bangladesh to tackle their projected and ongoing youth bulge.[12]

Figure 6: Different Stages of the Value Chain

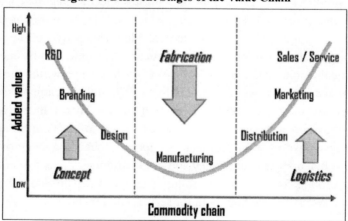

Source: Adapted from the Stan Shih "Smile Curve" concept.

12. Refer, Global Employment Trends Report 2014, International Labor Organization (ILO).

Promote Intra-regional Investment

Trade and investment go hand in hand; in South Asia, regional cooperation in investment lags behind the already low levels of trade in goods, as Figure 2 shows. While some countries like Nepal, Bangladesh and Sri Lanka have received a reasonable level of Indian investments (Kanungo, 2012), these are insignificant in relation to the large volumes invested outside South Asia by Indian firms. This means that the region has not been able to use its proximity advantage to create regional value chains or regionally-based platforms for exports, as has been done, for example, by ASEAN countries. Several studies show that under the right regimes, there is significant potential for intra-regional FDI.[13]

While there are general constraints to investment in South Asia, there are also political undertones that constrain intra-regional investment, and which have held back large as well as small and medium size companies from investing in the region.[14] Additionally, there are non-transparent regulatory restrictions on FDI, issues of land availability in many countries, specific restrictions on doing business with other countries in the region (till recently) as well as weak institutions. Furthermore, corruption, bureaucratic delays and property disputes create a sense of uncertainty in investment in the region. All this has prevented the region from benefiting from the fruits of cross-border investment which include technology transfer, reduction in investor risk, development of human capital, and formation of new markets.

In 2011, SAARC members agreed to promote greater flow of financial capital and long term investment. SATIS also has provisions related to investment in services in SAARC countries, including provisions on market access issues, progressive liberalisation, domestic regulations, recognition, dispute settlement, safeguard measures and subsidies. In 2007, an agreement was drafted under the SAARC umbrella on promotion and protection of investment of SAARC countries. The objective of this agreement was to ensure equal treatment of investments of South Asian countries without any restrictions, quotas or marketing limitations. Additionally, production resulting from such cross-border investments was not to be included in any

---

13. A well-functioning SAFTA will lead to a higher inflows of foreign direct investment and encourage vertically integrated FDI in the region (ADB and UNCTAD, 2008; Aggarwal, 2008). Kumar and Singh (2009) indicate that there is a great deal of potential for intra-regional FDI, especially in infrastructure (both cross-border and national), provided that credible regional regulatory harmonisation occurs.

14. See, Kathuria and Malouche (2015) for a discussion on this in a Bangladesh context.

sensitive list. However, the agreement draft has still not been approved. Even though the 17th SAARC Summit emphasised the "regional flow of financial capital along with promotion and protection of investment", there is a need to take concrete steps to (i) expand the coverage of investment promotion beyond services; (ii) implement investment-related provisions in SATIS; and (iii) harmonise investment procedures for all South Asian countries interested in investing in the region.

FDI, even more than trade, creates visible symbols of abiding cooperation. Taking steps to encourage FDI and facilitate value-chains in the region will be important in this regard. It is also important to encourage a few critical 'anchor investors': anchor investors from China and Japan played a key role in not only facilitating intra-regional trade in Southeast Asia but also in the formation of value chains. Similarly, if anchor investors from within South Asia could be encouraged to invest in the region, including from smaller to larger countries, it could help develop confidence and greater knowledge about the prospective market in the minds of potential investors – a 'crowding in' effect.

Enhance Connectivity

Facilitate Trade

Recent studies suggest that the lack of economic integration in South Asia arises largely from lack of progress in trade facilitation measures (customs, transport, checkpoint procedures, logistical bottlenecks etc.). Since border land regimes in particular have acted as major obstacles, particular focus should be given to easing trade through existing land routes, and opening new routes. Trade facilitation measures could lead to a decline in costs associated with NTBs, complement tariff reduction, promote production networks and value chains, and transport corridors. A recent study (De, Raihan, and Kathuria, 2012) found that under an India-Bangladesh FTA and improved connectivity between the two countries, Bangladesh's exports to India would increase by almost 300 per cent. Raihan (2012) found that the welfare impact of trade facilitation significantly exceeds those that arise from a full-fledged FTA in goods.

High transport costs are one of the major reasons holding back economic cooperation in the region—it currently costs more to trade within the region than with Latin America. Table 4 shows that during 2006-14, South Asian import costs rose more than 50 per cent for all countries except for India, where the cost of imports declined. Similarly, export costs rose for all countries except Pakistan and Sri Lanka. The landlocked countries (Afghanistan, Bhutan, and Nepal) face the highest trade costs in the region. There is also increasing divergence in trade costs among South Asian countries, highlighting the need for attention to LDCs and landlocked countries in the region. Moreover, there has also been a decline in the Logistics Performance Index (LPI) for most countries, especially LDCs, during 2010-14, as shown in Table 5.[15]

Table 4: Rising Trade Costs in South Asia

Country	Export Cost		Import Cost	
	(US$ per container)		(US$ per container)	
	2006	2014	2006	2014
Afghanistan	2500	4645	2100	5180
Bangladesh	902	1075	1287	1470
Bhutan	1150	2230	1780	2330
India	864	1170	1324	1250
Maldives	1200	1625	1200	1610
Nepal	1600	2295	1725	2400
Pakistan	996	660	317	725
Sri Lanka	647	595	639	775
South Asia	1232	1787	1297	1968
CV	0.47	0.74	0.46	0.73

Source: The World Bank, Doing Business Database.

Table 5: Falling LPI Ranks

Country	2010	2014	2010	2014
	Overall LPI Score		Overall LPI Rank	
Afghanistan	2.24	2.07	143	158
Bangladesh	2.74	2.56	79	108
Bhutan	2.38	2.29	128	143
India	3.12	3.08	47	54
Maldives	2.4	2.75	125	82
Nepal	2.2	2.59	147	105
Pakistan	2.53	2.83	110	72
Sri Lanka	2.29	2.7	137	89

Source: The World Bank.

---

15. The World Bank's Logistics Performance Index (LPI) reflects perceptions of a country's logistics based on efficiency of customs clearance process, quality of trade- and transport-related infrastructure, ease of arranging competitively priced shipments, quality of logistics services, ability to trade and trade consignments, and frequency with which shipments reach the consignee within the scheduled time.

The region can reduce trade costs through four elements of trade facilitation: (i) simplification and harmonisation of rules and procedures; (ii) modernisation and harmonisation of trade compliance systems; (iii) harmonised standards; and (iv) monitoring the progress of trade costs through institutional mechanisms. One particular method to achieve some of the above goals is through joint border posts with neighbouring countries, where customs and other clearance functions of both countries are co-located in the same facility. This will allow joint clearances or enable mutual recognition of clearances conducted by the other country, and allow data to be shared across the border to avoid duplication of time-consuming clearance functions. These measures would substantially reduce the costs and time for trade between neighbouring countries in South Asia. Zambia can provide important lessons in this regard, as the Government of Zambia initiated a state of the art construction of the Kasumbalesa border post at its border with the Democratic Republic of Congo (DRC). This is a single, common check post accepted by both the Zambian and DRC customs. It has reduced congestion, shortened the crossing time to desired levels, and has allowed Zambia to improve its monitoring and collection of customs duty and other fees, in its trade with DRC.

Facilitate the Formation of Economic Corridors
Given poor connectivity in the region, it is possible that transport corridors – eventually transitioning into economic corridors – could help partially overcome connectivity bottlenecks. Transport corridors are a set of routes that connect economic centers within and across countries. They can be thought of as enclaves that provide fast-track connectivity services.

To help develop economic corridors, it is important to integrate the different sub-regional corridors and modes of transport (railways, roads, air and shipping), overcome institutional constraints, and harmonise customs laws and processes across countries. Prioritising South Asian corridor projects and promoting regional integration through regional transit in a time-bound manner will enhance the process of forming economic corridors. Proper functioning of economic corridors would also require investment in soft infrastructure. In this regard, the region can learn lessons from a common regional structure, similar to the cross border transport agreement (CBTA) adopted by countries in the Greater Mekong Sub-region (GMS).

A transport corridor with improved infrastructure and logistics grows into an economic corridor, as it allows the integration of improved infrastructure with increased economic opportunities. A step-by-step approach is necessary for the development of an economic corridor. De and Iyengar (2014) had shown that corridor development goes through three main stages, evolving from a transport corridor to a trade corridor and finally to an economic corridor. Though economic corridors in South Asia are a relatively new concept, various studies[16] have identified different transport corridors in the region. Economic corridors can facilitate intra-industry trade by lowering trade costs and attract private-sector investment. For a vast region like South Asia, economic corridors, with their gateways and multimodal transport systems, can be the building blocks for a spatially integrated economic region.

Developing an economic corridor is a long-term undertaking. The few successful economic corridors that exist in developing countries start with a mapping of the sectors that could benefit from reducing the friction of distance.The chances of forming a successful economic corridor largely depend on the existing volumes of trade through that route, type and pattern of trade, and the potential to encourage development in the said area. In this context, developing those corridors that already witness high economic activity can have high payoffs. The most obvious and important corridor that can be developed is the SAARC Road Corridor 1, going from Lahore, Delhi, Lucknow, Kolkata, Dhaka to Akhaura/Agartala.[17] This corridor encompasses the heaviest economic activity in the region, is densely populated, and covers a route that has been used by traders for centuries. Other corridors can also link to this corridor. Within the context of economic corridors, an experimental transit regime may be considered along a specific corridor on a mutual basis.

Promote Services Trade

South Asia has a vibrant services sector that contributes to more than 50 per cent of the region's GDP, and is growing faster than manufacturing and

16. These studies include SAARC regional multi-model transport study, BIMSTEC transport logistics study, and Asian Land transport infrastructure development project.

17. The SAARC road corridor 1 covers most of the Grand Trunk Road; starting in Lahore (Pakistan), the corridor passes through India, and after cutting through Bangladesh culminates in India's north-eastern state Tripura's capital, Agartala. The corridor covers the two growth poles (both western and eastern) of South Asia, especially the eastern side. The route also spans regions that are some of the poorest in South Asia (excluding the Lahore-Delhi link).

agriculture. Yet, trade in services remains very low. To redress this, SAARC formed the SAARC Agreement on Trade and Services (SATIS), which came into effect in 2012. The goal of this agreement is a gradual and progressive liberalisation of services in line with national policy objectives, and the size and level of development of the country. However, developments in this regard have not been at par with the agreement's aspirations. General constraints that affect cross-border services cooperation relate to restricted mobility of people, an encumbered visa regime, and poor communication and transport links.

There is great potential for regional tourism in all South Asian countries due to their common history, culture, language, and traditions. This is why tourism has also been identified under SAARC as a priority sector for the promotion of intergovernmental cooperation. According to Chanda (2014), intra-SAARC travel accounts for only 20 per cent of all international arrivals among SAARC countries. And while in some neighbouring countries such as India and Sri Lanka, and Bangladesh and India, there is a high share of overall tourism inflows, much more can be done to exploit regional opportunities (see Table 6 for regional shares of tourist arrivals in India).

Table 6: Arrivals into India from South Asia and Other Regions

Region	No. of Arrivals			Proportion of Total (%)			Change (%)	
	2010	2011	2012	2010	2011	2012	2011-10	2012-11
Europe	1,977,992	2,113,293	2,165,752	34.2	33.5	32.9	6.8	2.5
North America	1,173,664	1,239,705	1,295,968	20.3	19.6	19.7	5.6	4.5
South Asia	998,179	1,096,260	1,130,526	17.3	17.4	17.2	9.8	3.1
Southeast Asia	850,990	997,706	1,076,536	14.7	15.8	16.4	17.2	7.9
West Asia	235,317	278,773	290,996	4.1	4.4	4.4	18.5	4.4
Africa	204,525	232,386	261,428	3.5	3.7	4.0	13.6	12.5
others	335,025	351,099	356,539	5.8	5.6	5.4	4.8	1.5
Total	5,775,692	6,309,222	6,577,745	100	100	100	10.9	5.2

Source: Ministry of Tourism, Government of India.

Tourism trade can be promoted both intra-regionally as well as through joint promotion of tourist attractions to those outside the region. Avenues for promotion include sports and recreational tourism, religious tourism, and medical tourism. Tourism cooperation at the bilateral level only exists between Maldives and India. The private tourism sector has also taken some steps, for example Taj Hotels, Oberoi Group, John Keells, etc., have presence across several South Asian countries through equity ownership, management contracts and joint ventures. But it can do more to tap the deep commonalities that exist between India and Pakistan; India, Nepal, Sri Lanka and Bangladesh; and so on. For example, religious tourism can potentially play an important role due to the presence of holy Muslim, Hindu and Sikh sites in both India and Pakistan.

One of the major obstacles to intra-regional services trade is the cumbersome visa regimes the countries (especially India and Pakistan) have for each other. Various surveys suggest that one of the major barriers people face in traveling from one place to the other are restricted visa regimes. Constraints related to security, infrastructure and connectivity also need to be addressed. These issues remain, despite several inter-governmental initiatives in the past to promote tourism, such as the SAARC working group on tourism (2004).

Healthcare is another sector that can act as a catalyst for regional cooperation. Cross-border regional investment in hospitals is currently being done by Indian hospitals providing services in Bangladesh and Nepal. Indian hospitals are also reportedly planning to expand to Bhutan and Sri Lanka in the near future. There are also substantial opportunities in medical tourism (mostly in India from other SAARC countries), given that patients would find treatment within the region to be more economical than other parts of the world. Telemedicine is another area that can be further explored. However, many constraints remain, including delays in visas, poor airline connectivity, and difficulties in pre- and post-consultations.

The telecom sector, which has grown significantly in all countries in the region, has seen some initiatives relating to cross-border cooperation. The South Asia Sub-regional Economic Cooperation (SASEC) programme has designated Information and Communications Technology (ICT) as one of the priority sectors for cooperation. A working group has also been established which would look into the common constraints faced by this sector, including lack of connections between member countries, lack of strong infrastructure, and poor human resource capacity in telecom services. Other initiatives at the industry level include an annual meeting of SAARC industry leaders in the telecom industry. Another initiative in this sector is the South Asian Telecommunication Regulators' Council (SATRC), formed in 1998, whose goal is to coordinate regulatory issues of common interest to the telecom regulators. SATRC intends to bring down telecom tariffs in the SAARC region as much as possible, promote inter-country direct calling services, and facilitate cellular roaming and liberalised leased lines and the use of either direct links or hubs or transit facilitates to promote intra-regional communications. The telecom sector, however, faces some challenges, including lack of institutional transparency, anti-competitive practices, lack of independence of telecom regulatory authorities, regulatory uncertainties and a monopolistic structure in certain segments of the sector.

Normalise Trade Between India and Pakistan

India and Pakistan make up 90 per cent of South Asia's GDP, more than 80 per cent of the region's intra-regional trade and 86 per cent of the population. Even though India's trade with Pakistan is less than half a per cent of its total trade and Pakistan's trade with India is about five per cent of its total trade, the potential is much higher. Various studies indicate that trade can increase by 10-27 times of the current level of US$ 2.6 billion. Both trade policy as well as trade facilitation measures are needed in order to realise this potential, the latter because of the long shared border between the two countries.

One powerful (albeit incomplete) indicator of trade potential is informal trade, which indicates that there is significant demand for Indian and Pakistani goods on either side of the border. Taneja *et al.* (2013) estimated informal trade between India and Pakistan at US$ 250 million to US$ 4 billion. The main import items from India that come through informal channels are cloth, tires, pharmaceuticals, textile machinery, while Pakistan's informal exports mostly include textiles. Most of this informal trade happens through third countries, i.e., Singapore, UAE, Iran and Afghanistan. However, the process of informal trade creates vested interests which become increasingly powerful; it also reduces revenue for governments. Hence, both governments should take steps to prevent this informal trade. This could be done by lowering tariffs and NTBs, eliminating sensitive lists, providing information to traders, and easing transport bottlenecks.

Fix the Trade Policy Regime

One of the most critical measures relates to the trade policy regime. Pakistan needs to provide Most Favoured Nation or Non-Discriminatory Market Access (NDMA) status to India, pending for over a decade. India needs to prune its sensitive lists in areas of interest to Pakistan; the same is true of Pakistan's sensitive list as well. For products where Pakistan considers itself vulnerable to Indian imports, a time bound regime could be considered, where such products are kept on the sensitive list for a limited and pre-defined period.

Eliminate NTBs

Traders on both sides of the border face multiple NTBs. Pakistani traders have expressed concerns in this regard, mentioning that many of the barriers they face in entering the Indian market are Pakistan specific. Recent studies, however, show that the barriers may not be Pakistan-specific, but there is a lack of awareness among Pakistani traders about Indian regulations. However, there have been complaints about country-specific NTBs, which cannot be ruled out since the border caters only to Pakistan-India trade.[18] Indian exporters have also complained about NTBs they face, especially those related to the export of live animals.

Apart from discussions relating to these barriers, the two governments can also create platforms for government-business and business-business interactions. Recent developments include a customs cooperation agreement to avoid arbitrary stoppage of goods at each other's ports, mutual recognition between 'Pakistan Standard and Quality Control Authority (PSQCA)' and 'Bureau of Indian Standards (BIS)', and an agreement on the redressal of trade grievances between India and Pakistan. However, not much progress has been made on implementing these.

Facilitate Movement of Goods

Most of the discussion of transport of goods between the two countries has focussed on the land route, primarily due to the restrictive maritime protocol between the two countries. Since the amendment of the protocol in 2005, trade was dominated by the sea route. This, however, does not necessarily

---

18. Ahmed *et al.* (2012) found that barriers include excessive checks at customs, over valuation of goods, tedious packaging and labeling requirements, access to limited number of ports in some cases, and lack of testing facilities. Indian goods also face some India-specific NTBs, which include stringent labeling and packaging requirements.

mean that the sea route is the most efficient and cost-effective. Trading through the land route (by rail or road) is more difficult owing to restrictions on the goods that can be traded through the land route, poor facilities on the land borders, trans-loading of goods at the border etc. Figure 7 shows mode wise trade between India and Pakistan.

Lahore and Amritsar, the two major cities close to the border, are only 54 km apart, which should make for low trade costs between northern Pakistan and northern India. However, Pakistan allows only 137 items to be imported from India via the Wagah border, which negates the proximity advantage. Allowing movement of all items via the land route would bring down the cost of trading significantly, and eventually benefit the consumer in both countries. Allowing trucks to move into each other's territory would also cut down costs, while reopening of the routes that were closed after the 1971 war, such as the Munabao-Khokhrapar road route, would further bring down costs.

Trade via rail is also restricted: currently there are only two routes (Attari-Wagah and Munabao-Khokhrapar), but even these routes face the problem of poor quality of rolling stock and restriction on the type of wagons (Taneja, 2006). Similar to cargo trucks, Pakistani cargo rail wagons cannot enter Indian territory and vice versa, thereby increasing the time and cost of trading substantially. Even though India opened an integrated check post (ICP), its benefits do not extend to trade via the rail route.

Figure 7: Mode-wise Trade between Pakistan and India

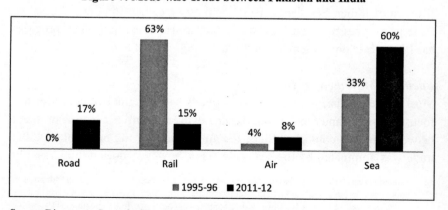

Source: Directorate General of Foreign Trade, Ministry of Commerce, India.

There is also a need for both countries to put 'goods transit' on their trade agenda, as currently neither India nor Pakistan allow transit of goods over their respective territories. Due to the lack of transit, India's exports to Afghanistan and Pakistan's exports to Bangladesh and Nepal turn out to be very costly.[19] The WTO Bali Package (2013) contains provisions that require countries to provide transit facilities to other countries. Under the agreement, countries including India and Pakistan would have to provide seamless transit facilities to each other. This would benefit both countries as India would gains access to Afghanistan and central Asia, whereas Pakistan would gain access to growing markets in Bangladesh, Bhutan and Nepal.

Strengthen Safety Nets

In any trade liberalisation process, there will be winners and losers. It is inevitable that some producers will lose (especially in the short-run); producers that export will gain through availability of better inputs; and many domestic producers will be induced to improve productivity. Consumers will be big gainers. However, it is important for Governments to anticipate and provide soft-landings for sectors that suffer job losses.

Even though adjustment costs might not be high at the national level, they are high for particular groups, giving those groups a strong incentive to organise, lobby and apply political pressure to maintain pressure. Therefore, it is important that the government steps in during this transition. Safety nets can be provided to those producers and workers who are at risk of losing from the liberalisation process. Such safety nets can serve dual purposes: (i) they can reduce the potential negative economic impact of such a transition; (ii) they can assuage concerns of the industries that are against the liberalisation process. A well-functioning safety net would provide a cushion to producers who will lose out during the liberalisation process and allow them to either feel less of an impact and/or rebound into the market after some time.

A survey of the literature reveals that the most important policies intended to compensate losers from trade liberalisation are unemployment benefits, information or training courses.[20] Also, it would be important for the region to

---

19. No transit agreement exists between India and Pakistan. India is seeking transit facility for its wheat export to Afghanistan, but the Pakistan agricultural industry has shown reservations on this due to the fear of Indian wheat finding its way into Pakistan and lowering wheat prices and, secondly, Indian wheat taking up the Afghani market of Pakistani wheat exporters.

20. See, Bacchetta and Jansen (2003) on how government can facilitate the adjustment process.

ensure that the liberalisation happens in a phased-in and predictable manner. A gradual and phased-in liberalisation would provide traders and affected workers more time to adjust, give the trade reform itself more credibility and therefore facilitate adjustment. The pace of reform could take into account factors such as country demographics, skill-set of the labor force, degree of government support for unemployed workers and rigidities in the labor market. The gradual liberalisation process should be coupled with export promotion efforts by the government in order to counter-balance any political pressure originating from the potential increased competition the import-competing sectors will face (Rodrik, 1989). Additionally, for countries like Nepal and Bhutan whose economies are heavily reliant on India (including a currency pegged to the Indian Rupee), their macroeconomic stability, both internal (inflation and employment) and external (balance of payments), should be a consideration in the pace of trade reform.

Conclusions

South Asia has significant untapped trade potential. It is seen that large gains in welfare and growth could be realised from closer regional cooperation in South Asia. However, there are many obstacles that stand in the way of the region reaching its true potential. These obstacles include: (i) high costs of trading within the region; (ii) absence of regional value chains (RVCs); (iii) complicated and non-transparent NTMs that hold back intra-regional trade; (iv) lack of intra-regional Foreign Direct Investment (FDI); (v) regulatory and other constraints to intra-regional trade in services; and (vi) political differences between the two largest economies in the region, India and Pakistan.

This paper proposes several interventions in the context of the mentioned obstacles. The proposals include moving towards an eventual customs union, incorporating steps like an elimination of tariffs and sensitive lists, reduction of NTBs through the creation of a mechanism for reporting, monitoring and eliminating NTBs, and moving towards a CET, including the harmonisation of rules and standards under an MRA. The paper also proposes the formation of value chains by focussing on the T&C sector as a pilot; promotion of intra-regional investment by pro-actively seeking flagship investors; improved connectivity through an experimental transit regime along a specific corridor on a mutual basis and exploring the idea of joint border posts with single clearances; promotion of services trade by focussing on a more liberal visa regime for specific categories of professionals as well as work visas. On India-Pakistan trade, specific steps include increasing the list of items traded through Wagah; and the simultaneous granting of NDMA status from Pakistan to India and India reducing the items on its sensitive list for Pakistan. Lastly, the paper suggests the strengthening of safety nets during the transition process, and ensuring that the liberalisation happens in a phased-in manner (even as the major obstacle to regional trade, i.e., costs of trading, are tackled with full speed and urgency).

References

ADB (2010). *BIMSTEC Transport Infrastructure and Logistics Study*, Asian Development Bank Manila

ADB and UNCTAD (2008). *Quantification of Benefits from Economic Cooperation in South Asia*, Asian Development Bank and United Nations Conference on Trade and Development, New Delhi: Macmillan.

Aggarwal, A. (2008). *Regional Economic Integration and FDI in South Asia: Prospects and Problems*. Working Paper No. 218. New Delhi: Indian Council for Research on International Economic Relations (ICRIER).

Ahmed, S., and E. Ghani (eds.) (2007). *South Asia: Growth and Regional Integration*. Delhi: Macmillan India Ltd.

Ahmed, S., S. Kelegama, and E. Ghani (eds). (2010). *Promoting Economic Cooperation in South Asia: Beyond SAFTA*. New Delhi: Sage Publications

Ahmed, M., N. Rehman, and S.Shahid. (2012). *Normalization of Trade with India: Opportunities and Challenges for Pakistan*. Trade Development Authority of Pakistan (TDAP), Pakistan and World Trade Advisors (WTA), Islamabad.

Arnold, J. (2007). The Role of Trade Facilitation in Export Growth in Sadiq Ahmed and Ejaz Ghani (eds.) *South Asia: Growth and Regional Integration*. New Delhi: Macmillan.

Bacchetta, M. and M. Jansen, (2003). *Adjusting to Trade Liberalization, The role of Policy, Institutions and WTO Disciplines*. WTO Special Study 7, World Trade Organization (WTO), Geneva

Baldwin, J.R. and B. Yan, (2014). *Global Value Chains and the Productivity of Canadian Manufacturing Firms*. Economic Analysis (EA) Research Paper Series, 11F0027M, No. 90 Statistics Canada, Analytical Studies Branch.

Banga, R. (2014). Integrating South Asia into Regional and Global Value Chains in S. Raihan (ed) *Moving towards South Asia Economic Union*, mimeo. Asian Development Bank (ADB), Manila.

Chanda, R. (2014). Services Liberalization in South Asia in S. Raihan (ed.) *Moving towards South Asia Economic Union*, mimeo. Asian Development Bank (ADB), Manila.

Chatterjee, B. and J. George, (2012). *Consumers and Economic Cooperation: Cost of Economic non-cooperation to consumers in South Asia'*. CUTS International, Jaipur.

De, P, S. Raihan and S. Kathuria (2012). *Unlocking Bangladesh-India Trade: Emerging Potential and the Way Forward*. World Bank Policy Research Working Paper No. 6155, The World Bank, Washington, D.C

De, P. and K. Iyengar, (eds.) (2014). *Developing Economic Corridor in South Asia*. Manila: Asian Development Bank.

De Rosa, D.A. and K. Govindan (1997). *Agriculture, Trade and Regionalism in South Asia*. 2020 Brief 46, International Food Policy Research Institute (IFPRI).

Gould, D., C. Tan, and A.S.S.Emamgholi (2013). *Attracting foreign direct investment: what can South Asia's lack of success teach other developing countries?* World Bank Policy Research Working Paper # 6696, Washington, D.C

Govindan, K. (1994). *A South Asian Preferential Trading Arrangement: Implications for Agricultural Trade and Economic Welfare.* Mimeo, Research report for Robert McNamara Fellowship, Washington, DC: World Bank.

Hirantha, S.W. (2004). *From SAPTA to SAFTA: Gravity Analysis of South Asian Free Trade.* Paper presented at the European Trade Study Group 2004. Nottingham. 9-11 September.

International Labor Organisation (2014). *Global Employment Trends Report.* International Labor Organization (ILO), Geneva

International Monetary Fund (2015). *Regional Economic Outlook: Asia and Pacific*, April.

Kanungo, A. K. (2012). *FDI Inflows into South Asia: a case study of India's investments in Bangladesh.* Social Science Research Network. Available on: http://ssrn.com/abstract=2140737 or http://dx.doi.org/10.2139/ssrn.2140737

Kathuria, S. and M. M. Malouche, (2016). *Toward New Sources of Competitiveness in Bangladesh: Key Insights of the Diagnostic Trade Integration Study.* World Bank, Washington, D.C.

Kathuria, S. and S. Shahid (2015). *Opening Up Markets to Neighbors: Gains for Smaller Countries in South Asia.* SARConnect Series, Issue 1, World Bank, Washington, D.C.

Kee, H.L. (2012). *Non-tariff barriers in South Asian countries and its trade impact.* Mimeo, World Bank, Washington, D.C.

Kumar, R and M. Singh,(2009). *India's Role in South Asia Trade and Investment Integration.* ADBI Discussion Paper No.32. Asian Development Bank Institute (ADBI), Tokyo

Pigato, M., C. Farah, K.Itakura, J.Kwang, W. Martin, K. Murrell, and T.G. Srinivasan. (1997). *South Asia's Integration into the World Economy.* World Bank, Washington, D.C.

Raihan, S. (2012). *SAFTA and the South Asian Countries: Quantitative Assessments of Potential Implications.* South Asian Network on Economic Modeling (SANEM), University of Dhaka, Dhaka

Raihan, S. (2014). Quantitative assessment of phases of regional economic integration in South Asia in *Moving towards South Asia Economic Union.* Mimeo, Asian Development Bank (ADB), Dhaka

RIS (2008). *Deepening Regional Cooperation in the Bay of Bengal: Agenda of the BIMSTEC Summit.* Policy Brief No. 38. New Delhi: Research and Information System for Developing Countries.

Rodrik, D. (1989). *Credibility of Trade Reform: a Policy Maker's Guide.* The World Economy, Vol. 12, No. 1, pp. 1-16.

SAARC Regional Multimodal Transport Study (SRMTS) (2006*). SAARC Regional Multimodal Transport Study Report.* Kathmandu: SAARC Secretariat.

Shakur, S., and A.N.Rae (2005). *Trade Reforms in South Asia.'* Discussion Paper No. 05. Department of Applied and International Economics, Massey University.

Srivastava, P. (2011). *Regional corridors development in regional cooperation.* ADB Economics, Working Paper Series, Manila.

Subramanian, U. and J. Arnold (2001). *Forging Subregional Links in Transport and Logistics in South Asia.* Washington, D.C.: The World Bank, Washington, D.C.

Taneja, N. and Sawhney, A. (2007). *Revitalizing SAARC Trade.* Economic and Political Weekly, Vol. 31, pp. 1081-1084.

Taneja, N. (2006). *India-Pakistan Trade.* ICRIER Working Paper No. 182, New Delhi.

Taneja, N., M. Mehra, P. Mukherjee, S. Bimal, and I. Dayal (2013). *Normalizing India Pakistan Trade.* ICRIER Working Paper No. 267, New Delhi.

UNESCAP (2007). *Regional Infrastructure Network Development and Trade and Transport Facilitation in Asia.* United Nations Economic and Social Commission for Asia and Pacific (UNESCAP), Bangkok.

Weerakon, D. and J. Tehnnakoon (2006). *SAFTA: Myth of Free Trade.* Economic and Political Weekly.

THREE

DEVELOPMENT OF REGIONAL TRANSPORT NETWORKS IN ASIA

Madan Bandhu Regmi

Introduction

The idea of linking Asia by road and railway networks in order to provide international connections not only among the countries of the region but also with the Middle Eastern and European countries was first expressed in 1959 and 1960, respectively. However, the progress was slow in formulating the broader regional transport networks and translating that to regional projects and their implementation due to the political and economic context at that time which was not conducive.[1]

Recognising the political and economic changes that had taken place in Asia from the mid-1980s onwards, under a renewed initiative of the United Nations Economic and Social Commission for Asia and the Pacific (UNESCAP), the Asian Land Transport Infrastructure Development (ALTID) project was launched in 1992. Development of region-wide transport infrastructure networks such as Asian Highway (AH), Trans-Asian Railway (TAR) and facilitation of land transport operation were included as core elements of the project.

The project provided a framework for the development of a region-wide integrated transport network comprising road and rail networks. Under the ALTID project a series of studies were conducted between 1994 and 2002 to identify and extend the AH and TAR routes. That led to the formulation of the Asian Highway and Trans-Asian Railway network covering all subregions.

---

* This chapter is a tribute to the leadership of Dr. Rahmatullah who was the Director of the Transport, Communications, Tourism and Infrastructure Development Division of ESCAP from 1994 to 2000. He was instrumental in implementing the ALTID project. Later these regional initiatives were formalised through respective intergovernmental agreements. Dr. Rahmatullah joined ESCAP on 17 May 1978 and retired from ESCAP on 31 May 2000. The views expressed in this chapter are those of the author and do not necessarily reflect the views of the United Nations.

1. Refer, for example, UNESCAP (1994, 2000, 2005)

These studies, together with a series of meetings of the member countries at the subregional level, helped to build consensus on an agreed network.

During 2009 the importance of intermodal logistics centres and facilities was recognised including the need to extend the reach of the AH and TAR networks to wider hinterland and facilitate their integration with other transport modes as well as bringing the facilities offered by seaports to inland areas and connecting them to seaports. Further, in order to realise the potential benefits offered by the intermodal transport, the intermodal interfaces such as dry ports or inland container depots need to be planned carefully to serve as efficient cross-over points where freight can switch modes without delays or damage. ESCAP supported Asian countries in negotiation, adoption and implementation of the Intergovernmental Agreement on Dry Ports.

The Asian Highway and Trans-Asian Railway play a pivotal role in fostering the coordinated development of regional road and rail networks. This collaborative work of ESCAP culminated in the formalisation of the two networks through the Intergovernmental Agreement on the Asian Highway Network[2] and the Intergovernmental Agreement on the Trans-Asian Railway Network,[3] which entered into force in July 2005 and June 2009, respectively. There are now 29 parties and one signatory yet to become a party to the Intergovernmental Agreement on the Asian Highway Network and 18 parties to the Intergovernmental Agreement on the Trans-Asian Railway Network. The Intergovernmental Agreement on Dry Ports entered into force on 23 April 2016.[4] Currently, it has 11 parties and 6 signatories yet to become a party.

The Asian Highway and Trans-Asian Railway are evolutionary by nature. Indeed, as per the terms of their respective Agreements, the formalised networks have been adopted as two coordinated plans for the development of highway routes and railway lines of international importance within Asia and between Asia and neighbouring regions to facilitate regional economic integration. To date, the Asian Highway comprises 143,000 km of highways in 32 countries, Trans-Asian Railway includes 117,500 km of railway lines in 27 countries and the agreement on dry port lists 240 dry ports of international importance. The development of the networks as well

---

2.   United Nations, *Treaty Series*, Vol. 2323, No. 41607

3.   United Nations, *Treaty Series*, No. 46171

4.   https://treaties.un.org/Pages/ViewDetails.aspx?src=TREATY&mtdsg_no=XI-E-3&chapter=11&clang=_en

as some of the dry ports of international importance has been incorporated into national plans or strategies in a number of countries.

However, there are still some sections of international highway that do not meet minimum specified standards and are missing links in the regional railways[5]. Further, many dry ports and logistics centres need to be developed and operated. In addition to these infrastructure gaps, the regional transport networks suffer from non-physical and procedural barriers that impede seamless regional transport operations in Asia.

In this context this chapter, outlines the progress in development of different elements of regional transport network, challenges and issue in improving regional connectivity and suggest possible way forward in development of regional transport network in Asia. Following the introduction, Section 2 elaborates status of different components of regional transport network; and Section 3 makes policy suggestion to overcome those challenges and provides way forward.

Core Building-Blocks of Regional Transport

Asian Highway, Trans-Asian Railway, development of dry ports of international importance such as intermodal facilities and facilitation of land transport operation are core building blocks of regional transport network in Asia. This section provides brief detail on these initiatives.[6]

Asian Highway (AH)

The Asian Highway network is a regional transport cooperation initiative aimed at enhancing the efficiency and development of the road infrastructure in Asia, supporting the development of Euro-Asia transport linkages and improving connectivity for landlocked countries.

In 1959, the Asian Highway project was initiated at Broadbeach, Australia during the 15th session of the Economic Commission for Asia and the Far East (ECAFE) with the aim of promoting the development of an international road transport system in the region. At that time, it extended over 11,200 km reaching from Thailand to Iran. From 1960 to 1970, potential routes were identified and analysed. However, the progress was slow until political and economic changes in the region spurred renewed interest in the network in the late 1980s and early 1990s.

5. Refer, UNESCAP (2016)
6. Refer, UNESCAP (2007, 2014, 2015)

The routes of the Asian Highway network have been identified and agreed through a series of studies; technical standards and guiding principle for the development of network was developed. Currently, the Asian Highway comprises 143,000 km of highways in 32 countries (Map 1). It extends from Tokyo in the East to Kapikule, Turkey in the West and from Torpynovka, Russian Federation, in the North, to Denpasar, Indonesia in the South.

Map 1: Asian Highway Network

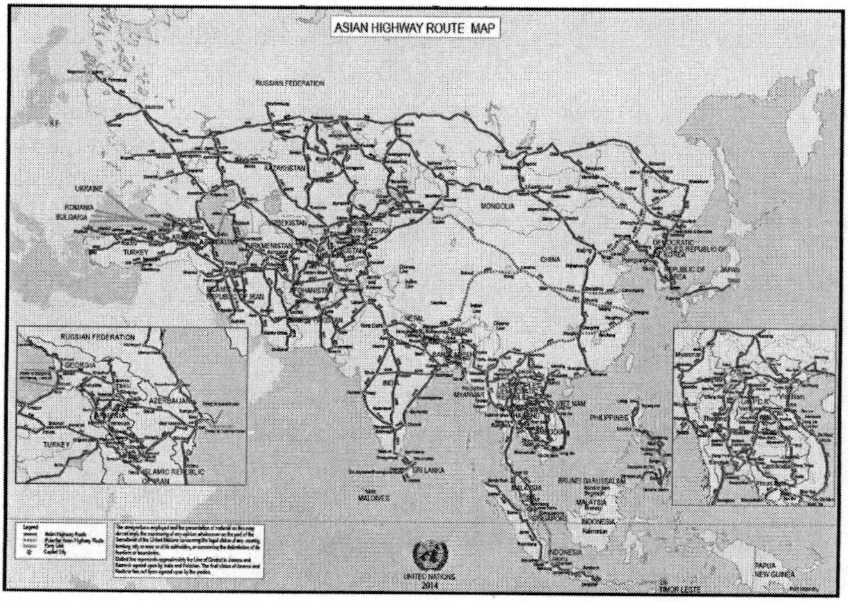

Source: UNESCAP

The Intergovernmental Agreement on the Asian Highway Network is the first treaty developed under the auspices of ESCAP and deposited with the Secretary-General of the United Nations. The agreement includes a list of Asian Highway routes, its classification and design standards and guiding principle for its development. The Agreement was opened for signature in Shanghai, China in 2004 and entered into force on 4 July 2005. Currently, there are 29 parties to the Agreement. The working group on the Asian Highway meet every two years to review process and policy issues on its development.

The 2015 update of the Asian Highway Database showed that to date about 10,147 km, i.e. 7.85 per cent of the Asian Highway network, do not yet meet the minimum desirable standards, while member countries have made substantial progress in upgrading Asian Highway routes between 2010 and 2014 as shown in Figure 1.[7] In too many instances, a same Asian Highway route falls into different groups of standard on two sides of a common border between neighbouring countries. This hampers the development of international cross-border road movements as road operators perceive poor infrastructure as posing a risk of injuries to drivers and damage to vehicles.

Figure 1: Status of Asian Highway Routes by Class, 2006, 2010 and 2014

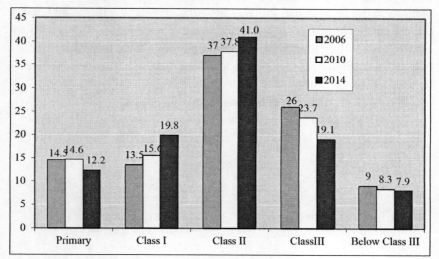

Source: UNESCAP

Trans-Asian Railway (TAR)

The idea of linking Asia by a railway network was conceived in 1960. The Trans-Asian Railway aims to serve cultural exchanges and trade within Asia and between Asia and Europe. From 1994 to 2001, the ESCAP collaborated with Asian countries to identify railway line of international importance through four corridor studies that covered all subregions. In addition to identifying routes, the studies reviewed minimum technical and commercial requirements for the smooth operation of the network. The consensual result of the studies became known as the 'Trans-Asian Railway' network.

---

7.   Refer, UNESCAP (2015). Figures have been sourced from UNESCAP (2016)

The Trans-Asian Railway network comprises 117,500 km of existing or planned railway tracks (Map 2) that have been selected by member countries for their current or future potential to carry international trade; of which 11,500 km are missing, i.e. 9.8 per cent of the network (Map 3). This total is the sum of cross-border line sections which, if constructed, would provide inter-country rail connectivity. The total investment required to put in place these missing links is estimated at US$ 69.5 billion. The lack of rail inter-country connectivity is particularly acute in Southeast Asia, including its links to other subregions, which account for 42 per cent of the missing sections in the Trans-Asian Railway network. Beyond the financing issue, a critical challenge that needs to be addressed is for countries concerned for each of the missing links to accord them the same level of priority in their respective development plans and coordinate their construction schedule.

Map 2: Trans-Asian Railway Network

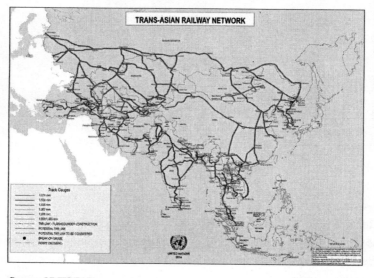

Source: UNESCAP

The Northern Corridor presents a high level of operational readiness due to the existence of continuous rail infrastructure, adequate inter-operability between railway organisations of neighbouring countries, even when a break-of-gauge exists at the border, and a high level of operational and technical competence. Since the completion of the Trans-Siberian main line, this corridor has traditionally been used for cross-border rail movements and the introduction of more market-oriented economic policies in China and the Russian Federation has intensified its use in recent years with an increasing number of new international container-block train services being launched along the corridor every year.

Poor rail infrastructure, insufficient number of rolling-stocks, lack of rolling-stock inter-operability across borders and low operational capabilities of railway organisations in some of the countries along the corridors hamper seamless operations of the railway corridors. Most importantly, the absence of continuous rail infrastructure across borders remains an obvious obstacle to the development of international services in some parts of the region.

Recognising that the network would reach its full operational capabilities through greater harmonisation of standards and acknowledging the need for a regional framework to discuss related issues, ESCAP supported negotiation, adoption and implementation of the Intergovernmental Agreement on the Trans-Asian Railway Network. The Agreement was opened for signature on 10 November 2006 in Busan, Republic of Korea and entered into force on 11 June 2009. Currently, there are 18 parties to the Agreement. This will facilitate coordinated development of the railway network and rail lines of international importance.

Map 3: Missing Links in the Trans-Asian Railway Network

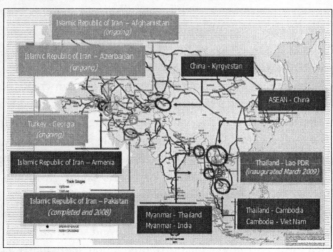

Source: UNESCAP

High speed railway construction is gaining popularity recently. In China, a major drive is underway to ensure that rail continue to assist the country's future economic development. China's high-speed rail network reached 10,000 km in 2014 with an additional 12,000 km being planned or under construction. India is also planning to develop 1745 km high speed lines linking Delhi, Bhopal, Nagpur and Chennai and a 508 km high speed line linking Ahmedabad and Mumbai.

After the establishment of ASEAN Economic Community in 2015, ASEAN has updated the ASEAN Connectivity Master Plan, which is known as ASEAN Connectivity Master Plan 2025. ASEAN countries are planning major investment in high speed rails. Planning for a 330 km high speed link between Singapore and Kuala Lumpur under PPP model is progressing. Thailand is also planning major railway upgradation projects to link Bangkok and Chiang Mai and Bangkok with Nongkhai. China is funding rail link to Vientiane, Lao PDR from Southern China at a cost of US$ 7 billion. Lao PDR and Vietnam are also planning high-speed rail link costing US$ 5 billion.

Dry Ports and Logistics Facilities

Due to high reliance on road transport, many Asian countries have recognised the deficiencies in transport and logistics infrastructure that are required to seize global market and remain competitive. The three essential components of an intermodal transport system are the transport network, intermodal nodes, and provision of transport services. While there has been renewed focus to develop transport networks, the development of logistics centres and intermodal transfer points needs priority attention.

Indeed, developing logistics centres or dry ports can create economic stimuli by attracting manufacturing, agricultural processing and associated activities. Transport and related services, such as freight forwarding, logistics, customs and sanitary services, would be available at these facilities. Other value-added services would include storage, warehousing, packing, grading, labeling and distribution. In addition, dry ports could grow into special economic zones with a much broader industrial and service base. Similar growth potential has existed around seaports that have brought prosperity to coastal areas by clustering economic activity and services, which have in turn attracted further economic factors of production, particularly a constant pool of mobile and well-trained labour, in a self-perpetuating process.

Dry ports offer facilities provided by seaports in inland areas. As Asia is home to 12 of the world's landlocked countries, the development of dry ports, in particular, rail-connected dry ports could play a major role in promoting intermodal transport. The most essential requirements of dry ports are connectivity to a seaport, preferably rail, customs clearance services, freight distribution and intermodal transshipment facilities. Dry ports can offer modal shift opportunities with long haul railway routes to seaports and distribution of goods in wider inland areas by improving operational efficiency.

In addition, dry ports can play an important role in rebalancing the transport task of land transport modes. Well-managed dry ports, particularly those located at a significant distance from a seaport, help reduce transportation costs and total transit time. Experiences from outside the region show that successful dry ports have increased logistics efficiency and allowed a modal shift from roads onto rail or inland waterways, thereby supporting policies aiming to reduce carbon emissions within the logistics chain. When distances between dry ports and seaports are relatively short, such as in Southeast Asia, it is proving more difficult to sustain rail transport. Although, some countries still build dry ports for the purpose of reducing traffic congestion and pollution in and around seaports.

Recognising the value of intermodal facilities in extending the reach of the Asian Highway and Trans-Asian Railway Networks as well as facilitating their integration with other transport modes, ESCAP supported the negotiation, adoption and implementation of the Intergovernmental Agreement on Dry Ports. The Intergovernmental Agreement on Dry Ports entered into force on 23 April 2016. To date 17 Member States have signed the Agreement and 11 have become parties to it.

The Agreement includes a list of 240 dry ports of international importance[8] (Map 4) and basic guiding principles for development and operation of dry ports. The main objective of the agreement is to promote the efficient movement of goods by: (i) promoting the development of dry ports of international importance; (ii) facilitating recognition of dry ports and investment; (iii) improving operational efficiency of intermodal freight; and (iv) enhancing environmental sustainability of freight transport through a modal shift.

---

8.   Among them, 110 have been identified as having a potential to develop into future dry ports.

Map 4: Dry Ports of International Importance

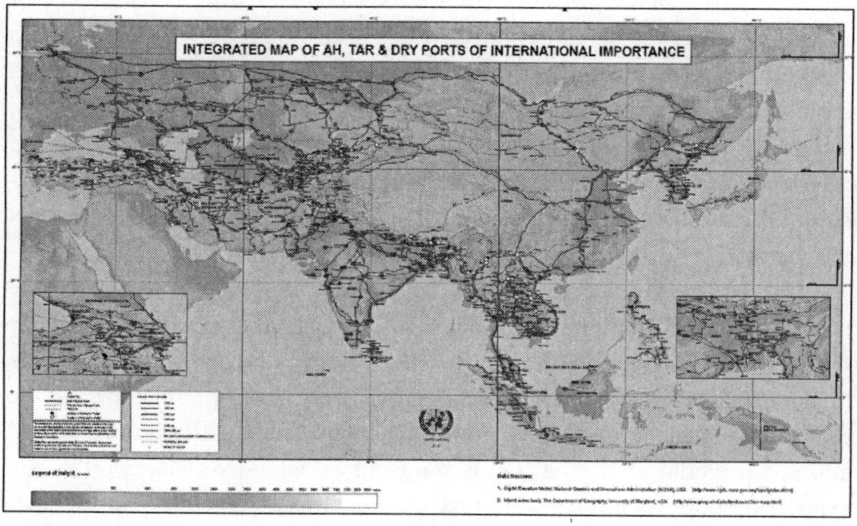

Source: UNESCAP

The Agreement will, in the long-term, offer the benefit that trade consignments will be directly transported and customs cleared between an inland port in one country and another inland port in another country. However, considerable investment will be required to upgrade existing dry ports and build new dry ports at the potential locations.

While the economies of ESCAP Member States are still reliant on exports to developed countries, intra-Asia trade is playing an increasingly important role in the region's overall exchanges. In this context, for the region to keep its economic vitality, it is important that a collaborative vision leads to the establishment of an efficient region-wide transport and logistics system that match new intra-regional trade flows.

The three intergovernmental Agreements are only part of the efforts developed by ESCAP to push the development of transport networks and intermodal facilities in Asia. In addition, ESCAP also extends support to Asian countries in implementing the agreements through technical cooperation and capacity-building activities.

Cross-border Transport Facilitation

Another important aspect of regional transport is the operation of the network as development of regional transport infrastructure "hardware" need to be complemented by "software" measures to facilitate cross-border and transit transport. The main objective of developing regional transport networks is increasing economic activity whilst at the same time maximising their usefulness and ensuring their sustainability. This infrastructure provision needs to be coordinated with solving the issues related to legal and regulatory barriers to transport across borders and increase use of ICT and other technologies for the facilitation of international road or rail transport. Trade and transport facilitation issues are seen as obstacles to enhance trade and tourism. Improving transport operations in accord with the logistics industry is necessary to bring down total transport costs and enhance the reliability of services.

Improving regional transport operation involves more efficient use of border crossing points. Usually these border crossing points pose a threat to the smooth flow of goods and people. The level of smoothness of transport operation can vary widely depending on the location of borders and the cooperation of the neighbouring country, existing agreements, and on origin and destination and type of cargoes. The border clearance process can also vary along the transport routes. The review of development in cross-border and transit transport shows that international transport still faces substantial difficulties in Asia region due to various non-physical barriers. Some of the commonly found non-physical barriers are:

- Inconsistent and time consuming, costly border crossing formalities and procedures;
- Restriction/limitation on entry of vehicles;
- Transshipment needed at the border;
- Different standards of vehicles and drivers;
- Restrictive visa requirement;
- Difficult and different process for transit traffic;
- Differential/reciprocal tariffs/charges;
- Incompatible working hours at borders;
- Coordination among various stake holders; and
- Excessive security checks.

Many of the above soft issues can be improved through accession and implementation of related international transport conventions and concluding bilateral and subregional agreements between/among the countries. Many studies have recognised the above barriers to trade and among others have recommended enhancing cooperation, improvement of border crossings, establishment of single-window at inland borders, improvement of trade corridors, and introduction of pilot demonstration runs of container trains. Recognising these difficulties, ESCAP continues to support the efficient and smooth movement of goods, passengers and vehicles by road and rail in Asia. A regional network of legal and technical experts for transport facilitation has been established. A set of facilitation models, along with model bilateral and subregional agreements, have also been developed to assist countries in removing non-physical barriers with innovative institutional, operational and technological solutions.

Subregional Transport Initiatives
There have been many regional and subregional efforts to promote subregional development and transport is a major sector of development within these programmes. In addition, many subregional organisations of Asia also have transport development programmes among their members. Transport infrastructure links between sub-regions of Asia, such as South-East, Central, East and South Asia, are being planned or implemented. Usually, these initiatives also have overlapping country membership. The sub-regional organisations and initiatives in Asia are:
* Association of Southeast Asian Nations (ASEAN);
* Brunei Darussalam-Indonesia–Malaysia-the Philippines East ASEAN Growth Area (BIMP-EGA);
* Bay of Bengal Initiative for Multi-Sectoral Technical and Economic Cooperation (BIMSTEC);
* Central Asia Regional Economic Cooperation (CAREC);
* Economic Cooperation Organisation (ECO);
* Greater Mekong Subregion (GMS);
* Indonesia-Malaysia-Thailand Growth Triangle (IMT-GT);
* Mekong-Ganga Cooperation (MGC);
* Shanghai Cooperation Organisation (SCO);
* South Asian Association for Regional Cooperation (SAARC);
* South Asia Sub-regional Economic Cooperation (SASEC);
* Subregional Economic Cooperation in South and Central Asia (SECSCA); and
* Greater Tumen Initiative (GTI).

Most of these subregional initiatives take corridor based approach for developing projects/programmes and largely use the Asian Highway, Trans-Asian Railway routes and dry ports of international importance as a basis to define subregional transport corridors. These programmes have made substantial progress in improving physical connectivity, however, despite various activities focusing on facilitation issues through development of framework agreements, single window system – cross-border movement of traffic is not encouraging as anticipated. This is the area where much policy attention and collaborative efforts of countries will be required.

The member States of the Shanghai Cooperation Organisation (SCO) signed the Intergovernmental Agreement of the SCO Member States on the Facilitation of International Road Transport in September 2014. In South Asia, Bangladesh, Bhutan, India and Nepal (BBIN) signed a Motor Vehicle Agreement (MVA) in June 2015. China, Mongolia and the Russian Federation have recently finalised negotiations of the Intergovernmental Agreement on International Road Transport along the Asian Highway Network. ASEAN has also updated its connectivity master plan.

ESCAP has established four subregional offices in the Pacific, North and North-East Asia, South and South-West Asia and North and Central Asia, with a mandate to look at subregional dimension of regional cooperation and development. Whilst the issues of transport connectivity in the Pacific are mainly related to air and maritime transport, for other subregions the land transport connectivity is a major focus. The transport connectivity within and among the subregions need to be improved. Connectivity is being increasingly addressed by subregional cooperation programmes and projects of these subregional organisations. However, there remains a need to have renewed focus to improve inter-subregional connectivity.

The Way Forward

The development of regional transport networks and connectivity is gaining prominence in Asia. Many policies, initiatives, and projects are being implemented by countries to enhance regional transport connectivity[9]. The chapter outlined historical perspective of regional transport, reviewed

---

9. Refer, ASEAN Secretariat (2016).

emerging trends and efforts of Asian countries to improve regional transport connectivity and put forward some policy proposals to improve physical transport infrastructure and their cross-border operation. Varying infrastructure standards, missing links in railway lines, need to develop and operate dry ports, financing their development, existing non-physical and procedural barriers at borders and transport routes are some of the challenges faced by Asian countries.

Despite these challenges, Asian countries with the support of their development partners have made substantial progress in developing regional and domestic transport infrastructure to enhance connectivity. Many sections of the Asian Highway and Trans-Asian Railway networks have been improved; upgrading and building of some portions of missing links have been planned. There is some progress in improving cross-border transport such as BBIN MVA among Bangladesh, Bhutan, India and Nepal, signing of SCO transport agreement to name few. Now, in order to better utilise these vast regional transport networks and offer intermodal transport opportunities, it is necessary that substandard sections be upgraded, missing links of railway be plugged in and dry ports and intermodal transit facilities at key strategic locations be developed.

Improving regional transport networks and bridging the infrastructure gap is a complex and challenging task that will continue to require the active involvement of all the stakeholders and development partners and a strong political commitment and collective efforts. Based on the review of the progresses achieved and the challenges and opportunities to develop regional transport infrastructure in Asia, the following policy suggestions can be considered to improve regional transport connectivity: (i) utilise existing infrastructure and facilitate cross-border connectivity; (ii) promote regional intermodal transport; (iii) prioritise maintenance of transport infrastructure; and (iv) increase investment in railways and intermodal infrastructure.

ESCAP will continue to promote the development of the regional transport connectivity as part of its overall goal to see the development of an international, integrated, intermodal transport and logistics system for the region, with the Asian Highway and Trans-Asian Railway networks and dry ports of international significance as well as facilitation of cross-border transport as major components.

References

ASEAN Secretariat (2016). *Master Plan of ASEAN Connectivity 2025*. Jakarta.

UNESCAP (1994). *Infrastructure Development as Key to Economic Growth and Regional Economic Cooperation*. Bangkok.

UNESCAP (2000). *A Review of Regional and Subregional Agreements on Land Transport Routes: Issues and Alternative Frameworks*. Bangkok.

UNESCAP (2005). *Toward an Asian Integrated Transport Network*, Monograph Series on Managing Globalization, No. 1 (First Edition). Bangkok.

UNESCAP (2007). *Toward an Asian Integrated Transport Network* (Second Edition). Bangkok.

UNESCAP (2014). *Regional Connectivity for Shared Prosperity*. Bangkok

UNESCAP (2015). *Review of Developments in Transport in Asia and the Pacific 2015*. Bangkok

UNESCAP (2016). *Asian Highway Database*. Bangkok

FOUR

CROSS-BORDER CONNECTIVITY INITIATIVES ACROSS SOUTH ASIA: WOULD THE BROADER REGION-WIDE CONNECTIVITY BE ENSURED?

Khondaker Golam Moazzem

Introductiosn

South Asia is one of the least physically connected regions in Asia. Establishing cross-border physical connectivity is being considered as one the major priorities of South Asian countries with a view to enhance trade and investment as well as to improve people to people contact within and beyond the region.[1] Over the last several decades various initiatives have been undertaken at individual, bilateral, sub-regional and regional levels across South Asia. Through such connectivity initiatives, the historical link of South Asia with rest of Asia and Europe through Southern Silk Route could be revived (Sobhan, 2000). The UN-led initiatives of Asian Highway and Trans-Asian Railway are the two most important initiatives to connect Asia with Europe. With growing importance of Asia in terms of trade and investment, particularly after 2000, South Asian countries, particularly India and its neighbouring countries especially China, took·additional initiatives for strengthening their connectivity within and beyond the region (De, 2015; Moazzem and Rayan, 2014). While some of those initiatives are extension of the UN-led initiatives, while others are new in terms of bilateral, sub-regional and regional connectivity. Such multiple initiatives indicate that countries in the region are being strategic in terms of connectivity and have opted for various alternate options to build regional networks.

The multiple initiatives on cross-border connectivity have diverse implications in ensuring region-wide broad-based connectivity (Rahmatullah, 2006; 2010). In fact, multiple initiatives would create alternate options

---

*   Author would like to register deep appreciation to Ms Monica Tasneem, Research Intern, CPD for her able research support. Views are personal. Usual disclaimers apply.
1.   Refer, for example, ADB-ADBI (2009, 2013), De (2013).

and would widen opportunities for countries to develop cross-border links through different routes. However, multiple initiatives would push countries to set their priorities, while taking decision for implementing related projects. Consequently, different level of priorities in implementing multiple initiatives would divert countries from achieving the common goal of building regional connectivity. In this context, it is important to examine relative merit of diverse strategies, followed by South Asian countries from the perspective of building cross-border connectivity across South Asia. This chapter reviews existing cross-border initiatives in South Asia with a view to appreciate the extent of alignment of different such initiatives towards achieving region-wide connectivity.

Overview of Cross-border Connectivity Initiatives across South Asia

Regional Connectivity Initiatives
There are a number of bilateral, sub-regional and regional initiatives of cross-border connectivity initiatives undertaken by South Asian countries. These initiatives appear to develop multi-modal connectivity, both within and outside the region.

Asian Highway and Trans-Asian Railway
As mentioned, the two most important initiatives led by the UNESCAP are the Asian Highway and the Trans-Asian Railway (Figure 1). The main objective of these two connectivity initiatives is to establish physical links between Asia and Europe by improving existing structures of highways and railways. According to the UNESCAP, the Asian Highway covers a total of 140,479 km road network, of which South Asia covers 24,832 km (17.6 per cent of total length of the road network). A total of nine highways (AH41 to AH51) aim to connect South Asian countries with other neighbouring countries such as Myanmar and China.

Trans-Asian Railway, on the other, is a project, which aims to create integrated freight railway network across Asia and Europe. The network is designed to be built in four corridors, of which, Southern corridor is being planned to develop linkages between Europe and South Asia and Southeast Asia. A total of 21 countries have signed the agreement, including all the countries of South Asia except Bhutan.

Figure 1: Asian Highway and Trans-Asian Railway

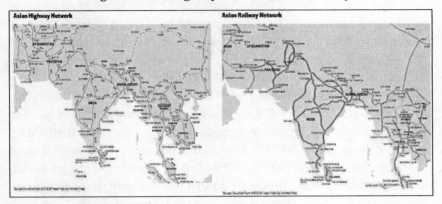

Source: National Transport Development Policy Committee (2013)

SAARC Motor Vehicle Agreement

Based on the Asian Highway Network, South Asian countries have undertaken various projects, both individually and collectively. At regional level, SAARC Motor Vehicle Agreement (MVA) has been drafted with a view to ensure free movement of motor vehicles across the region. A framework agreement is at final stage of negotiation in the SAARC process. The draft of the framework agreement has been prepared based on the findings of the Regional Multimodal Transport Study, conducted by the SAARC Secretariat.[2] The main suggestions of the study are developing transport and transit agreements in SAARC region for movement of freight, improvement of roads and rail corridors including maritime gateways (Rahman *et al.*, 2015). According to the Declaration of the 18th SAARC Summit 2014, member countries have agreed to finalise the framework agreement within

---

2. The SAARC Secretariat conducted the Regional Multimodal Transport Study to enhance transport connectivity amongst member countries through strengthened transportation, transit, and communication links across the region (SAARC Secretariat, 2006). In the case of regional road corridors, the study put forward suggestions to develop transport and transit agreements between India, Bangladesh, and Pakistan for the movement of freight; improvement of roads to reduce transit costs; and development of modern border crossings between India and Bangladesh to facilitate transit. In the case of rail corridors, the study proposed standardising technologies including track, rolling stock, and signaling and coordination (SAARC Secretariat, 2006). Regional inland waterways are to be developed through the signing of a protocol between Bangladesh and India which will be effective for long term; alongside this, more ports of call are to be introduced in Bangladesh to ease inter-country traffic. Maritime gateways are to be developed through the expanding capacity of Chittagong port, planning and augmenting rail, road and pipeline connectivity in all ports, and dredging to maintain water depth in Chittagong. With regard to regional aviation gateways, suggestions were put forward for the promotion of the low-cost carrier concept.

the shortest possible time. The draft agreement has highlighted on allowing the vehicles of other member states for transport of cargo and passengers in their respective territories subject to different terms and conditions.

BBIN Motor Vehicle Agreement (BBIN-MVA)

Bangladesh-Bhutan-India-Nepal (BBIN), a sub-group of SAARC countries, have signed MVA in 2015 (Figure 2). This framework agreement aims to facilitate movement of cargo and passengers across the sub-region. BBIN-MVA essentially draws on the SAARC-MVA and is prepared on the basis of same 17 Articles that of SAARC MVA. BBIN-MVA will facilitate cargo, passenger, non-regular passenger and personal vehicular traffic among the four countries (Rahman *et al.*, 2015). The agreement aims to permit regular passenger transportation and regular cargo transportation on the basis of multiple entries, valid for one year. Agreement will not affect any existing bilateral agreements or arrangements between the contracting countries. The agreement will be implemented through bilateral and tripartite protocols, which will be reviewed every three years. Protocols will need to have details of route, route maps, location of halts, rest or recreation places, tolls and check posts for passenger and cargo transportation. According to an estimate by Asian Development Bank (ADB), a total of 30 road projects worth US$ 8 billion would be required over a period of five years to fill and upgrade critical connections in the BBIN zone. According to the initial timeline, a six-month long (July-December, 2015) work plan has been finalised and officials of respective countries had discussed various issues and had finalised a number modalities related to movement of vehicles.

Figure 2: Routes Agreed under BBIN Motor Vehicle Agreement

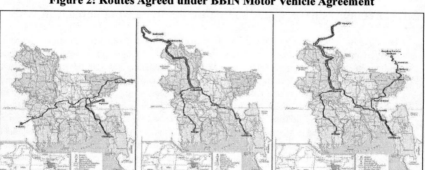

Source: Rahman (2015)

BIMSTEC Connectivity

The Bay of Bengal Initiative for Multi-sectoral Technical and Economic Cooperation (BIMSTEC) focusses on technological and economic cooperation among South Asian and Southeast Asian countries along the coast of the Bay of Bengal (Weerakoon and Perera, 2014). BIMSTEC has fourteen priority sectors including those of cross-border connectivity.[3] With a view to build and strengthen connectivity, the BIMSTEC Transport Infrastructure and Logistics Study (BTILS) came up with a strategy to promote transportation links to BIMSTEC member countries (ADB, 2008).[4] According to the study, strategies are to be pursued towards development of integrated regional rail networks that would facilitate access to Myanmar and Thailand.

BCIM Economic Corridor

Bangladesh, India, China and Myanmar have agreed to establish an economic corridor (Figure 3). Bangladesh-China-India-Myanmar Economic Corridor (BCIM EC) will be a sub-regional initiative with a view to develop a corridor among regions, which are geographically proximate areas of the four countries, of which, two are big developing economies (India and China) and two underdeveloped economies (Bangladesh and Myanmar). Most parts of this BCIM-EC, compared to other parts of these countries, are relatively backward, poor and partly land-locked. Poor domestic and cross-border connectivity has resulted in less external trade and low level of investment, which are also responsible for lack of development in the region. The BCIM-EC aims to establish a new path for cross-border connectivity, which could facilitate intra-regional and extra-regional trade and investment among BCIM countries, thereby accelerating production and employment including development of small and medium-sized enterprises (SMEs) in this sub-region, which would accelerate economic growth in the region. A joint study has been carried out to identify potential areas of cooperation including trade, investment, connectivity, energy cooperation, tourism and people-to-people connectivity, etc.

---

3. These sectors include commerce, investment, technology, tourism, human resource development, agriculture, fisheries, transport and communication, textiles, leather, etc.

4. BIMSTEC Transport Infrastructure and Logistics Study, conducted by Asian Development Bank (ADB) in 2008, has come up with a strategy for development of integrated regional rail networks within the region.

**Figure 3: Proposed Route for Movement of Transports in the
BCIM Economic Corridor**

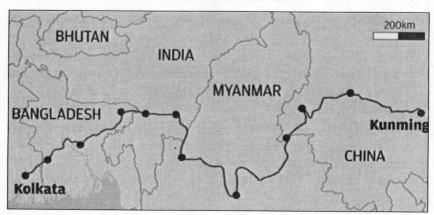

Source: Moazzem, Bashak and Raz (2014)

Bilateral Connectivity Initiatives Across South Asia

Bangladesh–India Connectivity

The scope for strengthening connectivity between Bangladesh and India was established through the signing of joint communiqués by the respective government heads in 2010 and 2011 (Figure 4). According to the first communiqué signed in 2010, both countries agreed to extend cooperation in roads, railways, ports, and waterways. The communiqué states that Bangladesh will allow the use of Mongla and Chittagong seaports for movement of goods to and from India through road and rail. Bangladesh also conveyed its intention to give Nepal and Bhutan access to Mongla and Chittagong ports. It was agreed that the construction of the proposed Akhaura–Agartala railway link will be financed by grants from India. A team of railway authorities from the two countries was to identify the alignment for connectivity. Both countries indicated interest in resuming road and rail links. Both the Prime Ministers have agreed that the Rohanpur–Singabad broad gauge rail link would be available for transit to Nepal. Bangladesh has informed about its intention to convert the Radhikapur–Birol railway line into broad gauge and requested that a railway transit link shall be established with Bhutan as well. India gave Bangladesh a line of credit worth US$ 1 billion for a range of projects, including the development of railway infrastructure, supply of broad gauge locomotives and passenger coaches, rehabilitation of Saidpur railway workshop, procurement of buses and dredging of rivers. The agreement also stipulated that Ashuganj in Bangladesh and Silghat in India would be additional ports of call. Furthermore, it has talked of amending the inland water transit and trade protocol through the exchange of letters and removing tariff and non-tariff barriers. Subsequent developments also include signing of the coastal vessels agreement to facilitate bilateral trade through coastal waterways. In 2015, a second India's line of credit of US$ 1 billion has been agreed to support a number of infrastructure and social projects.

Figure 4: Bangladesh-India Protocol Routes

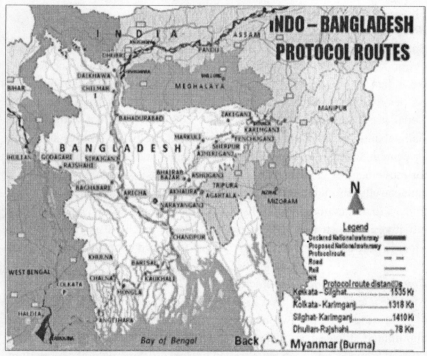

Source: Summary of Protocol available on the Bangladesh Inland Water Transport Authority website: http://www.biwta.gov.bd/website/?page_id=892

Bangladesh–Bhutan Connectivity

Bangladesh and Bhutan are keen to establish better connectivity between them. In April 2013, a joint statement signed by the foreign secretaries reiterated the stand of the two countries to put in place better connectivity to foster trade, commerce, and investment. It was agreed that connectivity between the two countries would be discussed in a subregional context involving Bangladesh, Bhutan, and India. Both countries agreed to form a joint working group (JWG) for finalising a transit agreement and a joint committee to study the utilisation of the protocol on inland water transit and trade between Bangladesh and India for transportation of Bhutanese cargo. They also emphasised the need to strengthen the role of SAARC, BIMSTEC, and other regional organisations to exploit potential benefits. In addition to the existing Burimari–Chengrabandha and Tamabil–Dawki land customs stations (LCSs), it was also agreed to establish additional LCSs viz. Dalu–Nakugaon and Gobrakura and Koraituli in Haluaghat, opposite Ghoshuapara in India.

Bangladesh-Nepal Connectivity

Bangladesh and Nepal signed a transit protocol in 1976 to facilitate movement of goods. However, this was not implemented as there were concerns from the Indian side regarding the movement of goods through Indian territory.[5] As per the Bangladesh–India joint communiqué, trucks from Bhutan and Nepal are now allowed to enter about 200 meters to the zero point at Banglabandh at Banglabandh–Phulbari LCS. The two countries signed an agreement to set up a timeframe for the conclusion of operational modalities for movement of vehicles between them. Emphasis was laid on promoting connectivity through the Rohanpur–Singhabad railway and the Kakarvitta–Fulbari road and maximum utilisation of these routes. Bangladesh is taking initiatives to open a new land route to Nepal and is also going to offer Mongla port for export of goods by Nepal to a third country.

Bangladesh-Myanmar Connectivity

A joint statement was issued in connection with the meeting of the heads of governments of the two countries in Myanmar in 2012. The statement highlighted bilateral cooperation in trade, investment, and connectivity. Myanmar and Bangladesh have signed two accords on bilateral cooperation: (i) an agreement to establish a joint commission for bilateral cooperation between the two governments; and (ii) a memorandum of understanding on setting up a cooperation commission office between the federations of chambers of commerce and industry. To develop connectivity between

---

5   According to the protocol, designated entry and exit points were mentioned for traffic-in-transit. The protocol also clarified import and export procedures for traffic-in-transit.

Bangladesh and Myanmar, an agreement was signed to construct a road from Gundum, Bangladesh to Bawalibazar, Myanmar (25 km). While a project on construction of link road from Bangladesh to Myanmar (135 km) was planned and Bangladesh made necessary allocation in its national budget, the project was not realised within the stipulated time due to lack of adequate steps for realising the project from both the governments.

India-Myanmar Connectivity

India and Myanmar have been jointly implementing Kaladan multi-modal transit transport project (Figure 5). The project will connect Kolkata to Sittwe by sea, Sittwe to Paletwa (Myanmar) through Kaladan River, then on Paletwa to India-Myanmar border (in Myanmar), and from there to Lawngtlai on NH 54 in India by road. The work of the project began in 2008 and is expected to end in 2016-17. However, the work was delayed resulting from various problems mainly in Myanmar side and some in Indian side as well. On the Tamu- Kalewa-Kalemyo Road, a total of 69 WW II bridges on Myanmar side make the road transportation difficult. The project is being built by India, and in October 2015 Indian government has revised the overall cost of the project at Rs. 29.04 billion.[6]

Figure 5: India-Myanmar Connectivity

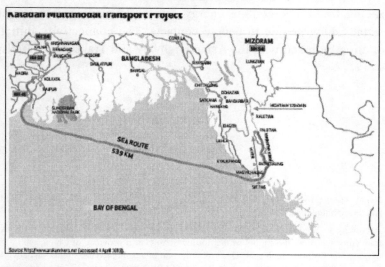

Source: Chatterji et al. (2015)

---

6. Construction of the project was approved by Indian government in 2008 with initial investment of Rs.5.36 billion.

Nepal-China Connectivity

Nepal and China are developing road and rail connectivity projects (Figure 6). The China-Nepal Friendship highway is an 800 km) route, connecting the capital of Tibet, Lhasa, with the Chinese-Nepalese border through the Sino-Nepal Friendship Bridge between Zhangmu and Kodari. The 2015 earthquakes in the region closed the highway and caused many evacuations. By 2016, there were some repairs but trading on the route was not restored to pre-quake levels.[7] Chinese railway connection via Nepal is a new route proposed for doing business with China. This will be a 540 km long railway passing through a tunnel to be built under Mount Everest. This railway line would provide Nepal an alternate route to transport goods to other countries. In China the railroad is expected to reach the Nepal border by 2020. There is also the possibility of connecting China to India via this railway line.[8]

Pakistan-China Connectivity Initiative

China-Pakistan Economic Corridor (CPEC) covers 2,000 km transport route, connecting Kashgar in Northwestern China to Pakistan's Gwadar port on the Arabian Sea via roads, railways and pipelines (Figure 7). Once completed, this corridor will contribute to both the economies by enhancing trade, overcoming energy crises, developing infrastructure and establishing people to people contacts. The connectivity initiative is not directly linked with the Asian Highway and Trans-Asian Railway Network.

---

7. Nepal exported food, silver, chili pepper, spices and garlic, and imported wool, cloth, gold and salt through this road.

8. According to Sigdel (2016), "May 11, 2016, marked the first ever departure of a freight train from Lanzhou, the capital of the northwestern Gansu province of China, with a cargo designed for Kathmandu, Nepal. This link is the part of a combined transportation network via Shigatse (Xigaze), Tibet Autonomous Region (TAR), where cargoes are moved from rail to road transport. Nepalese loaded trucks will be crossing from there over the Himalayan passes through Kyirong to reach Rasuwagadhi, Nepal, and then to the capital Kathmandu. The whole journey takes 10 days, 35 days less than traditional maritime routes would take."

Figure 6: Nepal-China Proposed Connectivity

Source: India Today at: http://indiatoday.intoday.in/story/
a-train-from-beijing-to-bihar-china-wants-to-extend-its-
nepal-rail-link-to-india/1/676239.html

Figure 7: China-Pakistan Economic Corridor

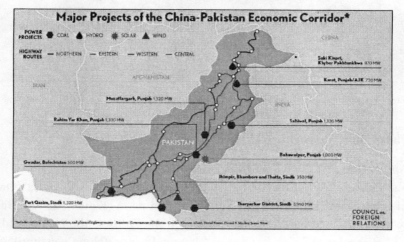

Source: Markey and West (2016).

Afghanistan-India Connectivity Initiative

India, Iran and Afghanistan have signed a tripartite agreement to turn the Iranian port of Chabahar into a transit hub bypassing Pakistan, which has been the only route for war-stricken Afghanistan to the Indian Ocean (Figure 8). Once the project is completed it will connect India to Afghanistan and Central Asia, whereas Afghanistan will get an alternate route to the Indian Ocean. The deal is crucial for the landlocked Afghanistan as it changes the geopolitics of the region and is seen as a way out of its dependency on Pakistan. Chabahar is not very far from the Pakistan port city of Gwadar, which is being developed by China.

Figure 8: India-Afghanistan Connectivity (via Iran)

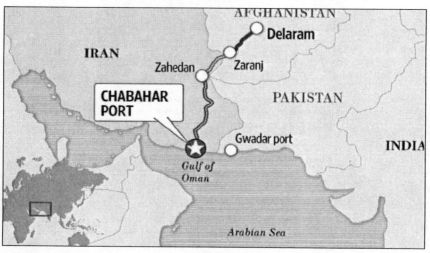

Source: LiveMint at: http://www.livemint.com/Politics/pI08kJsLuZLNFj0H8rW04N/India-commits-huge-investment-in-Chabahar.html

Other Country-Specific Initiatives

China's One Belt One Road Initiative (OBOR)

The Maritime Silk Road initiated by China is widely known as 'One Belt One Road' initiative and comprises two parts (Figure 9). The Belt encompasses land-based regions starting from China to the Netherlands. The belt begins at Xi'an in Central China before stretching west through Lanzhou (Gansu province), Urumqi (Xinjiang), and Khorgas (Xinjiang), which is linked with Kazakhstan. The Silk Road then runs Southwest from

Central Asia to Northern Iran before swinging West through Iraq, Syria, and Turkey. The Silk Road then crosses from Istanbul to the Bosporus Strait and heads Northwest through Europe, including Bulgaria, Romania, the Czech Republic, and Germany. Thereafter, it reaches Duisburg in Germany, and then swings North to reach Rotterdam in the Netherlands. At the end, the path from Rotterdam runs south to Venice, Italy. The proposed route of the belt will have no direct connecting point in Bangladesh. The only possibility would be Xi'an's link with Kunming, Yunnan, where Bangladesh would be connected through proposed Bangladesh, China, India and Myanmar (BCIM) Economic Corridor. Even connected with Xi'an, Bangladesh's traded products have to pass the distance about 2143 km from Kunming to reach Xi'an – the initial point of the Belt before it bound for Central Asia. Moreover, Bangladesh's trade through the BCIM EC would happen by road, whereas trade through the Belt would largely occur by rail. Overall, the belt of the Silk Road initiative would have limited implications for Bangladesh unless an efficient multi-modal connectivity is established with less lead time and cost for trading with Central Asia and Europe.

Figure 9: China's Belt and Road Initiative

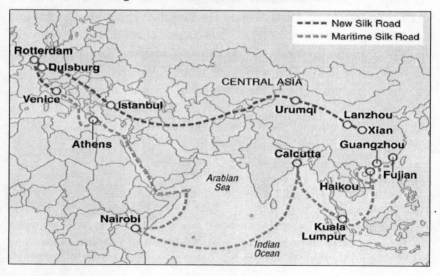

Source: http://www.sirjournal.org/op-ed/2016/3/20/ngd5k90acafjinn80ah0u8gxq48mp3

Maritime route (usually called 'road'), on the other hand, will begin in Quanzhou in Fujian province and hit Guangzhou (Guangdong province), Beihai (Guangxi), and Haikou (Hainan) before heading South to the Malacca Strait. Then through Kuala Lumpur, the Maritime Silk Road heads to Kolkata, India then crosses the rest of the Indian Ocean to Nairobi, Kenya.[9] From Nairobi, the Maritime Silk Road goes north around the Horn of Africa and moves through the Red Sea into the Mediterranean, with a stop in Athens before meeting the land-based Silk Road in Venice. The proposed route recognizes one stop in India (i.e. Kolkata). A number of other stops have been included, which are situated in nearby locations including one in Myanmar and one in Sri Lanka.

India's Maritime Connectivity in the Indian Ocean

India is actively pursuing maritime connectivity across the Indian Ocean through multiple means. The Indian Ocean Rim Association (IORA) in which India is a member along with 20 other states located in the Indian Ocean Rim has been considering maritime connectivity.[10] IORA countries are geographically located in different regions across the Indian Ocean – Southeast Asia, South Asia, East Africa, Eastern and Southern Africa, Australia and Gulf region. The issue of maritime connectivity between member countries is one of the major initiatives of the IORA. In this connection, a Maritime Transport Council for IORA has been proposed, which will work as a regional specialised agency that promotes and defends the interests of member states to facilitate maritime transportation. It strives towards strengthening of the maritime transport cooperation in the IORA region.[11] India has been assessing the possibility of maritime connectivity with ASEAN countries (Figure 10). It is also planning to develop link through sea route with East African countries.

---

9. The *Xinhua* map does not include a stop in Sri Lanka.

10. The Indian Ocean Rim Association was established in March 1997 with membership of countries located at the Indian Ocean Rim. At present, a total of 21 Member States and 7 Dialogue Partners comprise the Association.

11. Currently, the Sultanate of Oman is in an advance stage of implementing the text on Maritime Transport Council. Sultanate of Oman has offered to host the Headquarters of the Maritime Transport Council.

Figure 10: India's Proposed Shipping Routes with ASEAN

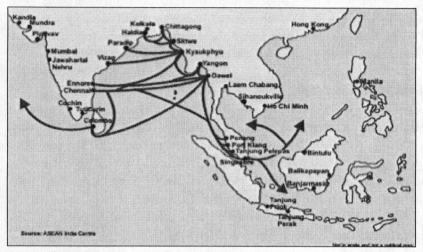

Source: AIC (2014)

Status of Implementation of Connectivity Initiatives

Status of Regional Projects

Despite the fact that regional connectivity projects in South Asia have been initiated early but the progress of implementation appears to be rather slow. SAARC Motor Vehicle Agreement (MVA) is a major connectivity initiative for South Asian countries, but has not yet signed. During the 18th SAARC Summit held in Kathmandu, the draft of SAARC MVA was discussed. and it was decided to finalise it immediately. However, till date not much progress happened towards finalising this agreement. Interestingly, Bangladesh, Bhutan, India, Nepal, a sub-group of SAARC countries, has signed a MVA called BBIN MVA in September 2015. The follow up process of SAARC MVA has been slowed down due to various internal and external reasons raised by the member countries. BIMSTEC connectivity initiative has been limited within a logistic assessment study undertaken by the ADB. Another initiative, BCIMEC has made slow progress till date – a joint study group has been preparing sector-specific recommendations for the respective governments. The follow up activities of the Joint Study Group (JSG) has not yet been finalised. Despite having a broader commitment of countries towards establishing Asia-wide connectivity under Asian Highway and Trans-Asian Railway initiatives, as part of which various regional and sub-regional initiatives have been planned, the progress till date appears to be slow. Lack of equal level of political commitment of member countries towards implementing region-wide connectivity seems to be a major concerning factor behind making slow progress of those initiatives.

Status of Bilateral Projects

Different bilateral projects are found to be at different stages of implementation. However, progress of these projects is better, compared to those of regional ones. Bangladesh-India connectivity projects have made considerable progress over the last several years. While a part of the connectivity projects are related to Asian Highway and Trans-Asian Railway, a number of other projects are not associated with those initiatives. India-Myanmar connectivity projects have made progress over the last several years and these projects are targeted to be completed by 2016-2017. Similarly, China-Pakistan Economic Corridor has made significant progress over the last several years. Over the last one year, a number of new bilateral initiatives have been undertaken, which include Afghanistan-India connectivity via Iran, for which a tripartite agreement has been signed between India, Iran and Afghanistan. On the other, Nepal and China are exploring possibilities to develop a railway link between them.

In contrast, a number of bilateral projects have made limited progress over the last several years. Despite initiated quite early, Bangladesh-Myanmar connectivity project has not made much progress. Bangladesh-Bhutan and Bangladesh-Nepal connectivity measures have made slow progress. And, connectivity with these countries is now discussed under sub-regional connectivity of BBIN MVA. Bangladesh's road connectivity with Thailand will hinge on connectivity with Myanmar.

Status of Implementation of Other Initiatives

China's OBOR initiative has made considerable progress particularly in the part which links China with Europe. Improvement of road part of the initiative is under progress. India, on the other hand, is actively pursuing the development of maritime connectivity under the India Ocean Rim Association. While, the progress so far has been slow, India is assessing the possibility to develop maritime connectivity with ASEAN countries. Presently, the liner shipping between major ports of India and ASEAN follows 'hub and spoke' model (AIC, 2015). Besides, India is actively thinking of developing maritime connectivity with East African countries connected through the Indian Ocean.

Perspective of Implementing Connectivity Projects

Differences in the Pace of Implementation

Different connectivity projects are at different stages of implementation. A general observation is that projects which are being implemented bilaterally have made more progress (except few), compared to those which are to be implemented regionally. In other words, countries are taking more interest on projects where bilateral interest are better matched in terms of trade, investment and other economic purposes. However, various other reasons have been identified as regards diverse level of implementation of different projects. A possible consequence would be that some of the regional projects may lose their importance to respective countries. This might affect other countries dependent upon the regional initiative.

On the other hand, a major challenge in implementing regional connectivity project is lack of adequate cooperation among regional countries towards implementing region-wide cross-border projects. Such situation has emerged owing to political, economic and security aspects among countries of the region.

Countries Opted for 'Second or Third Best' Solutions

Various bilateral connectivity projects appear to be 'second or third best' solution that countries aspire to achieve. Selected routes for the bilateral projects in some cases appear to be long distance, require huge additional investment, more time and cost to transport in comparison with the regional ones. In other words, these projects despite their advantage in terms of creating alternate routes are not necessarily always efficient in terms of cost and time to transport goods.

Countries of the region are at different stages of development. Hence, their capacity to undertake different projects may not necessarily be the same. A number of developing countries have their own priorities and these countries put their effort accordingly. Capacity to finance cross border projects need not necessarily be the same for all countries of the region; more specifically, finance has become available where big countries are involved. Consequently, there may be a 'vacuum', where countries/regions have some projects which are not priorities to both sides and where there is not adequate financing to implement the project as per the timeline. Without giving proper importance, these projects would be subsided and would hamper ensuring of region wide connectivity.

Less Strategic Interest in Implementing Regional Connectivity Projects

Countries sometimes may find it less worthy to invest in some regional connectivity projects because of their different perspectives in consideration of their priorities. Hence, implementation of some of the regional projects is delayed. Such a situation would adversely affect its neighbouring countries on their connectivity initiative. Given the constraints of resources as well as binding commitment of repaying huge debt for credit-financed projects, poor countries would set priorities in projects, which are of immediate importance to them. Moreover, countries reactive attitude towards implementing such projects would constrain realising the potential regional projects. Such reactive attitude develops due to various political, economic and security reasons. Finding a quick fix solution to such problems is very difficult. Hence, countries opt for alternate routes for connectivity.

Proactive Attitude for Building Strategic Connectivity Network

A number of cross-border connectivity initiatives are currently ongoing, which are being inspired by few South Asian and neighbouring countries with a view to further strengthening their connectivity links mainly outside the region. Parts of these projects may have linkages with Asian Highway and Trans-Asian Railway projects. Such connectivity projects have strategic interest to few countries and benefit accrued through implementing those projects would be much higher for those countries compared to those of other participating countries.

Conclusions

South Asian countries have undertaken various projects to develop cross-border connectivity. Parts of these initiatives are linked with existing regional and bilateral economic integration accords. Most of the connectivity initiatives, particularly related to rail and road, have been aligned with Asian Highway and Trans-Asian Railway initiatives. However, a number of bilateral projects emerged later with growing demand of additional and/or alternate route for connectivity. Interestingly, the progress of implementation of bilateral projects is much higher compared to that of the regional ones. While these bilateral projects create more opportunities for cross-border connectivity, a number of issues have been raised as regards to these initiatives More specifically, how countries could move to the 'first best solution' of establishing broad-based connectivity instead of opting for second best ones is to be seen.

It is natural that countries will explore the most feasible connectivity options. Such options may not necessarily be the most efficient one for economic activities. There are short term as well as long term issues with regard to achieving efficiency of different cross border projects. Do such bilateral initiatives are supportive towards ensuring cross-border regional connectivity across the region and ensure similar level of connectivity for all countries? Therefore, it is important to review the progress of various cross-border projects under broader regional connectivity framework. Such review should highlight on a number of issues which include (a) assessing the level of contribution of existing connectivity initiatives towards ensuring broader regional connectivity; (b) identifying connectivity projects which are being of less priority to some countries, reasons behind putting them as less priority projects and possible consequences on regional connectivity; and (c) exploring the possible solution for ensuring region-wide connectivity across South Asia.

References

ADB-ADBI (2009). *Infrastructure for a Seamless Asia*. Asian Development Bank (ADB), Manila and Asian Development Bank Institute (ADBI), Tokyo.

ADB-ADBI (2013). *Connecting South Asia and Southeast Asia. Interim Report*. Asian Development Bank Institute (ADBI), Toyko.

ADB. 2008. *Bay of Bengal Initiative for Multi-Sectoral Technical and Economic Cooperation (BIMSTEC) Transport Infrastructure and Logistics Study (BTILS)*. Technical Assistance Consultant's Report. Asian Development Bank, Manila. (TA 6335-REG).

AIC (2014). *India-ASEAN Maritime Connectivity Report*. ASEAN-India Centre (AIC) at RIS, New Delhi.

Chatterji, R., A.B. Ray Chaudhury, and Pratnashree Basu (2015). *India-Myanmar Connectivity: Possibilities and Challenges*. Observer Research Foundation (ORF), Kolkata.

De, Prabir (2013). *Connectivity, Trade Facilitation and Regional Cooperation in South Asia*. Commonwealth Secretariat, London.

De, Prabir (2015). India's Emerging Connectivity with Southeast Asia: Progress and Prospects in *Connecting South Asia and Southeast Asia*, ADB-ADBI Working Paper Series No.507, Asian Development Bank Institute, Tokyo.

Markey, D. S. and James West (2016). *Behind China's Gambit in Pakistan*. Expert Brief. Council on Foreign Relations. Available at: http://www.cfr.org/pakistan/behind-chinas-gambit-pakistan/p37855

Moazzem, K.G., and Kashfi Rayan (2014). *21st Century Maritime Silk Road Initiative: Perspective of Bangladesh*. Paper presented at the International Conference held in China.

Moazzem, K.G., K.K Bashak and S. Raz (2014). *Investment and Financing in the BCIM EC: Opportunities, Challenges and Policies*. BIISS and CPD, Dhaka.

National Transport Development Policy Committee (2013). *Promoting International Transport Connectivity between India and the South and Southeast Asia.*

Rana, P.B. and Binod Karmacharya (2014). *A Connectivity-Driven Development Strategy for Nepal: From a Landlocked to a Land-Linked State.* ADB-ADBI Working Paper Series No.498, Asian Development Bank Institute (ADBI), Tokyo.

Rahman, M., K.G. Moazzem, M. I. Chowdhury and F. Sehrin. 2015. *Connecting South Asia and Southeast Asia: A Bangladesh Country Study.* ADBI Working Paper Series No.500, Asian Development Bank Institute (ADBI), Tokyo, September.

Rahman, M., K.G. Moazzem, M. I. Chowdhury and F Sehrin. 2016. Bangladesh: perspectives on deepening cross-border links in M.G. Plummer, P.J. Morgan and G. Wingaraja (eds) *Connecting Asia: Infrastructure for Integrating South And Southeast Asia.* UK: Edward Elgar Publishing Limited.

Rahman, Mustafizur, Khaleda Akhter and Naimul Gani Saif (2015). Trade and Transport Facilitation; An Audit of the State of Play in Mustafizur Rahman (ed) *Towards Regional Integration in South Asia: Promoting Trade Facilitation and Connectivity.* Centre for Policy Dialogue (CPD), Dhaka.

Rahman, Mustafizur, Zafar Sadique and Nirman Saha (2015). Trade Facilitation in South Asia through Transport Connectivity: Operationalising the Motor Vehicle Agreements in Mustafizur Rahman (ed) *Towards Regional Integration in South Asia: Promoting Trade Facilitation and Connectivity.* Centre for Policy Dialogue (CPD), Dhaka.

Rahmatullah, M. (2006). *Transport Issues and Integration in South Asia.* Available at: http://www.ips.lk/saes/conference_material/downloads/rahamathullah_full_paper.pdf┌

Rahmatullah, M. (2010). *Strengthening Physical Connectivity in South Asia.* Paper presented at the International Conference on "SAARC @25" organised by RIS on 16-17 September 2010 in New Delhi New Delhi.

Rahmatullah, M. 2009. *Regional Connectivity: Opportunity for Bangladesh to be a Transport Hub.* Journal of Bangladesh Institute of Planners, 2: 13–29.

SAARC Secretariat. 2006. *SAARC Regional Multimodal Transport Study.* Kathmandu. www.saarc-sec.org.

Sigdel, Anil (2016). *Nepal-China Connectivity and the Need for Regional Cooperation.* Asia Pacific Bulletin, No. 347, June. East West Center, Washington.

Sobhan, R. (2000). *Rediscovering the Southern Silk Route: Integrating Asia's Transport Infrastructure.* Centre for Policy Dialogue (CPD). Bangladesh: The University Press Limited. ISBN 984 05 1519 5.

Weerakoon, Dushni and Nipuni Perera (2014). *The Role of Sri Lanka in Enhancing Connectivity between South Asia and Southeast Asia.* ADB-ADBI Working Paper Series No.487, Asian Development Bank Institute, Tokyo.

Web links referred

http://www.biwta.gov.bd/website/?page_id=892

http://indiatoday.intoday.in/story/a-train-from-beijing-to-bihar-china-wants-to-extend-its-nepal-rail-link-to-india/1/676239.html

http://www.cfr.org/pakistan/behind-chinas-gambit-pakistan/p37855

http://www.livemint.com/Politics/pI08kJsLuZLNFj0H8rW04N/India-commits-huge-investment-in-Chabahar.html

http://www.chinausfocus.com/finance-economy/one-belt-one-road-a-new-source-of-rent-for-ruling-elites-in-central-asia/

FIVE

TRADE FACILITATION IN SOUTH ASIA THROUGH TRANSPORT CONNECTIVITY

Mustafizur Rahman, Md. Zafar Sadique and Nirman Saha

Introduction

There is wide recognition that efficient transport connectivity not only facilitates trade but also an important driver of trade competitiveness. Good connectivity reduces cost of doing business and raises competitive strengths of trading partners within regions and sub-regions, enabling them to operate on the basis of comparative advantages. In view of this, in many regions, countries with common borders have signed Cross-Border Road Transport Agreements (CBTAs) to facilitate the movement of vehicles across borders. These agreements are also seen to be critical in terms of strengthening regional cooperation and integration. However, despite the existence of basic infrastructure, albeit not to the extent required, surface transport network in South Asia continues to be highly fragmented. Because of lack of integration of the transport system and absence of seamless connectivity, logistics costs incurred in conducting intra-regional trade in South Asia tend to remain significantly high. This in turn undermines the competitive strength of traders interested to carry out export-import business with neighbouring countries in South Asia. This also discourages intra-regional investment in spite of the fact that potential opportunities of cross-border investment are significant. Lack of seamless connectivity also undermines the possibilities of reaping the benefits of some of the positive initiatives that have been undertaken to deepen regional cooperation in South Asia. Some of these initiatives include duty-free, quota-free (DF-QF) offer of India to all least developed countries (LDCs) of the South Asian Association for Regional Cooperation (SAARC); Bangladesh's offer to allow the use of Mongla and

---

* This paper is an abridged and updated version of the contribution made by the authors in Rahman, M. (*ed.*) (2015) *Towards Regional Integration in South Asia: Providing Trade Facilitation and Connectivity* published by the Centre for Policy Dialogue (CPD), Dhaka.

Chittagong ports by India, Nepal and Bhutan; allowing Nepal and Bhutan to use Indian territory for trade with Bangladesh and third countries; proposed special economic zones (SEZs) for India in Mongla (Khulna) and Bheramara (Kushtia); and Coastal Shipping Agreement, to mention a few. Also, establishment of seamless connectivity will allow drawing synergies from other transport linkages such as in the context of the Asian Highway (AH) (AH1, AH2, AH41 in case of Bangladesh) and the Bangladesh-China-India-Myanmar (BCIM) Economic Corridor. These will also help reap the benefits of mega projects such as the construction of the Padma Bridge, proposed sea and deep seaports at Matarbari, Paira and Sonadia, and envisaged plans to develop water and rail connectivity.

In the absence of any bilateral road transport Agreement between Bangladesh and her neighbouring SAARC partners, goods are currently transshipped at the border points from truck to truck under the existing standard operating procedures (SOPs). As regards passenger transport between Bangladesh and India, Dhaka-Kolkata and Dhaka-Agartala cross-border passenger bus services have been in operation for some years now. No inter-country freight train moves across the border, although a passenger train runs between Dhaka and Kolkata. It is from this perspective that the sub-regional Motor Vehicle Agreement (MVA), signed in June 2015 by Transport Ministers of four SAARC member countries, i.e. Bangladesh, Bhutan, India and Nepal (BBIN), is of critical importance for deepening not only transport, but also trade, investment and people-to-people connectivity within the BBIN sub-region of the SAARC region.

Lack of inter-country multimodal and seamless connectivity is one of the main reasons why intra-regional trade in South Asia hovered around a lowly 5 per cent of South Asia's global trade; intra-regional investment has also been discouraged, to a large extent, for the same reason. A number of studies have established this relationship (SAARC Secretariat, 2006; Rahmatullah, 2012). In contrast, regional Agreements such as the European Union (EU) and the Association of Southeast Asian Nations (ASEAN) have been able to deepen economic cooperation and raise intra-regional trade by establishing closer transport connectivity within the region. The EU countries, particularly, have been able to set up a wide-range of transport networks for speedy movement of both goods and people within the region. The issue of connectivity has also featured in the World Trade Organization (WTO), where issues of cross-border movement of goods have been seen as an important driver of strengthened regional and global integration of developing economies.

At the political level, it has been recognised by the SAARC leaders that there is a need to significantly deepen transport connectivity, if regional economic integration is to be given concrete shape. This was also reflected in the successive Joint Communiqués signed by leaders of Bangladesh and India. Maximisation of the potential benefits originating from the DF-QF offer by India to SAARC LDCs also hinges, to a large extent, on more effective communication and connectivity. A study of the Centre for Policy Dialouge (CPD) on Bangladesh's export possibilities in the Indian market indicates that a large part of the estimated US$ 1.25 billion worth of trade potential remained unrealised because of lack of trade facilitation, particularly because of the high costs incurred on account of transport of goods to the Indian market (Rahman and Akhter, 2014). Same is the case for Bangladesh's trade with Bhutan and Nepal also. High transport costs undermine competitiveness of traders and the resultant foregone benefits to the economy are significantly high.

The Bangladesh-India Joint Declaration of June 2015 following the Indian Prime Minister's visit to Bangladesh has put emphasis on transport connectivity as a driver of regional cooperation and economic integration. Twenty two Agreements, Protocols and Memorandums of Understanding (MoUs) were signed during this visit. It may be recalled here, in 2012, India had sent a revised draft of Agreement for the Regulation of Passenger and Cargo Vehicular Traffic to Bangladesh with the proposal to sign a bilateral Motor Vehicle Agreement (MVA) between the two countries to facilitate cross-border movement of both passenger and cargo vehicles. However, progress had been slow, in part because Bangladesh had some concerns regarding some of the provisions in the proposed draft text. In this backdrop, the aforesaid June 2015 Joint Communiqué mentions the following: *"To commence negotiations on a Multi-Modal Transport Agreement between the two countries and to constitute a Joint Task Force for this purpose"* (Article 36). Bangladesh-India bilateral trade Agreement was earlier amended to allow for cross-border road transport movement between two points in India, through Bangladesh, in addition to the already existing water protocol. The Agreement was renewed keeping the provisions for use of water, roadways and railways for the purpose of commerce between the two countries and for passage of goods between "two places in one country" and "to third country" (Article VIII of the Protocol).

Prior to the Eighteenth Summit of the SAARC leaders in November 2014 in Kathmandu, the SAARC Secretariat took a move to sign a framework Agreement titled 'Motor Vehicle Agreement for the Regulation of Passenger and Cargo Vehicular Traffic amongst SAARC Member States' (SAARC MVA). Regrettably, the Agreement had to be deferred at the last moment.[1] Transport Ministers of the SAARC countries were given the responsibility to revise the draft suitably for subsequent signing and ratification by member countries. In parallel, initiative was taken to design a sub-regional MVA as part of the BBIN network. The recently signed BBIN MVA has put this idea into concrete shape.

Experiences of other Regional Trade Agreements (RTAs) such as in Greater Mekong Subregion (GMS) and ASEAN show that MVAs could play a crucial role in broadening and deepening regional cooperation. Absence of seamless connectivity creates physical and non-physical barriers that impede trade, thereby creating disincentives for traders to undertake trade within the region because of the lengthy lead-time, wastage and demurrage. These result in overall cost escalation and undermine competitiveness. Consequently, the potentials of backward and forward linkages and regional value chains are affected, adversely impacting global competitiveness of regional producers. This also has direct cost implications at the consumers' end.

As the preceding section has noted, two concrete initiatives have now been put in motion towards better connectivity within the SAARC region – the recently signed BBIN MVA at the sub-regional level, which was signed on 15 June 2015, and the SAARC MVA which is likely to be signed in the near future. If these developments are read in relation to the amended Bangladesh-India Trade Agreement, one can discern that the idea of transport connectivity between western India and the north-eastern states of India, via Bangladesh, is implicitly present in these Agreements. For example, Article VIII of the Trade Agreement states: *"The two Governments agree to make mutually beneficial arrangements for the use of their waterways, roadways and railways for commerce between the two countries and for passage of goods between two places in one country and to third countries through the territory of the other under the terms mutually agreed upon. In such cases, fees and charges, if leviable as per international Agreements, conventions or*

---

1. As far as is known, one SAARC member expressed reservation as regards certain provisions in the draft Framework Agreement.

practices, may be applied and transit guarantee regime may be established through mutual consultations."

In view of the aforesaid recent developments, issues related to operationalising the MVAs have now assumed heightened practical significance and importance. A model MVA appropriate for South Asia should include appropriate protocols along with detailed annexes to elaborate the protocols, and should be in line with international best practices. Global best practices show that, a comprehensive MVA should include the followings: principles that would govern the agreement; ways of operationalising of the agreement; documentation and procedures; border crossing formalities; registration of vehicles; container customs regime; taxes, fees and other charges; institutional arrangements; technical matters; infringements; application of laws and regulations; and provisions for amendments to the agreement, among others. The present study has made an attempt to examine the South Asian MVAs taking into account these concrete elements in the global best practices with a view to draw the needed insights and lessons. The purpose of the present study, thus, is to examine the three aforesaid MVAs, analyse to what extent these match with some of the best global MVAs, and discuss the concrete steps that will need to be undertaken to operationalise these MVAs.

Rest of the chapter is organized as follows: Section 2 presents an overview of the current state of cross-border transport movement; Section 3 critically assesses various provisions in the BBIN MVA from the perspective of global best practices. Section 4 has attempted to identify, on the basis of information generated through field surveys and consultations, existing major barriers to cross-border vehicular movement and come up with operational modalities to implement and operationalise the MVAs. Section 5 articulates the major findings of the study and provides a number of policy recommendations.

Cross-Border Road Transport Movement: Potential Benefits and Current State

Theoretical Framework

Theoretical framework is useful to capture the impacts that a regional Framework Agreement for vehicular movement or a bilateral cross-border road transport Agreement is likely to have on the domestic economies of participating countries and also on those in the region. Successful implementation of a CBTA/MVA involving bordering countries could translate transport corridors into economic corridors[2], enhance regional economic cooperation and stimulate trade integration within the region. However, such an Agreement must be accompanied by necessary investments in developing road infrastructure and land port modernisation, simplification and harmonisation of customs regime and large-scale trade facilitation. Doing away with transshipment could bring significant benefits for traders in the form of reduction in transport cost and time, reduced damage to cargo and timely delivery of product. Consequently, these help raise market competitiveness of the participating countries. Benefits originating from better transport connectivity and higher levels of regional trade integration are also likely to stimulate foreign direct investment (FDI). Additionally, the MVA opens the door for development of ancillary sectors in services including, particularly, transport services, by creating business opportunities for transport operators. Indeed, the real value addition emanating from such Agreements could be generated from services rather than through revenue generated from transit fees and service charges. Besides, MVAs also facilitate transport movement within various points of the participating countries, and thereby reduce cost and time of domestic trading.

Implementation of an MVA is expected to bring dynamic changes in the local economy. However, this could have an adverse impact on some specific sectors involved with trade processes at the micro-level, in the short-run. In the absence of transshipment, storage and labour use in the port area would reduce significantly. As a result local transport operators may incur losses.

On the other hand, better transport connectivity is likely to have significant positive externalities and spillover effects both at the micro (local), and the sectoral levels and also on economy-wide levels. Increased economic activities will expand fiscal space in the form of import duties and port-related service charges, and hence could generate additional revenue for the government. Wide-ranging economic activities

---

2.   The concept 'Economic Corridor' was first mooted in the GMS Development Plan (Wiemer, 2009). Banomyong (2013) explained the differences between transport, logistics and economic corridors. A transport corridor only links regions physically. On top of providing physical links, a logistics corridor also harmonises the institutional frameworks between those connecting regions. However, an economic corridor attracts investments also for enhancing greater economic activities in the region. Hence, an effectively functional economic corridor requires physical links and logistics facilitation which need to be put in place upfront by all the participating countries.

and investment opportunities will likely spring up along the transport corridors; furthermore, employment opportunities will be created in the various related sectors.

An MVA would help to promote regional cooperation and development through the provision of transit which is critically important from the perspectives of particularly the landlocked countries (LLCs) in the sub-region such as Bhutan and Nepal, and also landlocked regions such as the North-East part of India. Facilitation of transit connectivity merits special mention in the context of the BBIN sub-region because of the significant benefits that could originate from this for all the member countries.

Governments will need to ensure that the needed infrastructure facilities were developed to reap the potential benefits of connectivity. Mobilisation of additional resources will be called for to address the challenges of financing the significant investment.

An illustration of the theoretical framework is presented in the Figure 1.

Figure 1: Theoretical Framework for a CBTA/MVA

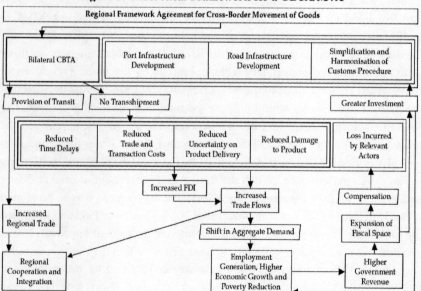

Source: Authors' elaboration.

Ongoing Initiatives for Cross-Border Road Transport Integration in the SAARC Region

Till date, three initiatives are in place to address the issue of deepening connectivity among SAARC member countries. The first is related to the formulation of a SAARC MVA. This was initially proposed by India, and then it was channeled through the SAARC Secretariat. Later, India proposed a bilateral MVA with Bangladesh to improve connectivity between the two countries. The third initiative is a sub-regional MVA to facilitate cross-border road transport in the sub-region embracing four countries – Bangladesh, Bhutan, India and Nepal. Of the three, as was seen, the BBIN MVA is the most matured one.

The provisions followed in the draft SAARC framework MVA and BBIN framework MVA entail that contracting parties will negotiate bilaterally or on a tripartite basis as would be called for concerning the various protocol and SOPs. These would state, among others, fees and charges, routes of operations, entry and exit points, technical requirements of vehicles, etc.

SAARC MVA

In the 14th SAARC Summit in 2007, the member states directed the Inter-Governmental Group on Transport (IGGT) to develop a regional MVA to facilitate cross-border movement of goods in the SAARC region. Following the directives, in the first meeting of the SAARC transport Ministers, member states examined the preliminary technical inputs by the Asian Development Bank (ADB) and the draft of the MVA prepared by India. It was decided that the SAARC Secretariat would prepare the final draft of the Agreement. The SAARC Transport Ministers in their second meeting in 2009 approved the recommendations of the IGGT to establish an Expert Group for negotiation and finalisation of the draft Agreement. In the third Expert Group Meeting in Rajasthan in September 2014, the draft Agreement was finalised and later endorsed at the fifth meeting of the IGGT. The Agreement was to be signed at the 18th SAARC Summit in November 2014. However, Pakistan informed the group that it was yet to conclude the internal process of approval. It was decided that the SAARC MVA would be finalised within the next six months.

An inter-Ministerial meeting in February 2015 asked for the opinions of the concerned Ministries and Departments including Roads and Highways Department (RHD), Foreign Ministry, Commerce Ministry, National Board of Revenue (NBR), banks and financial institutions. Based on this, a number of amendments were proposed. Important amendments included incorporation of a financial guarantee document for security of transit goods, determination of transit charges according to administrative expenses incurred, and inclusion in the text of other responsibilities of the customs sub-group. The amendments were to be placed at the next meeting of the SAARC Transport Ministers.

Bangladesh-India Bilateral MVA

The bilateral MVA between Bangladesh and India was first discussed between the Prime Ministers of both countries during the Indian Prime Minister's visit to Bangladesh in 2011. In January 2012, India sent the draft of a model MVA to Bangladesh. The bilateral MVA was discussed at various forums including at the Secretary-level meeting of Commerce Secretaries, meetings of Joint Working Group (JWG) on Trade, Joint Guidance Committee (JGC) and Joint Consultative Commission (JCC). Bangladesh had informed the Indian side that the Agreement was still under examination. Later on India shared a revised draft of the bilateral MVA with Bangladesh. At the 9th Meeting of the JWG on Trade at which the issue was discussed, it was informed by Bangladesh that the draft was going through inter-Ministerial consultation process because of transit-related issues in the draft MVA. India suggested Bangladesh to prepare its own draft through this consultation which then could be discussed at bilateral level. Subsequent developments in this regard remain unclear. However, a possible reason for this could be that the focus has now shifted to the BBIN MVA. As was pointed out earlier, the BBIN MVA will need to be operationailsed through bilateral and tripartite negotiations. There is a possibility that the two MVAs would be integrated at some future point of time.

BBIN MVA

It may be recalled that a Regional Technical Assistance (RETA) programme supported by the ADB worked as a consulting platform for economic cooperation at the sub-region level (Islam, 2003). Early on, South Asia Subregional Economic Cooperation (SASEC), initiated in 2001, financed a number of projects with support from the ADB, particularly to promote regional connectivity and bolster both intra-regional and inter-regional trade of the four member countries. In 2014, Maldives and Sri Lanka also joined the initiative. When the SAARC MVA could not be signed at the 18th SAARC Summit in Kathmandu, a parallel initiative was undertaken to formulate a sub-regional framework agreement with participation of four countries: Bangladesh, Bhutan, India and Nepal. The BBIN MVA, which was geared to link the four countries, was discussed at a meeting of the Transport Secretaries of the four countries held in February 2015. One of the distinctive features of the Agreement is that membership has been kept open. Presumably, this was done with a view to keep open the possibility of Myanmar and China joining the Agreement at some later stage (an idea that was mooted by Bangladesh). A draft of Terms of Reference (ToR) was also prepared for Joint Land Transport Facilitation Committee (JLTFC) and National Land Transport Facilitation Committee (NLTFC) to monitor the implementation of the agreement and prepare the protocols for the agreement. At the next meeting of the nodal officers in April 2015, the signing venue (Thimphu, Bhutan) was finalised, and the member states were asked to complete internal procedures before 15 June 2015.

The text of the draft BBIN MVA was finalised at the consultation meeting of the Transport Ministers on 14 June 2015; and the final draft was signed on 15 June 2015 in the presence of the Transport Ministers of the participating countries. A six-month work plan was drawn with activities to be covered and milestones to be reached over the next six months (July-December, 2015).

Assessment of the Draft MVAs

Components of an Ideal MVA: International Best Practices
This part of the paper looks at cross-country experiences in designing MVAs and attempts to find out the elements of what should be a model MVA.

Ideal Components of an MVA
Cross-Border Trade Agreement (CBTA) is one of the key tools to administer and regulate the movement of road traffic across borders and ports. Whilst a regional framework agreement sets out the ground rules for the MVA, mutually agreed bilateral or tripartite agreements are the preliminary steps towards operationalisation of such initiative. In most instances, bilateral CBTAs address particular issues that are then incorporated into multilateral agreements. Bilateral agreements also hold good in absence of multilateral region-wise system. However, a bilateral agreement has to be in conformity with existing national rules and regulations for its effective and smooth implementation.

The study has undertaken an assessment of the three MVAs (i.e. draft SAARC framework Agreement, draft bilateral Bangladesh-India Agreement and the BBIN MVA) based on the versions available. This was done from a comparative perspective of a number of important agreements in operation in different parts of the world. These are listed in Table 1. The team has reviewed a total of nine agreements – four of these are bilateral and five multilateral – to assess the aforesaid three MVAs in the SAARC region from a cross-country perspective. It may be noted here that many of the agreements reviewed are the best practiced ones in their respective regions.

Table 1: List of Agreements Reviewed

Bilateral Agreements
1. Agreement on Road Transport between the Government of the Republic of Belarus and the Government of the Kingdom of Belgium
2. International Road Transport Agreement between the Government of the Republic of Latvia and the Government of the Republic of Turkey
3. International Road Transport Agreement between the Government of the Republic of Turkey and the Government of the Republic of Iran
4. Agreement between the Government of the United Kingdom of Great Britain and Northern Ireland and the Macedonian Government on International Road Transport

Multilateral Agreements	Contracting Parties
1. Northern Corridor Transit and Transport Agreement	Kenya, Uganda, Rwanda, Burundi and Congo
2. ASEAN Framework Agreement on the Facilitation of Inter-state Transport	Brunei Darussalam, Cambodia, Indonesia, Lao PDR, Malaysia, Myanmar, Philippines, Singapore, Thailand and Vietnam
3. Tripartite Agreement on Road Transport – East African Community (EAC)	Tanzania, Kenya and Uganda
4. Greater Mekong Sub-region Cross-Border Transport Agreement (GMS-CBTA)	Lao PDR, Thailand and Vietnam; later Cambodia, China and Myanmar
5 ECO Transit Transport Framework Agreement	Afghanistan, Azerbaijan, Iran, Kazakhstan, Kyrgyz Republic, Pakistan, Tajikistan, Turkey, Turkmenistan and Uzbekistan

Source: Authors' compilation.

The study has classified the components under eight broad areas which constitute some of the key components (Figure 2). The purpose of the exercise was to arrive at a model MVA.

The following section presents a brief review of the key provisions in each of the areas of the MVA identified earlier.

a. Definitions and Objectives

An MVA should define the important terms used in the agreement in a concise and transparent manner. The 'Definitions' section should be prepared in a manner that facilitates a clear understanding of the provisions defined in the agreement. Majority of the reviewed agreements feature a complete set of definitions listed at the very beginning of the agreement. Indeed, it is important that the objectives of the agreement are presented explicitly at the very beginning. There is a wide diversity in the objectives of different agreements, but an important focus of all such agreements is to facilitate transport and transit of goods across borders and create better opportunities for trade by reducing unnecessary delays. For example, major objective of the EAC Tripartite Agreement is to reduce tax evasions, while the ASEAN Framework Agreement on the Facilitation of Inter-State Transport (AFAFIST) focused on supporting implementation of the ASEAN Free Trade Area (FTA).

b. Scope of Coverage and Principles of Governance

Ideally, an MVA should specify the geographical scope of coverage of the agreement; it should also mention about the type of operations that would be covered by the agreement. Geographical limitation is considered to be a barrier to trade which could constrain potential access to certain regions of the contracting parties. Geographical scope of the agreement must be informed by the importance of potential land routes from the perspective of facilitating trade and commerce. In addition, a liberal agreement should specify a clause to gradually open up new transport routes. The Bilateral Agreement between Lao PDR and Vietnam in 2012 opened three new routes for trucks and buses to reach destinations inside each other's territory to promote both trade and tourism in the GMS area (ADB and AusAID, 2013). Certain operations such as 'admission of third country traffic' may be incorporated within the scope of a bilateral MVA, to facilitate trade and transport not only between contracting parties, but also with other neighbouring countries. Macedonia FYR-UK (2005) and Belarus-Belgium (1995) bilateral agreements have kept this provision. With adequate security provisions, cabotage operations are also allowed in some Agreements (EU multilateral arrangement[3]) within the scope of an MVA. On the other hand, a standard agreement explicitly states the principles that will govern operations. Principles of consistency, simplicity, efficiency, non-discrimination, fair competition, transparency and mutual cooperation create the foundation for guiding the implementation of the agreement. The AFAFIST

---

3. This provision is provided in EC's new Regulation No. 1072/2009 which replaced the old Regulations No. 881/92 and 3118/93.

(2009) and Northern Corridor Transit and Transport Agreement (2007) are good examples of this. However, the four bilateral agreements under review did not clearly feature the principles of operations.

Figure 2: Components of an Ideal Cross-Border Road Transport Agreement (CBTA)

Definitions and objectives	• Defintion of key terms • Objective of the Agreement
Scope and principles of operations	• Scope and coverage of the Agreement • Principles of governance
Enabling criteria for road transport movement	• Types of vehicles permitted • Criteria for licencing of transport operators for cross-border transport operations • Registration of vehicles • Identification of routes/corridors • Permit and quota requirements • Documentation and procedures
Technical specifications	• Vehicle weight and dimensions specification • Roads, bridges designs and construction standards and specifications
Customs regime	• Transit and inland customs clearance regime • Commodity classification system • Customs duties and charges
Revenue requirements	• Taxes, fees, tolls and other charges (including road user charges) • Exemptions
Facilitation measures	• Facilitation measures for border clearance • Facilitation measures for transport operators • Facilitation of frontier cross formalities
Other issues	• Applicable laws and regulations • Border security management • Institutional and implementational arrangements • Dispute settlement • Modification, amendments and review mechanism • Validity of the Agreement

Source: Authors' elaboration.

c. Enabling Criteria for Road Transport Movement

An ideal agreement has a number of enabling criteria such as identification of routes, types of permitted vehicles, registration of vehicles, licensing of transport operators, other permits, documents and quota requirements. The practice is to articulate the criteria in general terms in the main Agreement, whilst detailed specifications are issued in supplementary annexes and protocols. Many agreements keep provisions relating to plying of cargo vehicles, passenger vehicles, and also personal vehicles in the host territory. The idea is to stimulate both trade and tourism. In most cases, the agreements accept movement of foreign haulers through some of designated (identified as having trade enhancing potential) routes to reach importer's warehouse. Transit cargoes are generally permitted in covered cargoes, and are allowed to stop at some designated frontier posts. As regards transport operator's license, the GMS-CBTA experience shows that it is some competent authority in the 'home country' which is authorised to issue the license. Issuance criteria include, in many instances, financial soundness and no criminal record of the operator, safe operations management capacity and fair competition. Similarly, in many cases, national registration of vehicles is a criterion that allowed travel through the host territory without hassles. Additionally, vehicles should have the registration certificate, and registration plates on the front and rear. A sign unique to the country of registration should also be deployed. This is important to distinctly identify vehicles undertaking cross-border operations and ease border crossing through simplified procedures. Finally, some agreements followed limited access (quantitative restriction) of vehicles over a specified period of time. Sometimes, priority consignments (i.e. perishable goods, pharmaceutical supplies or medical patients) may receive special exemptions.

d. Technical Specifications

Technical issues such as vehicle weight and its dimension, in line with the standards and specified designs of designated roads and bridges in the host country, need to be spelt out clearly in the agreement. For example, a major part of Bangladesh's roads have a capacity of not more than 8.2 tonne in single axle load, while the same is 10 tonne in case of her other neighbouring countries such as Bhutan, India and Nepal. The Northern Corridor Transit and Transport Agreement specified that the maximum axle load limits for multiple axles would be within 53 tonne. On the other hand, GMS-CBTA articulates the highway standard and pavement types according to the vehicle loads. Such specifications are important to regulate and manage road traffic movement in a manner compatible with the road conditions and infrastructure of the participating countries.

e. Customs Regime

Customs procedures and customs duty/tax payment are an integral part of cross-border operations for vehicular movement. A good agreement contains detailed structure of customs formalities starting from the entry at the zero point to the point of customs release. The agreement identifies the port of entry, articulates cross-border formalities and specifies the documents that will be needed for border crossing and also for other clearance procedures (including tax/fees/ duty structure[4] and payment mechanism). All these should help smooth customs transition. For transit traffic, customs formalities are separately stated.

Ideally, an MVA incorporates articles as regards simplification and harmonisation of the customs control procedure that also include commodity classification system. This is particularly important from the perspective of charging duties on imported goods, to reduce unnecessary procedural delays and guard against possible illegal practices of tariff evasion.

f. Revenue Requirements

An ideal MVA should charge reasonable and proportionate amounts of taxes, charges and fees, and also provide necessary exemptions[5] on road freight transports. The general practice is that only the charges applicable for the domestic vehicles are imposed on the foreign road transport of goods. These may include taxes incorporated in the price of vehicles, road charges, highway tolls and user fees for designated bridges, ferries and tunnels. However, practices vary across agreements. There are provisions for charging unsubsidised rates for fuel purchased in the host country so that the benefits enjoyed by domestic companies at the cost of national exchequer are not enjoyed by vehicles of operators from other contracting parties. Additional charges on account of building new roads, costs of road maintenance, noise and air pollution, etc., are also imposed as part of some agreements.

---

4. Many road transport agreements, both bilateral and multilateral, feature exemptions from import duties in case of temporary admissions for maintenance and recovery of vehicles, for fuel stored in tanks, spare parts of vehicles and accessories, etc. This is done to keep the corridor competitive and attractive for traders.

5. Exemptions may include taxes on ownership, registration, permit fees and other operations.

g. Facilitation Measures

Typically, an MVA may feature a priority order of clearance of goods and passengers in cases of emergency. Such clearance may take the form of clearing sick passengers first, then perishable foodstuffs, followed by livestocks, and then other merchandise (GMS-CBTA). In case of emergencies, the border clearance documents may be exchanged in advance between the customs officials of the contracting parties. In case of hazardous goods or chemical products, the ideal MVA should also specify clear instructions for handling and quarantining. If certain ports do not have quarantine facilities, the MVA may specify priority clearance of such consignments to avoid contaminating other passing cargoes.

For transport operators, standard provisions should be in place to allow establishing branch offices in the host country to ensure smooth operation and to allow opening of bank accounts for emergency remittance of funds. Interestingly, the Agreement between Macedonia, UK and Northern Ireland does not feature such facilitation measures for transport operators, although no permit authorisation is specifically required for operation.

For simple, easy and efficient border crossing formalities, an agreement can provide necessary pointers and directions to facilitate smooth border crossing formalities. The suggested measures may be completed in phases depending on capacity of partner countries and resources available. The MVA should specify gradual implementation of such frontier formality measures. These may include: (i) Single-stop inspection, (ii) Single window customs procedure, (iii) Full automation of customs procedure, (iv) Cooperation, coordination and harmonisation of documents and procedures across borders.

To execute the single window system, an MVA may propose for coordination and cooperation between the contracting parties. Coordination is desirable in case of integrating the customs process and also for matching the hours of operations of the adjacent frontier border guard authorities. The GMS-CBTA includes provision for coordination of working hours; in absence of this, vehicles may be held up for long hours waiting for the border authorities of the partner countries to begin working in tandem. This is a real problem in respect of working at Bangladesh-India border with Friday and Saturday being holidays on the Bangladesh side, and Saturday and Sunday being holidays on the Indian side.

h. Other Issues

Vehicles and their operators moving across borders must abide by applicable laws and regulations which are mentioned in the agreement. First, an MVA should state the rules and regulations that the immigrants, transport operators and vehicles (drivers) must follow while crossing the territory of the host country. Additionally, it must be specified that any laws outside the scope of the agreement will be governed by rules and regulations mutually agreed by the contracting parties. Second, there should be penalties associated with infringement of laws. Also, competent authorities of the two parties must cooperate as regards investigations concerning violations. They must also cooperate to prevent further occurrences of similar violations in future. Such provisions are included to transmit a sense of warning to the transport operators who pass through the territories of the host countries. Third, a clause on extension of validity of permit for overstay due to *force majeure* conditions may also be included. This flexibility is particularly relevant for transport operators. In some MVAs security issues are also given due attention. Lastly, provisions ought to be there to discourage movement of prohibited goods and guard against illegal trade. These should clearly forbid goods that are prohibited by the laws of the host country. This is particularly important to discourage illegal trade in drugs and prevent customs duty evasion. All international vehicular Agreements contain such provisions.

In addition, some of the other issues that a good MVA should include are: (i) issues as regards security management during border crossing and during stay of the vehicle in the host territory; (ii) institutional arrangements for coordination and implementation of the agreement[6]; (iii) dispute settlement clause to settle any issue caused by differences in interpretation of the clauses stated in the Agreement; (iv) modification, amendment and review mechanism pertaining to the Agreement; and (v) timeframe of the validity of the Agreement.

---

6.   The AFAFIST (2009) introduced the National Transit Transport Coordinating Board (NTTCB) as an agency responsible for the coordination and implementation of the agreement. It was entrusted with the responsibility of overseeing the coordination and implementation and following guidelines from other coordination bodies and ASEAN Ministerial bodies. The NTTCB was also required to come up with periodic progress reports. The ASEAN Secretariat was designated to provide assistance to the Board and also prepare evaluation reports for the Board.

Overview of the Draft MVAs

An evaluation of the bilateral Bangladesh-India MVA draft is useful in terms of identifying the strengths and weaknesses of the MVA provisions. The draft bilateral MVA (January 2012) sent by the Indian Government to the Government of Bangladesh (GoB) follows a hierarchical structure with individual chapters and articles broken further into different clauses. The draft has 17 articles under five chapters. There is provision for protocols in the agreement; these are to be prepared through mutual consent of the two negotiating countries. The draft MVA also articulates road development system, incident management system, third party liability and insurance, customs formalities and transport documentation.

Although the Ministry of the Road Transport and Highways has been identified as the relevant competent authority of India, the Bangladeshi counterpart was not been identified in the draft MVA. The relevant authority in Bangladesh should perhaps be the Ministry of Road Transport and Bridges. More bilateral consultations are needed to give final shape to the draft. The draft appears to be in its initial stage of development and lacks details on technical requirements, routes of operation and fees and charges which are to be there in the subsequent protocols. Given the fact that road conditions in the two countries are widely varying, it is felt that the draft did not address the technical requirements concerning the vehicles adequately. However, the draft does feature an institutional arrangement for effective implementation of the Agreement with a JWG to be put in place. Also, environmental impact of road transport has been given consideration which is important to promote the cause of environmental sustainability. Development of road traffic information system has also been incorporated in the draft which is important from the perspective of maintaining a secure transport system.

In line with the bilateral draft, the SAARC MVA has 17 different articles with individual titles and a preamble at the beginning. However, the articles were not structured according to chapters as in the bilateral Agreement. Despite several revisions of the SAARC MVA draft, many weaknesses still remain. In contrast to the bilateral MVA, the draft did not mention about provisions for road quality development system or environmental control. Permit forms relating to different types of transport and three annexures focusing on designated routes, competent authorities and a form for helper's document card have been added at the end of the Agreement. As in the bilateral agreement, technical requirements on the basis of varying road conditions were not adequately addressed in this agreement. Moreover, there are no provisions as regards protocols. Indeed, issues such as designated routes for selected transit traffic will need to be featured under a separate protocol. On a positive note, no quota system for road traffic has been featured in the SAARC MVA, and third country transport has been allowed. It may be noted here that, the BBIN MVA largely corresponds to the SAARC MVA, but in addition it has provision for new membership.

The major weakness in all the MVA drafts is that not enough attention has been paid to designation of frontier posts and installation of facilities at border crossings. Permit requirements also appear to be rather complicated. A comparison between the reviewed MVAs is provided in Table 2.

Table 2: Draft Agreements at a Glance

Issue	Bangladesh-India Bilateral MVA	SAARC Framework MVA	BBIN Framework MVA
Permit requirement	All vehicles	All vehicles	All vehicles
Quota restriction	Quota restricted	Unrestricted	Unrestricted
Cabotage operation	Prohibited	Prohibited	Prohibited
Special traffic exemption	No special consideration	No special consideration	No special consideration
Third country traffic	Prohibited	Allowed	Allowed
Routes of operation	Prescribed routes	Prescribed route	Prescribed route
Vehicle registration	Registration in home country	Registration in home country	Registration in home country
Driver licensing	National/international driving permit	National/international driving permit	National/international driving permit
Passenger identification	Internationally recognised travel document	Internationally recognised travel document	Internationally recognised travel document
Visa for crew members	No clause	Multiple entry valid for at least one year	Multiple entry valid for at least one year
Prohibited goods	Restricted/prohibited list of host country	Restricted/prohibited list of host country	Restricted/prohibited list of host country
Fees and charges	Independently decided by destination country	Independently decided by destination country	Independently decided by destination country

Facilitation measures for transport operators	Permission for opening branch offices and bank accounts in the other country	Permission for opening branch offices and bank accounts in any of the countries	Permission for opening branch offices and bank accounts in any of the countries
Insurance requirement	Insurance required for passenger, crew, cargo and vehicle	Insurance required for vehicle only	Insurance required for vehicle only
Right of inspection	Authority designated by government of each state	Authorised officials	Authorised officials
Environmental impact	Considered.	Not considered	Not considered
Institutional arrangement	Joint Working Group	No Joint Committees	Joint Land Transport Facilitation Committee
Inclusion of new members into the contract	Not allowed	Not allowed	Other countries will be allowed to join (perhaps China, Myanmar and others)

Note: Shaded rows indicate issues that were either not at all addressed in the MVAs or addressed in different ways.
Source: Authors' elaboration.

Bangladesh-India Bilateral MVA: An Assessment About Openness

Degree of market openness of countries as provided in the bilateral agreements may be assessed based on the scope and coverage of the operations permitted in the agreement and the rights of operation that are granted to the participating countries. Market openness in trade is especially important, because although the contracting parties may enjoy a high degree of tariff concessions from trade agreements, trade may be undermined by restrictions imposed by provisions in CBTAs in the form of Non-Tariff Barriers (NTBs). Such restrictions add to trade costs and may even erode the competitiveness gained from tariff concessions.

Openness score pertaining to bilateral MVAs is a measure of the liberty traders enjoy in terms of ability to economise on trade costs in relation to transportation, opportunity to diversify product market and expand operations. The score also takes into consideration specific facilitation measures available to the operators involved in the trading process. In this backdrop, this section attempts to undertake an assessment of the various provisions in the three MVAs under consideration: the recently signed BBIN MVA, the SAARC MVA (under consideration) and the proposed bilateral Bangladesh-India MVA. This exercise is expected to assess the potential of the agreements to generate further trade. A detailed methodology developed by the World Bank (Kunaka *et al.*, 2013), which has been widely used, was deployed in evaluating the MVAs. The methodology stipulates that for every restrictive measures articulated in the agreement, penalty points are to be deducted from the score (100 being the maximum). The scores of the three MVAs, with their ranking in reference to 77 bilateral agreements and eight multilateral agreements studied by World Bank, is presented below.

Evaluation of the BBIN MVA reveals a relatively high degree of openness compared to the other agreements. The BBIN MVA was penalised on grounds of cabotage restrictions, special authorisation in the form of permit requirement along with absence of any stipulated timeframe for permit approval, route restriction, partial tax exemptions, lack of facilitation measures for goods and vehicle transport and transparency issues. Notwithstanding the restrictions on openness, there are particular features in the agreement which do provide an opportunity for facilitated trade operations. Features such as no restrictions on any type of transport, transit facilitation measures for transport operators and institutional arrangement in the form of a JLTFC were some of the strengths of this Agreement. In reference to the 77 bilateral Agreements, the BBIN is ranked 15th (Table 3). Indeed, this conforms to BBIN's high degree of market openness which alludes to a good opportunity to make use of the agreement. In the context of the eight multilateral agreements in the World Bank database, only the GMS-CBTA received a higher score of 75. With no institutional arrangements or any Joint Committees to oversee implementation, SAARC MVA's score was rather low. Furthermore, the BBIN MVA scored high in terms of market opportunities compared to the other MVAs because of its provision to allow new members into the grouping (although this had no bearing on the openness score).

Table 3: Openness Scores of Reviewed MVAs

MVA	Openness Score	Ranking	
		Among Bilateral Agreements	Among Multilateral Agreements
Bilateral MVA	42-51	29-43	
SAARC MVA	61	18	2
BBIN MVA	64	15	2

Source: Authors' calculation based on Kunaka et al. (2013)

The proposed bilateral MVA received a score in the range of 42-51, lower compared to BBIN MVA. This lower score may be attributed, in part, to the quota system incorporated in the bilateral MVA. Owing to the ambiguity in this regard, separate partial scores were also computed. Articles 3.e and 9.1 of the bilateral MVA stipulate limitations on vehicles plying; however, the quota system was not explicitly mentioned. In case of transit traffic and quota exemption, separate partial scores were reported where maximum score was given when there was no quota limitation, while minimum score was given in case of quota restrictions. A caveat is called for here though. The quota system is a restriction to openness. However, in view of the road conditions in Bangladesh it may become necessary to allow transport movement with this restrictive provision, at least for a certain time period. It is reckoned that the quota system to be followed will be more clearly spelt out when the agreement is given final shape.

In relation to the bilateral agreements considered in the World Bank study, based on the minimum score of 42, the Bangladesh-India bilateral MVA would be ranked 43rd (44th percentile), whereas the maximum score of 51 would put the agreement at 29th position (64th percentile). This range of score, however, puts the bilateral MVA behind the average Asia-Asia bilateral agreement score of 58.[7] Compared to the other regions, the bilateral MVA scored considerably higher than the average score of Africa-Africa bilateral agreements (29). However, the minimum score was lower than the average scores of both Asia-Europe (50) and Europe-Europe bilateral agreements (51).[8]

---

7. The Asia-Asia bilateral Agreement score was based on the average score of nine such agreements in the World Bank study.

8. The World Bank study considered seven Africa-Africa bilateral agreements, 29 Asia-Europe bilateral agreements, and 18 Europe-Europe bilateral agreements.

Addressing the Weaknesses of the BBIN MVA

A dissection of the recently signed BBIN MVA helps to identify initiatives and measures that could help enhance the degree of openness. Areas that have not been adequately addressed and components that restrict openness have also been identified, and these could also be helpful in this regard (Figure 3). Following are some areas where further attention will be called for to bring in more clarity in the provisions of the agreement and to make the MVA more user-friendly:

- There is some ambiguity as regards the issue of transit. It is not explicitly mentioned whether vehicles could ply between North-East India and the rest of India through Bangladesh.
- The agreement does not spell out any plan for convergence of transport structure in the context of varying road conditions across the BBIN countries. No remedies in the form of road-wise axle load limit have been mentioned in the agreement. A protocol should be dedicated to address this concern.
- There is no reference to the development of a joint special utility vehicle (SUV) for transportation of goods in containerised vehicles. This is important to prevent damage to goods since most of the consignments are transported in open trucks in this region.
- There is a need to limit the adverse environmental impact of intensive vehicular movement. This is important from the perspective of sustainable development of the emerging post-MVA road transport system. In contrast to the Bangladesh-India MVA, these concerns have not been incorporated in the BBIN MVA.
- The agreement does not address issues of development of road infrastructure through cooperation among the BBIN members.
- The dispute settlement clause does not mention any third party arbitrator to resolve disputes in case no solution can be reached by the parties in conflict.
- Rates of taxes, fees, surcharges and the SOPs at the borders will need to feature in a separate protocol, and should be set in line with capital costs, recurring costs and the administrative expenses that are to be incurred on account of operationalising the BBIN MVA. A possible guideline here could be the principle of *benefit sharing* (in view of the significant benefits to be accrued to the operators, there is a scope to share the incremental benefits according to an agreed formula that can then be reflected in the various charges).

Figure 3: A Dissection of the BBIN MVA

Open	Needs to be Detailed Out	Restrictive
• Open for new membership • All types of vehicles permitted • Third country traffic allowed • Mutual recognition of vehicle registration • Facilities for transport operators • Insituitonal arrangemnent • Review system in place	• Standard operating procedures • Vehicle weight, axle load and dimension • Road design and construction standard • Prescribed routes • Commodity classification system • Rates of tax and fees • Transit: needs clarity • Dispute settlement clause	• Cabotage restriction • Permit requirement • Harmonisation and simplification of documentation and procedure • Measures to ease frontier crossings such as Single Window system, electronic data interchange (EDI) • No provision for priority clearence or green channel

Source: Authors' elaboration.

Indeed, some of these concerns may be subsequently addressed in the course of operationalising the BBIN MVA.

- Cabotage restriction is a restrictive component which may be gradually lifted through consultation among the contracting parties.[9]
- Review mechanism should gradually sort out the permit requirement. In its existing form, it is rather complex and needs to be addressed adequately to facilitate vehicular movement.
- Installation of frontier posts at the borders and associated facilities were not incorporated in the agreement. These may be covered by a separate protocol.
- Priority-based clearance in case of emergencies such as carrying of patients and movement of hazardous chemicals and perishable foodstuffs should be addressed in the protocols. Express way facilities or *green channels* for priority consignment may be considered in this connection.

---

9. Representatives of the Freight Forwarders' Association have pointed out that such restrictions may increase the costs of transportation for the transport operators. Indeed, this concern may compel them to stick to the practice of transshipment which will undermine the objectives of the BBIN MVA.

- The JLTFC which is responsible for effective implementation of the MVA should seriously address the issues of reducing the burden of documentation and procedural complexities. Attention should be geared to harmonisation of the involved procedures and documentation.

Operational Modalities for Implementing Cross-Border Road Transport Movement

Barriers to Cross-Border Transport Operation

This sub-section reflects information and experience gleaned from the field surveys carried out at different ports of Bangladesh for the purpose of the current study. The study has tried to identify the physical and non-physical barriers that restrict seamless movement of cross-border traffic in South Asia. This exercise is pertinent from the point of view that the proposed MVAs will need to address, tackle and resolve the attendant barriers and problems that inhibit cross-border movement of goods and people. Field experience revealed various transport-related barriers to deepening intra-regional cross-border trade, which include:

Absence of an MVA

Field visits revealed that absence of a regional MVA was perceived to be a major impediment to facilitating hassle-free cross-border movement of road transport. However, it also emerged that the involved stakeholders at the field level had only a limited knowledge as regards the MVAs and recent developments in this regard.

Port-centric Barriers (Hard, Infrastructure Issues)

Development of required infrastructure at the border areas and at the land ports was found to be a critical element for smooth cross-border vehicular movement. Among the port-specific micro-level physical problems that restrict the use of full capacity of a land port, some of the problems identified in the course of field visits are: lack of adequate space in the port area; problems of land acquisition; inadequate warehouse/shed facilities; narrow approach roads; underdeveloped internal roads; lack of weighbridge scale and other physical facilities; absence of adequate residential/working facilities for officials; lack of banking facilities within reasonable range; uninterrupted availability of telecommunication network; lack of alternate power source for automated customs processes; and absence of laboratories/ quarantine facilities.

Port-centric Barriers (Soft, Regulatory Issues)

A number of non-infrastructure related barriers, particularly relating to regulations, processes and procedures were also identified in the course of the survey. The barriers (soft) to cross-border trade and transport processes that were identified included: delay in customs procedure; documentation of cargo; documentation of trucks; legal restrictions/ barriers to trade at specific border points; and delays on the part of importers to claim products resulted in congestion and efficiency loss. Lack of cooperation of customs officials from the Indian side was also mentioned. It needs to be mentioned here that, in many land ports in Bangladesh, LCSs were established within the same administrative area but with independent functionality. Lack of coordination among the concerned authorities often led to significant delays in cross-border trade processes.

Customs Procedures

Bangladesh Customs is now using Automated System for Customs Data (ASYCUDA) World software for customs automation. In recognition of the fact that non-physical barriers are a major challenge to growth in intra-regional trade and transport, major land ports, seaports and inland container depots (ICDs) were put under the coverage of automated operations. Currently, land ports in Bangladesh are also going through phases of customs automation. Two major land ports, viz. Benapole and Hili, have come under the coverage of automation; Banglabandha Port is expected to join the network soon. In other land ports that were visited customs procedures were found to be kept in manual form and cumbersome in nature. These led to considerable time delays at the border check points. In some border points efficiency of the concerned customs officials were also questioned by the service recipients.

Implementing the MVA

In the preceding section, an attempt has been made to identify the key implementation-related barriers that inhibit the realisation of full potentials of the underlying sub-regional road transport agreement, the

BBIN MVA. The upshot of the discussion above is that, if the major hurdles are adequately addressed, the envisaged objectives of the agreement could be appropriately addressed and intra-regional trade and connectivity could be significantly improved. The purpose of initiatives such as the MVA should be to reduce hassle, allowing speedy movement of vehicles and facilitating trade and tourism. This section outlines the implementation framework needed to operationalise the newly signed BBIN MVA.

Preparation for Operationalisation

It has been noted earlier that, a six-month work plan has been agreed upon by the four member countries, with time-bound goalposts. The protocols and the SOPs will need to be designed in a manner that facilitates the implementation of the BBIN MVA. For preparing the needed protocols and SOPs, the implementing agencies may consult with international best practices such as the GMS-CBTA.

Formulation of protocols in the areas of identification of potential corridors and routes, specification of the technical requirements of vehicles, setting up of the structure of taxes and fees, documentation and procedures, development of frontier cross formalities and customs clearance regime will call for particular attention. An Expert Group Meeting may be conducted with participation of different stakeholder groups. The Expert Group Meeting could help identify suitable corridors, and measures to facilitate vehicular movement and movement of people along those corridors. They would also identify ways and means to maximise the potential benefits of the MVA. In the context of establishing technical specifications, consideration needs to be given to the state of varying road conditions in the sub-region. Specifications should be articulated in a route-specific manner based on road capacities. Whilst designing the taxes and fee structure, factors that will need to be considered should include cost recovery, efficiency in collection of the charges, sharing of potential benefits, revenue concerns and the opportunity cost of alternative modes of transport. A detailed plan of action as regards formulation of the needed protocols is provided in the Section 5.

Following the drafting of protocols, opinions of different Ministries may be sought for vetting purposes. This will require establishment of a coordination mechanism with inclusion of key stakeholders involved. When the country positions are finalised, negotiations among partners can begin for a comprehensive and coordinated sub-regional stance.

Institutional Strengthening

Along with measures to facilitate implementation of the MVA on the ground, initiatives will need to be taken to strengthen both adequate institutional and human resources to help operationalise the MVA in an adequate way. Imparting of technical knowledge to the staff at border points will be critically important. Given the timeframe of only six months, a dedicated team should be set up to execute the drafting of the protocols and to complete the preparatory works. The NLTFC, composed representative of individual Ministries and Departments in each of the member countries is responsible for drafting of the protocols. Strengthening of the NLTFC will call for inclusion of appropriate representatives from the involved Ministries, close cooperation among the Ministries, effective allocation of human, technical and financial resources and improved capacity of relevant agencies. Technical assistance may be sought from international organisations, such as the ADB, in the drafting process.

Issues of Financing and Financial Institutions

Indeed, a major implementation-related challenge concerns mobilisation of adequate financial resources to underwrite the costs for the needed upgradation of roads to four-six lane high-quality expressways, and also for improvement of facilities at land ports. One may recall that Rahmatullah (2012) have identified 17 road sections within Bangladesh which required immediate rehabilitation that called for an investment requirement of about Tk. 12,000 crore (US$ 1.5 billion). An additional Tk. 200 crore (US$ 25.2 million) was also estimated for land port development.

The study team also assessed the cost of upgradation of important road sections within the Bangladesh territory along three of the possible routes that may be incorporated in the BBIN MVA. The assessment was based on the reference value of Tk. 25-30 crore (about US$ 3.7 million) of investment requirement for upgradation of one km of roads to international standard. The summary is presented in Table 4.

Table 4: Investment Required to Upgrade Important Road Sections
within Bangladesh

Routes and Road Sections	Estimated Investment (US$ billion)
Banglabandha to Chittagong Port	1.6
Banglabandha to Mongla Port (excluding common road sections)	1.1
Burimari to Mongla or Chittagong Port (excluding common road sections)	0.5
Benapole to Dhaka	0.8

Source: Authors' estimation.

The investment required to upgrade Bangladesh road section for two of the important routes connecting Kathmandu to Chittagong/Mongla and Thimphu to Chittagong is estimated to be US$ 3.27 billion. An additional US$ 0.8 billion is estimated for upgradation of the Benapole to Dhaka section of the Benapole to Agartala route. It may be noted here that, in the context of the BBIN MVA, seven important road projects have been identified that may be prioritised for operationalising the MVA.[10]

A suitable financing strategy must be developed by the GoB and governments of other member countries. Among many other options, the GoB may earmark certain priority projects to private sector/international agencies/entities on a public-private partnership (PPP) basis. There will be a need to prioritise and fast track the most important projects and look out for assistance from international funding agencies, in addition to resources generated from the domestic economy. A joint BBIN infrastructure fund may also be established. A part of the proposed US$ 2 billion Indian line of credit (LoC) can also be deployed toward this. Fees and tax structure must be integrated with the investment plan so that the cost can be recouped over the years of operation of the relevant services. The government should also design a comprehensive fees collection strategy to prevent revenue leakages and also enhance the efficiency of fees/charges collection. Digitisation and automation at all stages should be the catchwords.

Financial institutions of the region including banks and insurance companies can play a proactive role in coordinating efforts to mobilise

10. These road projects include the four-laneing of Dhaka-Chittagong highway; four-laneing of Joydebpur-Elenga-Hatikamrul-Banglabandha/Burimari road; the Padma Multipurpose Bridge Project and four-laneing of connecting roads; four-laneing of Jessore-Benapole road; Kantchpur (2nd Phase); construction of Meghna and Gomoti Bridge; four-laneing of Dhaka-Sylhet-Tamabil-Jaflong and four-laneing of Baraiyarhat-Ramgarh road.

the needed financial resources. These actions are necessary both from the perspective of long-term investment, and also to conduct day-to-day smooth operation regarding transport movement.

Addressing Security Concerns

Incident management system and road traffic information system embedded in the Bangladesh-India bilateral MVA may be replicated while operationalising the BBIN MVA. Measures such as installation of tracking equipment in vehicles are already included in the agreement. Road traffic information system will facilitate easy detection of vehicles and drivers in case of violation of law, while the incident management system will facilitate rapid actions in case of emergencies or accidents and pave way for smooth traffic by mitigating the consequences of accident. Also, security check posts need to be established along the sections of the road that are included in the BBIN MVA route. In this case, adequate Border Guards Bangladesh (BGB), Ansar Guards and police mobilisation will be required.

To ensure the security of transit goods, financial guarantee document may be incorporated as a pre-requisite. Financial guarantee document will be deposited at the point of entry of a transit country, and will only be released to the trucks at the exit point of the same country after unloading the goods in the destination territory.

Amendments of Legal Framework

Existing policies in the participating countries will need to be seriously evaluated and necessary reviews should be carried out and if required amendments should be made to national policies for these to be integrated with the BBIN MVA regulations. In this context, existing road transport legislation will need to be reviewed (Motor Vehicle Ordinance, 1983 for Bangladesh) and updated through necessary amendments. Some of concerned areas in this context are vehicle registration requirements, axle load limits and vehicle dimensions, driver licensing requirements and road traffic regulations. Protocols and conventions on cross-border road traffic movement will need to be developed. Agencies such as the Ministry of Road Transport and Bridges, Ministry of Shipping and the Customs Wing of the NBR will have to work closely with a view to design the necessary protocols and conventions. International conventions for cross-border traffic movement will need to be ratified by the participating countries. Harmonisation issues in case of road traffic law enforcement and also customs regime will need to be addressed.

Joint Collaboration

Various institutional arrangements will need to be put in place to facilitate implementation of the BBIN MVA. Joint institutions that will need to be developed to facilitate Bangladesh-India trade has been highlighted in Section 2. A collaboration mechanism will have to be developed among the four countries to address the issue of simplification and harmonisation of rules and regulations and to promote investment in infrastructure development. The BBIN MVA directed the proposed Joint Land Transport Facilitation Committee (JLTFC) to harmonise the different standards of operation existing in the four countries. Harmonisation of traffic legislation may not always enhance the efficiency of cross-border movements, particularly if the harmonisation induces conflict among members due to differences in national legislations (Nick Poree and Associates, 2010). Movement of motor vehicles is generally regulated by respective national laws and regulations, and harmonisation of these will need to be done very carefully. Harmonisation will mean identifying common elements or withdrawing some components and replacing those with new ones. Some members could feel that harmonisation of documentation and procedures and transport law enforcement would mean erosion of the power of their own national laws and regulations. Thus, these will need to be dealt with due sensitivity.

Harmonisation is difficult to achieve particularly because the contracting parties have to come to common terms with respect to the issue of enforcement of transport law. This is reflected in the lack of harmonisation of rules, legislation and procedures evident in many of the international bilateral and multilateral Agreements; this continues to remain a concern in many of the existing CBTAs. In this respect, the EU serves as the best example of harmonisation of legislation. According to the UNESCAP (United Nations Economic and Social Commission for Asia and the Pacific) guidelines, the process of harmonisation can be done by way of three possible routes: legal transplantation, legal harmonisation and legal unification. The EU countries have gone for all the three processes. In case of transport, harmonisation refers to setting common standards for technical requirements for vehicles, driver and crew formalities, etc. Legal unification has also been adopted by the ASEAN in the ASEAN Framework Agreement of Multimodal Transport

(2005). Harmonisation thus obligates the contracting parties to go for joint collaboration to settle disputes and conflicts arising on different grounds. It is important to note that, for effective implementation of initiatives and agreements such as the BBIN MVA, political commitment at the highest level is an essential pre-requisite. Once this is guaranteed, other things generally tend to fall in place. The EU is the best example of this.

Cross-Border Management and Use of ICT

To manage cross-border movement in a coherent and comprehensive manner, development of adequate infrastructure and use of information and communication technology (ICT) must be put at the forefront of the implementation design. In many regional arrangements, use of single window system and EDI at border crossing points is a common practice. ASEAN countries have developed regional single window along with respective national single windows. In a single window system all documentation and cross-border formalities are carried out at a dedicated one-stop point which helps avoid duplication and reduces clearance time significantly.

Challenges of single window should also be kept in mind and be adequately addressed. Some of the concerns relate to the following:
- A single point of access could also mean a single point of failure,
- Security and ownership of trade data,
- Duplication of technical modules, features and functionalities between a centralised single window and the various national single windows,
- Designated authorities to operate the centralised single window within the sub-region,
- Cost sharing between national single window and centralised single window, and
- To act with impartiality.

In some of the CBTAs conflicts have arisen because of diverse approach and attitude towards the above on the part of respective authorities of the participating countries.

Enabling Implementation Environment

An ongoing mechanism should be in place to monitor the implementation of the BBIN MVA. This would involve two types of monitoring: process monitoring and outcome monitoring. Process monitoring would ensure smooth functioning of the MVA, whilst outcome monitoring will assess, as to whether the results are commensurate with expectations.

Changing Dynamics of the 'Actors' Involved in Cross-Border Movement
Evidently, the MVA will rope in new actors in the SAARC intra-regional trade process. The reducing time delay and trade costs will depend on the efficacy of delivery of the services of the relevant factors involved in the vehicular movement processes. Importance of the Road Transport and Highways Division (RTHD) of the Ministry of Road Transport and Bridges, the signatory of the BBIN MVA, will rise significantly. The representatives of the RTHD in the JLTFC will have to coordinate with their counterparts of the other BBIN countries to establish the routes that will come under the coverage. The RTHD and the BRTA will be actively involved in setting the road charges, highway tolls and other charges that are applicable for vehicular movement on Bangladesh's territory. Considering the diversity in road infrastructure between participating countries, technical specification and road traffic rules will need to be harmonised through coordination by the BRTA. For transport law enforcement, security agencies such as the BGB, Ansar, Bangladesh Police, etc., will need to be adequately prepared. Check posts for inspection of vehicles coming from other countries will have to be set up along the routes authorised for movement. This will require deployment of considerable forces by these agencies. In this respect, the government will have to establish a designated authority for inspection and approval of the vehicles. The government will also need to take up the responsibility to develop the infrastructure of roads and ports so as to ensure smooth flow of traffic. In this case, the RHD, under the RTHD will play a key role. It will be the responsibility of the government to ensure that transport operators, customs officers and security agencies are adequately prepared to implement the various provisions of the MVA. It will also be important that all the relevant actors and agencies involved in the implementation of the MVA take their own initiatives to do the needful in this context. This will in turn require significant strengthening of institutional and human resource capacities of all involved agencies.

While the MVA will increase importance of some government agencies, there may be a declining importance of some of the traditional actors at the LCSs. If unimpeded traffic movement is allowed through the MVA, some of the functions at the LCSs will likely decline, for example, warehouse, storage and truck terminal facilities will become largely redundant. Workers, loading-unloading operators may be adversely affected since cargo handling at the port will also become unnecessary. Transport operators may face difficulty to adjust to the emerging changes. Without cabotage provision and import consignments on the return journey, transport operators will need to adjust the rent of transporting trade consignments (upwards) to maintain profitability. All these may give rise to opposition, conflicts and disputes. These must be handled intelligently and with understanding. Alternative measures should be put in place to mitigate adverse implications. However, experience shows that, many new employment opportunities tend to emerge once MVAs are put into motion, particularly in construction and transport services areas. Negative effects are likely to be short-term though. Nonetheless, there will be a need to deal with possible difficulties of affected groups with sensitivity and care.

Conclusions and Recommendations

As the preceding sections have shown, there are three MVAs on the table at present where Bangladesh is a party. The BBIN MVA has been concluded in June 2015.[11] The SAARC MVA is expected to be concluded in the near future. The draft of the Bangladesh-India MVA has been there for quite some time and following the decision to set up a Joint Task Force on Connectivity, this may be brought back to the table once again. All the three MVAs will need to be seen and dealt with in a coordinated and comprehensive manner. Indeed, by all counts, the time for 'Connectivity' appears to have arrived in South Asia. With the signing of the BBIN MVA, issues of deepening transport connectivity in the BBIN sub-region have assumed both currency and urgency, and have gained heightened importance. There is also an increasing need for the MVA to be implemented in a way that ensures maximisation of potential benefits. As has been elaborated in the earlier sections, several developments are in the offing which will need to be coordinated with the MVAs. Investments in both infrastructure development

---

11. It is to be noted that, the first meeting after signing of the BBIN MVA has been held on 8-9 September 2015, in Dhaka. Protocol for passenger vehicle movement was to be finalised by 23 September 2015. Home Secretaries were to meet in the first week of October 2015 in Dhaka to ease visa formalities. ADB was to provide technical-financial support to set up electronic tracking system. BBIN Car Rally was to be held in the second week of November 2015. To test cargo vehicular movement, pilot trips were to be organised in the initial period, to be followed by finalisation of the protocols.

and also developments in the areas of trade facilitation and border crossing will need to be synchronised with MVA-related initiatives. Plans for developing railways and waterways and in the context of investments in connection with the Asian Highway and Trans-Asian Railway will need to be coordinated with MVA-related investments to ensure the seamless multimodal connectivity. Indeed, the routes of operationalisation of the MVAs should be considered as economic corridors that operate in a seamless manner. Development of river and sea ports and building of bridges will thus need to be coordinated with the operationalisation of the MVAs.

The task at hand at present is to operationalise the MVA with concrete steps including preparation of the protocols and SOPs, setting up the needed institutions, building human resources and undertaking the needed investment. Another important task is to ensure harmonisation of standards and procedures across borders and countries. The proposed NLTFC will be expected to take the lead in implementing the roadmap that the Ministers have agreed for the first six months (July-December, 2015).

It is hoped that MVA will have both direct and indirect economy-wide positive impact and externalities. The present study has pointed out that transport connectivity is at the centre of all four types of connectivities, namely trade, investment, transport and people-to-people connectivity. Various studies have undertaken quantitative exercises that show that significant gains could originate from the MVAs in the form of reduced lead-time, producers' benefits and consumers' welfare, cost reduction and increase in competitiveness.

The benefits of BBIN MVA are high also because it entails three types of movements: cargo vehicle; passenger carrying transport; and personal vehicles. However, these potential benefits will be accrued only if the needed tasks are addressed with due urgency and due diligence. The present study has made an attempt to anticipate these tasks taking cue from the aforesaid roadmap and the best practices. The experience of the GMS-CBTA was particularly relevant in this context. In view of the above, the study has articulated a number of tasks that are to be executed at the Bangladesh end.

The first task concerns preparation and adoption of the protocols and SOPs. International best practices may be consulted for this purpose. Priority attention will need to be given to identification of key routes, specification of technical requirements and axle specification of vehicles, harmonisation and standardisation of documentation and Agreement on coordination of border crossing formalities and customs clearance formalities, permissions and permits. Whilst in case of the Bangladesh, Bhutan and Nepal market access in India was duty-free, in other cases border crossing by vehicles, for the purpose of trade, will call for collection of customs duties. Thus, customs clearance facilities will also be critical in terms of ensuring smooth crossing of borders. Inter-Ministerial coordination within the country and reaching consensus on key aspects of protocols and SOPs across countries are the major challenges in this context.

The second task relates to mobilisation of the needed financial resources. This is particularly crucial since operationalising the MVA will entail significant investment in developing the needed road infrastructure (e.g. the BBIN Ministerial meeting has come up with the estimates of an investment requirement of US$ 8 billion for development of the identified 30 priority projects within the BBIN areas, of which seven are in Bangladesh). Financing of the border crossing infrastructure at the LCSs including building of single windows, putting in place EDI facilities and speedy customs clearance (including green channel and priority lanes of emergency vehicular movement and movement of vehicles with perishable goods) will also require significant resources. Both traditional financing institutions (World Bank, ADB) as well as new ones (Asian Infrastructure Investment Bank (AIIB), BRICS Development Bank[12]) are expected to contribute to this. Financial institutions including insurance companies of the participating countries will play an important role in this respect. Issue of long-term infrastructure bonds and promotion of public private partnerships could also play a positive role in mobilising the needed funds.

The third important task will entail strengthening of the relevant institutions with well-endowed human resources. MVAs are new to Bangladesh. Institutions will need to develop the required capacities to deal with attendant issues in the areas of development, coordination, harmonisation and standardisation of the protocols and SOPs, dispute settlement, fixation of fees, service charges and surcharges among others.

The fourth task, which is of critical importance, relates to fixation of fees, surcharges and user-charges. These will need to be fixed in a manner that ensures cost-recovery. Here, benefit sharing could be a key strategic approach for Bangladesh. Compensatory mechanisms to take care of

---

12. Now known as the New Development Bank (NDB)

subsidised fuel prices for refuelling of vehicles from other countries have been mentioned in the BBIN MVA. It will be important to come to at an agreed modality for fixing the fuel prices in this regard. The rates will also need to be competitive and take care of the opportunity cost. Reciprocity in allowing flexibilities will also need to be taken care of, as also support provided by partner countries to develop the infrastructure.

The fifth task will entail coordination among Ministries, alignment with connectivity strategies and allocations envisaged in the Five Year Plans and the Annual Development Programme (ADP) of Bangladesh. Formulation of a 'Comprehensive Regional Connectivity and Investment Plan' will also be called for. Such a plan will have to be coordinated with development of all transport/connectivity-related investment including development of road, waterways, railways, ports and border infrastructure.[13] Such an integrated approach will reduce costs, raise investment efficiency and enhance potential benefits. Development of containerised vehicular movement will also need to be aligned with investments to implement the MVA.

The sixth task relates to ensuring security of persons, vehicles and cargo during in-country movement and border crossing. Incident management system and road information system may be introduced to ensure security through installation of tracking equipment and vehicle and driver detection system, as also for safeguarding against violation of law and addressing and mitigating consequences of accidents and vehicular malfunctioning. Containerised vehicular movement, under seal, will need to be promoted and security check posts with adequate human resources will need to be deployed at border crossing points.

The seventh task, to be undertaken particularly by the private sector in Bangladesh, will entail development of business models whereby Bangladeshi operators can maximise the potential benefits accruing from the commercial and business activities which will be encouraged and stimulated consequent to operationalisation of the BBIN MVA.

---

13. The meeting in Dhaka held on 8-9 September 2015 has prioritised six routes for the purpose of BBIN MVA: (i) Kolkata-Benapole-Jessore-Dhaka-Chittagong; (ii) Chittagong-Dhaka-Hatikamrul-Bogra-Rangpur-Burimari-Shiliguri; (iii) Chittagong-Dhaka-Hatikamrul-Bogra-Rangpur-Burimari-Changrabandha-Jaigaon-Fuentling-Thimphu; (iv) Dhaka-Rangpur-Banglabandha-Phulbari-Panitank-Kakurvita-Kathmandu; (v) Kolkata-Dhaka Sarail-Sylhet-Tamabil-Dawki-Shilong-Gowhati-Samdrup Jongkhar; and (vi) Khulna-Jessore-Benapole-Kolkata.

It will be important for the BBIN MVA members to carefully assess the issue of inclusion of new members which has been provisioned in the Agreement. An appropriate Dispute Settlement Mechanism (DSM) will also need to be set up, with a clear and transparent ToR and mandate.

Participating countries will need to undertake a number of tasks, on an urgent basis, if the expected benefits originating from the BBIN MVA are to be reaped by producers, exporters, consumers and citizens of the countries of the sub-region.

The agreement has already been ratified by Bangladesh, India and Nepal; it is hoped that it will come into force once this is ratified by Bhutan where it has been passed by the Lower House of the Parliament and awaiting clearance in the Upper House.

Simultaneously, steps are being taken to finalise the Protocols. As of now, the Passenger Protocol is in a relatively advanced stage of negotiation. The Protocol includes regular (e.g. bus service), non-regular (e.g. occasional services during festivities) and personal (individual traveller) vehicular movement. The Cargo Protocol has made some progress with India making a trial run in Bangladesh (DHL and Bata being the conduits); Bangladesh is expected to do the same with respect to India. Once the experience of these trial runs are reviewed, and the necessary incorporations made, the Cargo Protocol will be finalised, hopefully at the next meeting of the concerned officials.

There is, thus, a need to undertake a number of additional measures to finalise the Protocols and to operationalise the BBIN-MVA. Proactive engagement of all concerned parties will be necessary to move the process forward with the urgency it deserves.

References

ADB. (2008). *Transport Infrastructure and Trade Facilitation in the Greater Mekong Subregion – Time to Shift Gears.* ADB Evaluation Study Reference Number: SAP: REG: 2008-86. Manila: Asian Development Bank (ADB)

ADB and AusAID. (2013). *Progress Report on Transport and Trade Facilitation Initiatives in the Greater Mekong Subregion.* Manila: South Asian Department, Asian Development Bank (ADB).

Banomyong, R. (2008). *Logistics Development in the North–South Economic Corridor of the Greater Mekong Subregion.* Bangkok: Center for Logistics Research.

Banomyong, R. (2013). The Greater Mekong Sub-region of Southeast Asia in J.H. Bookbinder (ed.) *Handbook of Global Logistics: Transportation in International Supply Chains.* New York: Springer.

CIE. (2010). *Economic Benefits of Trade Facilitation in the Greater Mekong Subregion.* Australia: Centre for International Economics (CIE)

Cousin, L. and Y. Duval (2014). *Trade Facilitation Potential of Asian Transit Agreements in the context of the WTO Negotiations.* TID Working Paper No. 01/14. Bangkok: ESCAP Trade and Investment Division.

De, P. and B.N. Bhattacharyay (2007). *Prospects of India-Bangladesh Bilateral Economic Cooperation: Implications for South Asian Regional Cooperation.* ADBI Discussion Paper 78. Tokyo: Asian Development Bank Institute (ADBI).

Hansen, P. and L. Annovazzi-Jakab (2008). *The Global Enabling Trade Report.* Geneva: World Economic Forum (WEF).

Hossain, S. M. (2009). *South Asian Free Trade Area: Implications for Bangladesh.* MPRA Paper No. 18517

Islam, D. M. (2003). *The Potential of Developing through Freight Transportation System for Cross Border Trade: The Case of Bangladesh.* Retrieved from: http://www.gfptt.org/sites/default/files/refread/bf3a4178-0194-4abe-a88e-f1cedb8c0547.doc (accessed on 30 June 2015).

Kunaka, C., V. Tanase, P. Latrille, and P. Krausz (2013). *Quantitative Analysis of Road Transport Agreements (QuARTA).* Washington, D. C.: The World Bank.

Miankhel, A. K. (2011). *Audit of Trade Facilitation Measures for Enhancing Pakistan Light Engineering and Made up Articles Exports to ECO countries.* Draft Report. Retrieved from: http://www.nttfc.org/reports/natrpts/Trade%20facilitation%20by%20Adil%20K%20Miankhel_311011.doc (accessed on 3 June 2015).

Nick Poree and Associates. (2010). *Facilitation of Road Transport Market Liberalisation in the SADC Region,* final report. Gaborone: South African Development Community (SADC).

Raballand, G., C. Kunaka, and B. Giersing, (2008). *The Impact of Regional Liberalization and Harmonization in Road Transport Services: A Focus on Zambia and Lessons for Landlocked Countries.* Policy Research Working Paper 4482. Washington, D. C.: The World Bank.

Rahman, M. (2012). *Trade-related Issues in the Bangladesh-India Joint Communiqué: Maximinisng Bangladesh's Benefits and Strategies for the Future.* Governance Working Paper 23145. Canberra: East Asian Bureau of Economic Research, Australian National University.

Rahman, M. and K. Akhter. (2014). *Trade Facilitation towards Export Promotion in the Indian market: Addressing the Emerging Gaps.* CPD Research Monograph 8. Dhaka: Centre for Policy Dialogue (CPD).

Rahmatullah, M. (2009). *Regional connectivity: Opportunities for Bangladesh to be a transport hub.* Journal of Bangladesh Institute of Planners, 2: 13-29. Retrieved from: http://www.banglajol.info/index.php/JBIP/article/view/9553/7079 (accessed on 3 June 2015).

Rahmatullah, M. (2010). Transport issues and integration in South Asia in S. Ahmed, S. Kelegama and E. Ghani (eds.) *Promoting Economic Cooperation in South Asia: Beyond SAFTA.* Washington, D. C.: The World Bank and New Delhi: SAGE Publication India Pvt. Ltd.

Rahmatullah, M. (2012). *Operationalisation of Regional Connectivity between Bangladesh, India, Nepal and Bhutan, including strategic infrastructure development to that end.* New Delhi: Indian Council for Research on International Economic Relations (ICRIER).

Rahmatullah, M. (2013). *Regional transport connectivity: Its current state.* The Daily Star, 20 March. Retrieved from: http://archive.thedailystar.net/beta2/news/its-current-state (accessed on 24 February 2015).

SAARC Secretariat. (2006). *SAARC Regional Multimodal Transport Study.* Kathmandu: SAARC Secretariat.

Scheerlinck, I., L.M.A Hens, and R. S'Jegers, (1998). *On the Road to Transport Liberalization: Belgian Road Haulers Policy Preferences.* Journal of Transport Economics and Policy, 32 (3): 365-376.

Smith, G. (2009). *Bangladesh: Transport Policy Note.* Final Draft. Transport Unit, Sustainable Development Department, South Asia Region. The World Bank. Mimeo.

Stone, S. and A. Strutt (2009). *Transport Infrastructure and Trade Facilitation in the Greater Mekong Subregion. ADBI Working Paper Series 130.* Tokyo: Asian Development Bank Institute (ADBI).

Thapar, K. L. (2009). *Forging Efficient and Economic Transport Logistics: Case Study India-Bangladesh*. Presentation made at a seminar on Overcoming Border Crossing Obstacles, 5-6 March, Paris.

Teravaninthorn, S. and G. Raballand (2009). *Transport Price and Costs in Africa: A Review of the Main International Corridors*. Washington, D. C.: The World Bank.

Wiemer, C. (2009). *Economic Corridor for the GMS*. EAI Background Brief 2009 No. 479. Singapore: East Asian Institute (EAI), National University of Singapore.

Wilson, J., C.L. Mann, and T. Otsuki (2004). *Assessing the Potential Benefit of Trade Facilitation: A Global Perspective*. World Bank Policy Research Working Paper 3224. Washington, D. C.: The World Bank.

World Bank. (2007). *People's Republic of Bangladesh Revival of Inland Water Transport: Options and Strategies*. Bangladesh Development Series Paper No. 20. Dhaka: The World Bank Office.

World Bank. (n.d.). *Bangladesh Transport Sector Review*. Dhaka: The World Bank Office. Mimeo.

SIX

BBIN MVA: GOOD BEGINNING BUT MANY CHALLENGES

Prabir De

Introduction

Three decades passed away since we agreed upon the South Asian Association for Regional Cooperation (SAARC); however, progress on the regional trade at the ground level has been rather limited.[1] At the same time, the ongoing political tension between some of the member countries of SAARC compels the rest of South Asian countries, particularly the geographically contiguous South Asia in the eastern part, to form a subregional initiative centering India that would help them to raise and solve the subregional economic and political challenges being faced by them. Also known as South Asian Growth Quadrangle (SAGQ), the Bangladesh, Bhutan, India and Nepal (BBIN), is a unique initiative, importance of which was felt by many commentators and organisations in the past.[2] Started between Bhutan, Bangladesh and India in late of the last decade, this sub-regional cooperation received further impetus once Nepal joined the group. BBIN today has received further impetus through several economic integration initiatives. Being part of SAARC as well as BIMSTEC, its multi-dimensional presence is crucial for success of both the integration initiatives. Being an integral part of India's Neighborhood First policy, BBIN is the "Bridgehead" in the Bay of Bengal area, which links South Asia with greater Southeast Asia and vice versa. In view of the above, this chapter discusses the challenges and opportunities in BBIN Initiative and presents a set of recommendations to take forward the integration ahead.

---

1. Till 2014, intra-regional trade was 5 per cent, making it world's one of the least integrated regions.

2. Refer, for example, Dubey *et al*. (1999), Ray and De (2003), etc. The SASEC initiative of the Asian Development Bank (ADB) has been drawn upon the South Asia sub-regional cooperation, which was launched by ADB in 2001.

Progress So Far

Countries out of the slow progress of SAARC have realised that narrowing the connectivity gaps among countries is must for facilitating regional trade. Not only trade, an improved connectivity is essential to provide cheaper access to goods and services, create more jobs including along trading corridors, and ultimately help reduce poverty at a faster pace.[3] BBIN initiative, therefore, has emphasised on building connectivity from its beginning. As a result, we find that the shared vision of BBIN is to increase trade and cooperation within eastern South Asia, create linkages within and beyond, ensure faster movement of goods and people, sustainable development through water resource management and protection of climate, etc. Mainly driven by the governmental activities with regular meetings of the Joint Working Groups (JWGs)[4], the BBIN initiative so far has dealt with water resources management, electricity exchange, and connectivity. Till date, three meetings of JWGs were held and the outcomes have been very positive. It is the BBIN Motor Vehicles Agreement (MVA) that has triggered the BBIN initiative.

The JWG on Water Resources Management and Power/Hydropower has the mandate of power trade and inter-grid connectivity cooperation in future power projects and water resources management between the four countries. The JWG on Connectivity and Transit looks after the BBIN MVA. At the 3rd JWG meeting, held in Dhaka on 19-20 January 2016, it has been agreed to commence discussion on the possibility of having a BBIN Rail Agreement drawing on the draft SAARC Regional Rail Agreement template. It was also agreed that land ports/ land customs stations crucial for sub-regional trade and transit would be given priority attention by all four countries.[5] Advantage of BBIN is that by starting late, it has learned from the mistakes of other regional integration initiatives. Illustrated in Table 1, BBIN's focus is not in the trade and investment agreement but in non-trade issues such as connectivity, energy, etc.

---

3. A great deal of works has been done by several scholars, commentators and practitioners. Refer, for example, Rahmatullah (2004, 2010), RIS (2008), Kathuria (2014).

4. BBIN has two JWGs such as Water Resources Management and Power/Hydropower, and Connectivity and Transit. The third meeting of the JWGs was held in Dhaka on 19-20 January 2016.

5 Refer, http://www.mea.gov.in/press-releases.htm?51/Press_Releases

Table 1: Features of BBIN

Particulars	BBIN	BCIM	BIMSTEC	SAARC	ASEAN
Location	South Asia	South - South East Asia	South - South East Asia	South Asia	South East Asia
Members	4	4	7	8	10
Year established	2013	1997	1997	1985	1967
FTA signed	No	No	Yes*	Yes	Yes
Investment agreement	No	No	No	No	Yes
Services trade agreement	No	No	Yes*	Yes**	Yes
Connectivity projects	Yes	Yes*	Yes*	Yes	Yes
Energy exchange	Yes	No	Yes*	Yes*	Yes*
Financial integration	No	No	No	Yes*	Yes
Trade facilitation	Yes	No	Yes	Yes	Yes
Initiative type	Track 1	Track 1.5	Track 1	Track 1	Track 1
Secretariat	No	No	Yes	Yes	Yes

Note: *Proposed.
Source: De (2016).

Trade Facilitation Priorities and Needs in BBIN

BBIN countries are relatively open economies, where, with the exception of Nepal, trade openness has increased during 1991 to 2014. India contributes to over 90 per cent of the sub-regional trade. In 2014, India's total export to BBIN was about US$ 11.7 billion, of which US$ 8.7 billion was export and remaining was import.[6] The trend in intra-BBIN trade has been influenced by recent growth of the Indian economy and the India's unilateral removal of tariff and sensitive list items for the least developed countries (LDCs) in recent years. Since a large part of BBIN's trade is India-centric, any improvement of connectivity and trade facilitation in the sub-region would, therefore, will lead to improving the competitiveness of BBIN export, thereby providing higher market access to exports of Bangladesh, Bhutan, and Nepal in India. BBIN MVA is primarily designed to serve this purpose

---

6.   Data source is Director of Trade Statistics (DOTS), International Monetary Fund (IMF).

– facilitate sub-regional trade, people to people contact and integration. However, the reality is that the BBIN countries are yet to connect each other through a comprehensive trade facilitation and connectivity measure. BBIN has a number of logistics handicaps. Except trade between India and Nepal and India and Bhutan, India's trade with Bangladesh or Bangladesh's trade with Bhutan and Nepal is not seamless. Goods are loaded or unloaded every time at the land border. Transit of goods exists, but partially.[7] Railways or inland waterways have been used for regional trade marginally. Roads are narrow with missing last-mile connectivity. Banking and financial instruments are weak, making pre- and post- shipment payment lengthy. Also adequate infrastructure is not available. For example, electricity is available at the border, but the quality of electricity varies. Trade in BBIN, therefore, continues to face higher costs and time.

Table 2 presents business procedures, time and costs in export and import and documents needed while carrying trade along select BBIN corridors. Trade involves a relatively higher number of procedures and documents in all the three BBIN corridors. Specifically, exports of oranges from Bhutan to Bangladesh face the highest number of procedures and second highest number of parties in corridor 2, whereas export of lentils from Nepal to Bangladesh witnesses the second highest number of procedures but highest number of parties in corridor 1. Corridor 3 is the most expensive corridor, both in terms of cost and time. A container load of carpets exported from Kathmandu to a third country costs around US$ 2260.60 per TEU and takes about 24 days to cover a distance of 1287 km to reach the port of Kolkata. The more time-consuming the export or import process is, the less likely it is that a trader in the BBIN will be able to compete in the regional and international markets.

Application of modern information and communication technology (ICT) to trade processes has been recognised as an important component of national and regional trade facilitation strategies. Many of the export and import documents along BBIN corridors are still not being submitted and/ or processed electronically. Submission of documents is largely handled manually (over 80 per cent of trade documents on average).[8] Exporters and importers (or their customs house agent (CHAs)) can submit customs

---

7. Refer, for example, De and Kumar (2014).
8. Refer, for example, ADB-ESCAP (2014).

declaration online, although a hard copy also often needs to be submitted at some point during the process. Automation of trade documentation is relatively a new process in BBIN except India. India has been successful in introducing an Electronic Data Interchange (EDI) system, called ICEGATE, which to a great extent has facilitated the submission of trade documents electronically.[9] The scope for application of ICT in trade process management in BBIN countries, particularly in Bhutan, Bangladesh and Nepal, is very large. Application of ICT in managing trade processes in India has gained immense popularity since the exporters and importers have found it increasingly beneficial. While the documents required for export and import were handled manually till only a few years back, today most of the export processes are dealt with electronically. Similar trends have been noticed in some South Asian countries like Maldives and Sri Lanka. Cargo insurance and payment are managed electronically in many of the BBIN countries, including India. The number of documents per se does not matter, but rather their nature (electronic vs. paper) and the procedures involved in their preparation and submission that make a difference. By making e-filling of documents mandatory, the documentary burden on the trade of goods along the BBIN corridors will be reduced undoubtedly. India's EDI system is a case in point, which offers important lessons to other BBIN countries to improve their electronic customs system.

Excessive documentation gives a scope for simplification of trade processes. The entire trade process becomes very cumbersome. Between export and import, the import process is highly dispersed, thereby indicating the need for simplification of documentary requirements. There is enough scope for simplification of documentary requirements and aligning the system with international standards. Besides, building highways, improving border infrastructure facilities, strengthening banking and financial infrastructure, establishing governance transparency along with trade facilitation measures would improve the competitiveness of BBIN countries globally. At the same time, the implementation of MVA would depend on the financial and technical capacity of the BBIN countries.

To meet the global and regional/sub-regional obligations, BBIN countries have to improve trade performance through enhanced trade

9. ICEGATE handles all e-filing, e-payments, drawback disbursal and message exchange with stakeholders -almost 98 per cent India's international trade. ICEGATE web portal provides comprehensive real time tracking and information services, and all services are provided free of cost.

facilitation measures, both soft and hard infrastructure. For example, countries need to regulate the trucks moving along BBIN corridors; encourage competition among service providers such as transporters, banks and insurances providers, etc.; build trade infrastructure such as testing laboratories; and improve the highway conditions and border-crossings infrastructures, etc.

In Bhutan and Nepal, the costs associated with completing documentary and other import and export procedures for international trade can account to a substantial part of the value of traded goods.[10] Costs of trade go up due to lack of regional (or sub-regional) insurance system for transit cargo. Therefore, raising the competition among logistics service providers would not only lead to fall in transaction costs but also improve the efficiency of service providers. Labour-intensive transport services will see the application of efficient technology at an increasing scale along the transit corridors. Besides, higher efficiency of ports of Kolkata, Haldia, Chittagong, etc., improvement of border infrastructure and corridors, and well-developed transit arrangements may transform transit corridors into economic corridors.

The Primal: BBIN Motor Vehicles Agreement (MVA)

South Asia witnesses eight cross-border passenger bus services and few cross-border freight services, which are limited in numbers, compared to potential. In a major bid to facilitate transportation and trade, BBIN countries signed the Motor Vehicles Agreement (BBIN MVA) for the 'Regulation of Passenger, Personal and Cargo Vehicular Traffic' amongst them on 15 June 2015.[11] The BBIN MVA, drafted in line with the SAARC MVA, aims to fulfill the need to accelerate cross-border transportation and deepen the regional integration through sub-regional measures as outlined in the declaration of the 18th SAARC Summit.[12]

---

10. Refer, for example, ADB-ESCAP (2014).

11. BBIN MVA is available at http://morth.nic.in/showfile.asp?lid=1715

12. Refer the Joint Statement of the Ministers of Transport of Bangladesh, Bhutan, India, and Nepal on the Motor Vehicles Agreement dated 15 June 2015, available at http://mea.gov.in

Table 2: Business Processes, Time and Costs in BBIN Countries

Corridor	Exporter	Importer	Products	Procedures (No.)			Time (Days)	Cost (US$/TEU)	Documents & Copies (No.)		
				Exporter	Importer	Total			Exporter	Importer	Total
Corridor 1: Kakarvitta-Panitanki-Phulbari-Banglabandha	Nepal	Bangladesh	Lentils	18	13	31	23.40	791.80	18 (44)	18 (71)	36 (115)
	Bangladesh	Nepal	LAA	12	16	28	29.26	1402.05	15 (50)	15 (33)	30 (83)
Corridor 2: Phuentsholing-Jaigaon-Hasimara-Changrabandha-Burimari	Bhutan	Bangladesh	Oranges	18	14	32	18.60	569.84	14 (26)	18 (69)	32 (95)
	Bangladesh	Bhutan	Fruit Juice	9	16	25	20.13	527.61	9 (30)	16 (44)	25 (74)
Corridor 3: Kathmandu-Birgunj-Raxaul-Kolkata	Nepal	Third country*	Carpets	23		23	26.00	2260.60	19 (44)		19 (44)
	Third country**	Nepal	CSO		21	21	18.00	689.74		22 (49)	22 (49)

Notes: *Excluding export processes. **Excluding import processes. Numbers in parentheses are copies needed for export and import.
Source: Author based on ADB-ESCAP (2014).

The primary objective of the MVA, as noted in the Joint Declaration, is to facilitate cargo movement across borders in BBIN countries and is expected to significantly reduce trade transaction costs in the sub-region. The MVA has 17 articles, four forms of permits of both passenger and goods traffic, and three annexures. Among the 17 articles, three articles are unique in nature such as Article VII, which talks about fees and charges, Article VIII which presents the road signs and signals and the compliance with traffic laws, and Article XI which provides arrangements of insurance.

Through this Agreement, the Contracting Parties (here BBIN countries) have agreed to allow the movement of registered vehicles in each Contracting Party to ply in territory of other Contracting Party(ies) including (i) cargo vehicles (including trucks, trailers, etc., that could carry containerized cargo) for inter-country cargo including third country cargo and (ii) passenger vehicles for both hire or reward; or personal vehicles. As per Article II, all regular passenger/cargo transportation will be allowed only through authorised operator(s).

Article III of BBIN MVA says that all the vehicles of a Contracting Party will require a permit for plying through the other Contracting Party(ies), where the permit will be issued after verification of all the required documents as mentioned in Article IV. Permits for regular passenger transportation and regular cargo transportation will be for multiple entries, valid for one year and renewable every year. A vehicle entering and plying into the territory of a Contracting Party or exiting from its territory under this Agreement will do so using authorised routes through authorised immigration checkpoints and land customs stations as notified by the Contracting Parties in the mutual agreement. Any deviation from the route will be treated as a violation of the permit conditions and of the relevant customs laws of the concerned Contracting Parties. Sector and the details of route, route maps, location of permitted rest or recreation places, tolls and check posts open for regular passenger or cargo transportation among the Contracting Parties as defined in the Protocol is at Annexure-I of the Agreement.

Article II of the BBIN MVA also talks about installation of a tracking system on motor vehicles as well as containers at the cost of entering vehicle/container will be introduced within two years from the signing of the agreement subject to the mutual consent of Contracting Parties.

Article IV states that the driver of the vehicle will have to carry a set of 11 documents written in English language.[13] Registration papers and other documents such as insurance policy, fitness certificates, etc., will be carried by the vehicle and made available for inspection on demand by the competent authority or any officer duly authorised. Article VI also indicates that vehicles registered in one Contracting Party and operating under this Agreement will not be permitted to transport local passengers and goods within the territory of other Contracting Party(ies). The Agreement provides an important role of border check posts, land ports/dry ports and land customs stations of the concerned Contracting Party(ies) which will endorse entry/ exit particulars of the vehicles on the permit and these will be treated as the date of entry/exit for the purpose of this Agreement. Vehicles transporting goods or passengers cannot move on any routes. Article VII of the MVA says that traffic between the two countries will be restricted only through existing notified land ports/dry ports and land customs stations/routes.

In relation to border, land port/dry port formalities, customs and quarantine formalities, taxation and fees, the provisions of internal laws or agreements between Contracting Parties will be applied in deciding matters which are not regulated by this Agreement. The Article VII says that all fees and charges for issue of permit for the vehicle of one Contracting Party will be levied only at the entry point of another Contracting Party. The rates of such fees and charges (including the fee for vehicle in transit) will be decided and notified from time to time by Contracting Parties and informed to one another. Fees and charges will be paid in the currency of the Contracting Party in which the vehicle is entering. Nothing in this clause exempts the vehicles of another Contracting Party from the commercial charges payable on the

---

13. The list of documents listed in BBIN MVA is as follows: (i) a valid registration certificate; (ii) a valid certificate of fitness (wherever applicable); (iii) a valid insurance policy; (iv) a valid permit; (v) a valid "Pollution Under Control" certificate issued by a Contracting Party, certifying emission level and pollution under control of that vehicle in the Contracting Party, which has issued the certificate. The compliance of PUC check of the transit or destination state will be decided by the concerned Contracting Party(ies); (vi) a valid driving license issued by a Contracting Party or an international driving permit; (vii) pre-verified passport of the crew containing inter-alia the photo identity of the crew; (viii) a passenger list (with details of their nationality) in case of regular passenger transportation and non-regular passenger transportation for hire or reward; (ix) an internationally recognized valid travel document as proof of identity for passengers; (x) way bill providing a brief description of the cargo and destination(s), commercial invoice and packing lists; and (xi) list of personal goods/articles in possession of the crew including accessories, spares and parts in the vehicle to account for customs duty exemption/assessment.

highways, toll-ways, etc., as long as the same are equally applicable to the vehicles of the destination or transit Contracting Party. Any other charges to cover the cost of services provided for cross-border transportation between the Contracting Party(ies) may be levied on a mutually agreed basis. It also tells that no additional charges such as octroi, or local taxes will be levied on transportation of passenger vehicles of one Contracting Party, while plying in the territory of another Contracting Party except those taxes/charges which are equally applicable to vehicles of the destination Contracting Party, and the transit fee applicable to vehicles of other Contracting Party(ies) in transit. The Article VII has proposed to set up a Customs subgroup having participation from all the Contracting Parties to formulate the required Customs and other procedures and safeguards with regard to entry and exit of vehicles. There is also an indication of convergence on road signs and signals, compliance with traffic laws, among the four countries under Article VIII.

The Article XI deals with insurance. The non-regular passenger transportation by vehicles to be operated under this Agreement will be insured by a registered Insurance Company against at least third party loss, in all the Contracting Party(ies) where the vehicle is allowed to ply. It tells that the regular passenger and cargo vehicles must have a comprehensive insurance policy.

According to Article XVI, the BBIN MVA will enter into force on completion of formalities, including ratification by all the Contracting Parties and upon issuance of notification through diplomatic channels. The provisions of this agreement shall be reviewed by Contracting Parties after a period of three years from the date of entry into force of this Agreement or earlier as mutually agreed by Contracting Parties. The review process will suggest amendments, modifications or improvements in the provisions of this Agreement.

Annexure-I of the MVA has provided a template on the protocol containing details of routes, route maps, location of permitted rest or recreation places, tolls and check posts for passenger or cargo transportation, which BBIN countries have to ratify on expeditiously. The competent authorities under reference in Article – III (12) of this Agreement will be the authorities to be specifically designated as under Annexure-II. List of Competent Authorities may be mentioned specifically by each Contracting Party. Annexure-III presents the formalities about the form of conductor's/cleaner's/helper's identity card/document.

Implementation Plan

The countries have agreed to carry out a six-month work plan for the implementation of the BBIN MVA in accordance with the following activities and milestones:

*   First, formalisation of the BBIN MVA, including the Protocols in Annexure 1 and 2, by August 2015. This has been done already.
*   Second, preparation of bilateral (and perhaps trilateral/quadrilateral) agreements/protocols for implementation of the BBIN MVA, by July 2015. This is completed.
*   Third, negotiation and approval of bilateral (and perhaps trilateral/ quadrilateral) agreements/ protocols, by September 2015. Yet to meet the deadline, and is under progress.
*   Fourth, installation of the prerequisites for implementing the approved agreements (e.g., IT systems, infrastructure, tracking, regulatory systems), by December 2015. BBIN countries are yet to meet the deadline, and this is under progress; and
*   Fifth, staged implementation from October 2015. This is not yet done.

Nodal officials or National Land Transport Facilitation Committees have been instructed to monitor the work plan, and bring to the immediate attention of Leaders any issues that may arise in the course of its implementation. Asian Development Bank (ADB) has been requested to continue providing technical support and other related arrangements necessary to ensure the effective and efficient implementation of the work plan. Besides, countries have identified 30 priority transport connectivity projects with an estimated total cost of over US$ 8 billion to rehabilitate and upgrade trade and transport corridors in BBIN.

Challenges, Concerns and Recommendations

The BBIN MVA is likely to generate economic dividends in the sub-region, more particularly for Bangladesh, Bhutan, and Nepal. This is true because the corridors would pass through underdeveloped parts of the world, generating relatively higher marginal returns from investment. No doubt, the Agreement would facilitate trade among each other through faster and uninterrupted movement of vehicles in the sub-region. Value chains offer immense opportunities for BBIN countries to strengthen the economic integration process. It is expected that BBIN MVA will facilitate value chains in the sub-region. However, we need to have an integrated approach to BBIN connectivity. An integrated approach is the only way to avoid decisions being prepared under wrong assumptions. We also have to remember that BBIN MVA cannot fulfill every demand or aspiration. Expectations of stakeholders from BBIN MVA are, therefore, very high. Addressing those expectations is itself a big challenge.[14]

Reaching a consensus on BBIN corridors may not be difficult among countries, but what matters most is commitment on auxiliary services attached to corridors such as permits for trucks and vehicle operators, vehicle registration, inspections, insurance, issuance of visa, etc., in expeditious manner within the given time limit. A properly integrated planning by BBIN countries delegating the responsibilities to concerned authorities should be carried out before the sub-region is opened up for cross-border passenger and cargo transportation.

Surge in traffic may cause damage to existing infrastructures since those are not equipped to take care of the additional load of cargo as expected from BBIN MVA. Therefore, investments in the development of hard infrastructure such as roads, bridges, border infrastructures, etc., must be scaled up in BBIN countries, particularly in Bangladesh. Although BBIN countries have identified US$ 8 billion investment in 30 transport connectivity projects, implementation of projects in priority sectors should be done expeditiously. In parallel, we need to introduce an enabling framework in order to scale up the investments, particularly for public-private partnership (PPP) projects.

Managing cross-border corridors is another challenge that BBIN countries are going to face since they have limited experiences. Learning from existing corridors being developed elsewhere such as Maputo corridor between South Africa and Mozambique would be very useful in managing BBIN corridors. Therefore, training and capacity building shall be another priority. This includes, among others, strengthening capacities of government officials involved in implementation of BBIN MVA to carry out priority reform programmes in the areas of customs modernisation and harmonisation of border procedures, automation of border processes, and provision of improved services and information to private sector. A BBIN Forum may be constituted to undertake research, advocacy, and training and

---

14. Refer, Summary of the Seminar on 'Motor Vehicles Agreement among the BBIN Group of Countries: Key Concerns, Challenges and Benefits', organised by CUTS in Geneva on 1 July 2015. Also refer, Rahman (2015), De (2015), a.o.

capacity building of officials in consultation with BBIN nodal ministries and in coordination with the proposed customs sub-group under the Article VII of BBIN MVA and the sub-regional joint committee, which is going to monitor the implementation of the agreement.

Electronic communication shrinks the distance between partners. Going for digitalisation in monitoring the movement of vehicles or payment of duties and toll taxes, etc., by BBIN countries will pave the way for faster clearances of goods at the border and also along the corridors.

Faster movement of goods and services is contingent upon harmonisation of rules and regulations of motor vehicles in the sub-region. By making an entry into international instruments such as the TIR Convention, harmonisation can be achieved quickly and so also the safety of goods in transit. At the same time, implementation of Revised Kyoto Convention (RKC) and WTO Trade Facilitation Agreement (TFA) would also help BBIN countries to achieve simplification and harmonisation of customs procedures, leading towards paperless trade environment. UNNExT offers many good suggestions and templates on cross-border harmonisation of customs procedures. Similarly, harmonisation of road standards shall be another priority. For example, parcel load of Indian and Bangladeshi roads are different, indicating Bangladeshi roads would not able to carry full-loaded Indian trucks or containers. It is suggested that specially designed container be created, which are adjustable with global standards for road and rail transportation in BBIN.

BBIN countries should support goods in container. There is a gap between containerised goods and goods in container. The BBIN MVA talks about containerised goods, but there is no mention about the movement of containers in the sub-region. For a safe and faster movement of goods, container movement shall be encouraged. It would also encourage multimodal transportation within the sub-region and also with rest of the world. BBIN Railway Agreement should take care of the railway movement in the sub-region.

To implement connectivity corridors in a timely fashion, effective coordination between countries and other stakeholders is vital. Without this, it is unlikely that an optimal connectivity will come into existence. Countries have recognised BBIN MVA as a complementary instrument to the existing transport agreements or arrangements at the bilateral levels. India and Nepal have already signed bilateral MVA. India and Bhutan have liberal transport arrangements. India and Bangladesh have also signed bilateral MVA in 2015. An effective coordination among the BBIN countries in implementing bilateral or sub-regional MVAs is required to minimise the wastage of resources and duplication of services.

Customs shall operate 24×7 in BBIN sub-region. At present, there are differences in working hours between customs. It is recommended that full automation and link-up between customs will reduce transaction time and cost. Simple, harmonised and standardised trade and customs processes, procedures and related information flows are expected to reduce transaction costs in the region, which will enhance trade competitiveness and facilitate the regional integration. BBIN countries need to align customs procedures and trade services among themselves through interoperability of Customs Single Windows.

Managing the export and import at border jointly would lead to saving our resources, time, and costs. For example, cargo scanner can be shared jointly by both the countries at the border. The One Stop Border Post (OSBP) allows neighbouring countries to coordinate import, export, and transit processes to ensure that traders are not required to duplicate regulatory formalities on both sides of the same border. This system may be implemented along selected corridors in the sub-region, to start with.

Concluding Remarks

The signing of BBIN MVA is a historic event. However, to maximise the regional welfare, a region-wide MVA is necessary. With BBIN MVA in place, western South Asian countries may replicate a mini version of the MVA among themselves. Adding Iran and central Asian countries in a gradual manner will pave the way for higher market access for South Asian LDCs. With the signing of agreement on development of Chabahar port in Iran, India, Iran and Afghanistan may consider signed transit and transport agreement for the trade between them as well as between South and Central Asia through Iran and Afghanistan. In the eastern side, India, Myanmar and Thailand have been negotiating the MVA for trade and transportation along the Trilateral Highway. Building a common template for running and maintaining the corridors and signing of mutual recognition agreement (MRA) on logistics and other transportation services between the participating countries would be essential for not only removing the barriers to trade but also sharing the benefits and risks.

The BBIN MVA does not explicitly talk about transit for third country trade, particularly between India's Northeast and the rest of India through Bangladesh. It did not propose any plan of convergence of transport structure and remedies such as axle load and tonnage. Neither, it talks about special and differential treatment (S&DT) for countries or areas within the region for revenue loss or environmental damage. Costs of non-cooperation may damage the whole great effort. Therefore, greater involvement of states or sub-national entities would make it an inclusive trade-transport arrangement, perhaps, the best and unique in the world.

Finally, improvement of infrastructure is not a sufficient condition for regional development. Improvement of infrastructure gives rise to both distributive and generative effects. Generative effects would tend to be higher than distributive effects particularly in our case. The success of BBIN MVA would depend how quickly BBIN countries build the physical connectivity in the sub-region. The beginning is good but challenges are plenty. BBIN countries continue to engaging themselves while dealing with these challenges. Measures to reduce transit costs and time are immensely important to strengthen regional integration process. BBIN MVA will entail in particular further preparation for the implementation of the trade facilitation priorities and strategies in WTO Trade Facilitation Agreement (TFA), in which all the four BBIN countries are members and some of them such as India and Bangladesh have already ratified the Agreement.

References

ADB-ESCAP (2014) *Trade Process Analysis Report for Subregional Cooperation in South Asia.* Asian Development Bank (ADB), Manila and United Nations Economic and Social Commission of Asia and the Pacific (UNESCAP), Bangkok.

De, Prabir (2012) "Why is Trade at Border a Costly Affair in South Asia? An Empirical Investigation", *Contemporary South Asia*, Vol. 19, No. 4.

De, Prabir (2015) "Regional Integration". *Economic and Political Weekly*, Vol. 50, No. 52.

De, Prabir and Arvind Kumar (2014) "Regional Transit Agreement in South Asia: An Empirical Investigation". SAWTEE Discussion Paper. South Asia Watch on Trade, Economics and Environment (SAWTEE), Kathmandu.

Dubey, Muchkund, Lok Raj Baral, Rehman Sobhan (1999) *South Asian Growth Quadrangle: Framework for Multifaceted Cooperation*, Macmillan India, New Delhi

Kathuria, Sanjay (2014) "Five lessons of regional integration from Asia, America, and Africa". The World Bank, Washington, D.C.

Rahman, Mustafizur (2015) "Trade Facilitation in South Asia through Transport Connectivity: Operationalising the Motor Vehicle Agreements (MVAs)", Presentation Made at the Roundtable on BBIN MVA, Held at Centre for Policy Dialogue (CPD), 20 June 2015, Dhaka

Rahmatullah, M (2004) "Integrating Transport Systems of South Asia" in Rehman Sobhan (ed.) *Promoting Cooperation in South Asia: An Agenda for 13th SAARC Summit.* Centre for Policy Dialogue (CPD) and the University Press Ltd., Dhaka.

Rahmatullah, M (2010) "Transport Issues and Integration in South Asia" in Sadiq Ahmed, Saman Kelegama, and Ejaz Ghani (eds.) *Promoting Economic Cooperation in South Asia Beyond SAFTA,* Sage Publications, New Delhi

Ray, Jayanta Kumar and Prabir De (2003) *Promotion of Trade and Investment in the Eastern South Asia Subregion*, Bookwell, New Delhi

Sobhan, Rehman. (2000) *Rediscovering the Southern Silk Route: Integrating Asia's Transport Infrastructure*, Centre for Policy Dialogue and the University Press Ltd., Dhaka.

Subramanium, Uma (2001) "Transport, Logistics, and trade Facilitation in the South Asia Subregion" in *Integration of Transport and Trade Facilitation: Selected Regional Case Studies.* The World Bank, Washington D.C.

SEVEN

TRADE AND TRANSIT COOPERATION WITH AFGHANISTAN: RESULTS FROM A FIRM-LEVEL SURVEY FROM PAKISTAN

Vaqar Ahmed and Saad Shabbir

Introduction

The objectives of this chapter are to inform academia and policymakers, on ways and means to first, increase trade with Afghanistan, and second, to discuss trade-related mechanisms, procedures and processes that could be streamlined for reducing the cost of doing business with Afghanistan.

Pakistan provides transit facility to Afghanistan. The Afghanistan Pakistan Transit Trade Agreement (APTTA), signed in 2010, allows Afghan trucks to use the seaports of Karachi, Port Qasim, and Gwadar via the Torkhum and Chaman border points. Replacing the Afghanistan Transit Trade Agreement (ATTA 1965), the APTTA allowed the Pakistani traders to export their goods to central Asia via Afghanistan. It was also agreed to constitute a joint coordination committee of government officials and private stakeholders from both countries to address any issues relevant to the transit trade agreement.[1]

The Agreement has attracted attention of other landlocked countries. More recently Tajikistan has requested to be part of this arrangement and an expert level group meeting on Trilateral Transit Trade Arrangement among Afghanistan, Pakistan and Tajikistan was held on 3 January 2015 in Islamabad. In the meeting of the Commerce Secretaries from 7 Central

---

*   The authors are grateful for technical and data related inputs from Sadika Hameed, Nohman Ishtiaq, Abdul Wahab, Asif Javed and Mohsin Kazmi. Views are personal. Usual disclaimers apply.

1.   Article 34, Section X of APTTA 2010. Afghanistan Pakistan Transit Trade Coordination Authority (APTTCA) shall be established to monitor, facilitate, and effectively implement APTTA 2010. APTTCA is co-chaired by Deputy Commerce Minister (Afghanistan) and Secretary Commerce (Pakistan). For further details please see: http://www.commerce.gov.pk/Downloads/APTTA.pdf

Asian countries (held on 7 March 2015 in UAE and facilitated by the World Bank), Pakistan has offered similar arrangement to these countries as well.

The latter sections in this paper discuss the emerging economic scenarios in Afghanistan and the corresponding effects on regional economies and businesses. It also examines Pakistan's role as a conduit, i.e. opportunities of scaling up efforts for South and Central Asia economic corridors and measures to mitigate these risks. Finally, we make a case for extending the bilateral economic cooperation to cross-border investment in supply chain linkages and trade in services.

Transit Trade Dynamics
Afghanistan's exports of goods and services were recorded around US$ 500 million in 2014, whereas the imports of goods and services increased from US$ 3 billion in 2009 to US$ 10.6 billion in 2014. The current account balance remained negative and decreased over the years. These statistics, however, do not account for the substantial informal trade between Afghanistan and Iran, and between Afghanistan and Pakistan. Trade has been on rise for the most part of the last decade. Pakistan remains the largest trading partner of Afghanistan with a share of 28 per cent, followed by the United States, which has a share of 17.8 per cent.[2] Afghanistan was the third largest destination for Pakistani exports in 2012-13.[3]

Since 2006 both trading nations have managed to keep collective export and import value above US$ 1.5 billion. While Pakistan's export to Afghanistan has slightly decreased since 2011, Afghanistan's export to Pakistan has steadily been on rise (Figure 1). There is, however, competition for Pakistan as exports from Iran and India have increased. Additionally, differential treatment by Pakistani authorities, longer clearance time at the port, high demurrage charges and issues related to transit guarantees in Pakistan are some factors which make transit via Iran relatively more attractive.

The top products exported from Pakistan to Afghanistan in the last seven years include milk, cream, sugar, animal and vegetable oil, cement, crude oil, wheat and rice, and household furniture. Analysis of a wider

2. Refer, Eurostat, European Commission (2013).
3. Refer, State Bank of Pakistan Annual Report (2012).

list of export items in 2014 reveals that cement, food and oil supplies are the dominant products. However, items in the export basket are subject to substantial variation due to the fast changing demand in Afghanistan.[4]

Figure 1: Export Patterns of Key Partners for Afghanistan

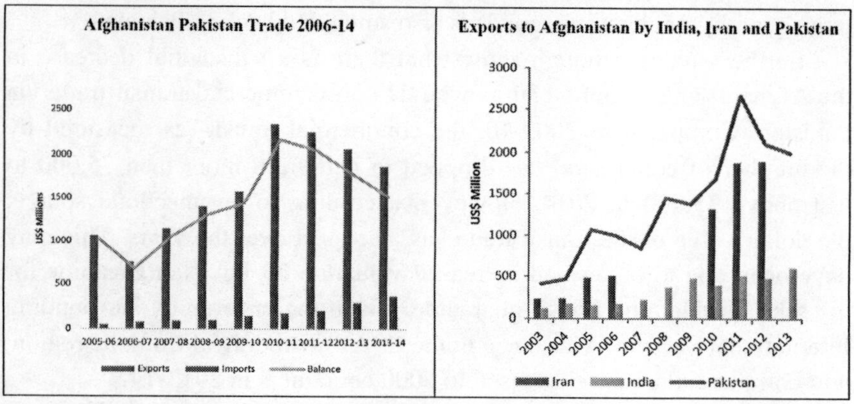

Source: World Development Indicators 2014, the World Bank, and the State Bank of Pakistan

A key challenge is whether the imports of Afghanistan from India or elsewhere are making their way into Pakistan through illicit or even legitimate means, posing a threat to the indigenous industries in Pakistan.[5] It has been reported that Pakistani traders with the help of Afghan traders, import goods under transit trade, ship them to Afghanistan and then smuggle them back into Pakistan. Another factor is that a number of cargo containers that were imported under transit trade go missing and their products end up selling in the Pakistani markets. The incentives to smuggle also arise because of Pakistan's trade restrictions on Indian imports. It is likely that once such restrictions are relaxed, informal imports or smuggling from Afghanistan may also decline.[6]

---

4. For example, a number of high-end food items were destined as supplies for the International Security Assistance Force (ISAF). The value of such items is subject to the number of ISAF personnel on-ground. Another example is Kerosene Type Jet Fuel, which had negligible export demand from Pakistan to Afghanistan in 2013 butthis jumped to US$ 83 million in the next year.

5. Interviews conducted with SAARC Chamber of Commerce and Industry (CCI).

6. Afghanistan has also complained regarding transit goods from Pakistan finding their way into Afghanistan's market. See Ahmed *et al.* (2015) for details.

Independent studies[7] point out that often the goods imported in Afghanistan are in excess in regard to demand and thus the surplus is sent into Pakistan through illicit trade. Black tea is not commonly used in Afghanistan as green tea is preferred. Yet, a large quantity of tea was reported to be imported in Afghanistan for sending back to Pakistan. Similarly, a large quantity of electronic goods is also smuggled back to Pakistan.

Further analysis though shows that there is a substantial decrease in the Afghanistan's commercial as well as non-commercial transit trade via Pakistan. Compared to 2009-10, the commercial transit (as measured by the number of containers) has dropped to half from more than 75,000 to just above 35,000 in 2014. However, according to an anecdotal source, the dollar value of the transit trade has increased over the years. This may have been due to better and increased valuation by Pakistan Customs for the sake of obtaining transit guarantee. Given the uncertainty surrounding International Security Assistance Force (ISAF) withdrawal from the region, non-commercial transit decreased to 6000 containers in 2013-14.[8]

Recent empirical literature points towards the following additional challenges in the way of expanding trade ties with Afghanistan:

* Higher compliance costs of trade and transit related documentation (PILDAT, 2012)
* Weak road and ports related infrastructure to support an increased transit flow (Shabbir and Ahmed, 2014)
* Frequent changes in on-ground customs regime specific to Afghanistan (Hussain and Masood, 2008)
* Thriving trade via informal channels reduces incentives for formal trade (Hameed, 2012). Estimates of informal trade between Afghanistan and Pakistan vary across anecdotal evidence. This amount is said to be equivalent to or greater than formal trade between both the countries.

Methodology

In this chapter, we adopt a methodology that directly surveyed the business community about the above mentioned issues affecting them and the specific reforms they would like to be put in place. Using a mix of desk review, qualitative and quantitative survey (Figure 2) this paper aims to:

7. Refer, PILDAT (2012)

8. The International Security Assistance Force (ISAF) was a NATO-led security mission, established by the United Nations Security Council for Afghanistan.

- explore perceptions regarding economic opportunities and major challenges in Afghanistan and their impact on Pakistan and other actors in Central Asia. The term 'actors' here is not limited to states or their institutions. Efforts of multilateral organisations and the private sector in the region were also explored.
- review estimates from recent studies highlighting expected changes in Afghanistan-Pakistan commercial and transit (commercial and non-commercial) trade flows following ISAF drawdown in Afghanistan.
- review perceptions regarding current arrangements and the future possibilities of strengthening bilateral trade arrangements and agreements between Afghanistan and Pakistan

The firm-level survey helped in estimating the firm income models as well as the investment and expenditure functions (of these firms).[9] In order to have a representative sample we interviewed 260 firms.[10] These firms were:
- split across exporters who are also producers (and not traders),
- owners of businesses falling under wholesale trade, retail trade, transport, distribution and warehousing, and
- firms acting as clearing agents (Table 1).

Such a sample distribution allowed observing both the impact of the ISAF drawdown on industries servicing the transit trade, and the impact of perceived political or security related upheavals on formal trade and commercial transit.

We have tried to ensure that the sample is representative of the firms currently trading with Afghanistan and Central Asia. As a starting point, we resorted to the directory available with the Pakistan Afghanistan Joint Chamber of Commerce and Industries. This directory was further augmented with information about 2013-14 memberships provided by the Chambers of Commerce in Karachi and Peshawar. This consolidated list was split into three categories: (i) exporters (manufacturing community), (ii) trade, transport, distribution and warehousing (TTDW) sector, and (iii) clearing agents. Next, we split each of these lists according to the cities where each category is concentrated. For example, the exporters'

---

9.   The list may be obtained from authors on request.

10.   Interested readers can request a copy of the questionnaire administered from the research team at Sustainable Development Policy Institute (SDPI).

list was split across Karachi, Quetta and Peshawar. Given the resource and time already invested to reach each of these cities, we acquired equal responses from each city. In our opinion, this should not influence our policy conclusions given the objectives of this survey were only to record current and future perceptions. Finally, under each category and city, random selection was ensured.

Figure 2: Study Methodology

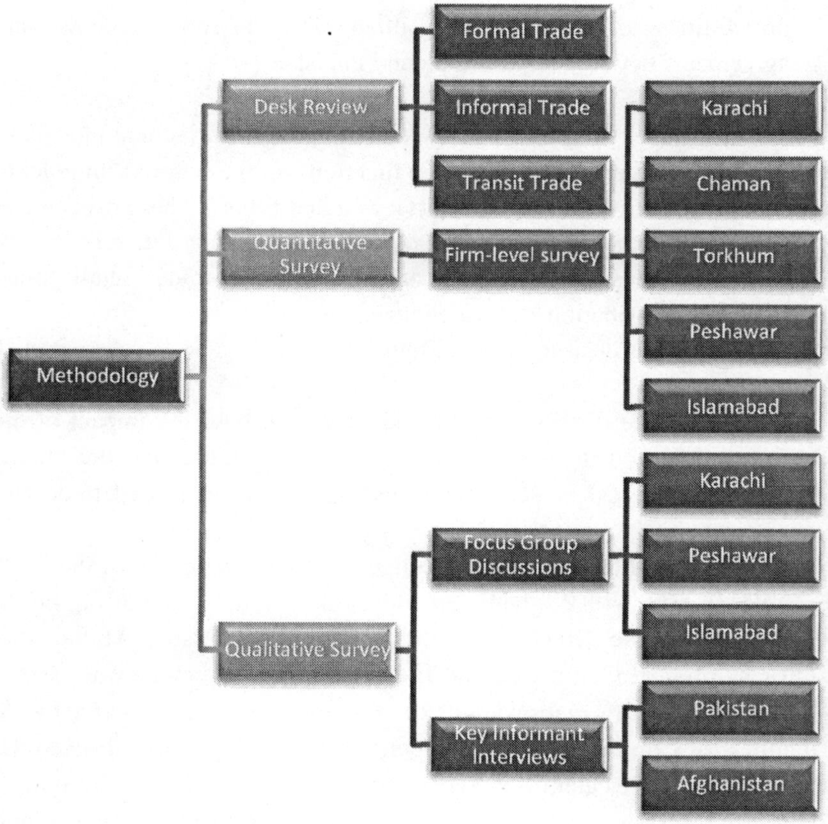

Source: Drawn by authors

Table 1: Number of Respondents by City and Category

City	Exporters*	TTDW** Sector	Clearing Agents	Total
Karachi	30	30		60
Chaman		20	20	40
Quetta	30	30		60
Peshawar	30	30		60
Torkhum		20	20	40
Total Sample				260

Notes: *These are producer-exporters,
          ** TTDW= Trade, Transport, Distribution and Warehousing.

Survey Results and Findings

Most respondents informed that to realise the US$ 5 billion target of bilateral trade between the two economies (as set by the Ministries of Commerce of the two countries), the share of manufactured products needs to increase.[11] For this to happen, one needs to start by looking at how Pakistani firms compete in Afghanistan.

• Around 25 per cent of the revenues of firms sampled are from sales abroad. Given the energy crisis faced by the firms in Pakistan, annual turnover and exports have decreased. This is particularly the case for firms in Balochistan and Khyber Pakhtunkhwa provinces. Most respondents reported highly increasing costs of doing business. Some of these costs are discussed below:

   ▪ There was a consensus that the cost of electricity is prohibitively high for doing business and efficiency. Both India and Iran (who are competitors for Pakistani products) heavily subsidize their energy sectors. However, Pakistan due to its weak budgetary position cannot match such subsidies. In a more recent reform under the IMF programme, Pakistan is expected to further phase out subsidies and increase both power and gas tariffs. However, subsidies should be phased out gradually as the energy sector is deregulated in order to allow the private sector to enter and create competitive pricing for consumers. This requires investing in longer-term energy needs

---

11. Pakistan's exports to Afghanistan still largely focus on agriculture and livestock while there is a growing industrial sector in Afghanistan which is projected to contribute to processed food manufacturing (particularly in the case of fruits and vegetables).

of firms wishing to scale up exports to Afghanistan. Most of these firms are still classified as SMEs and can be helped through export-related rebates on consumption of energy.

- About 52 per cent of firms reported that transportation costs have increased by 5-15 per cent during the past 12 months (Figure 3).[12] However, for 19 per cent of the firms the increase in these costs was between 15-25 per cent. Similarly, in the case of warehousing, 45 per cent firms reported an increase in such costs to the tune of 5-15 per cent and 8 per cent firms reported that these costs had increased between 15-25 per cent. Most of the latter firms were from the agriculture sector that faces a high risk of loss in perishable products.

Figure 3: Magnitude of Change in Logistics Costs

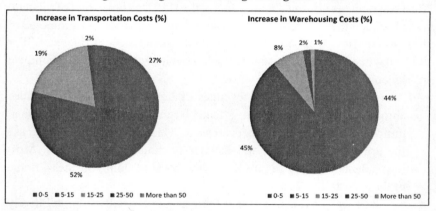

Source: SDPI Monitoring and Evaluation (M&E) Unit, 2014.

- In the past year (2013-14), the cost of inputs has risen more than 20 per cent as a result the prices of the finished products also increased.[13] For the same period, firms reported a rise in increased wage bills and spending on power and gas.
- Around 60 per cent of firms have outsourced transportation and warehousing services. The transportation costs of goods have increased due to increases in oil prices in the international

---

12. The survey team was mobilised in June 2014. Therefore, past 12 months refer to the period prior to June 2014.

13. Firms producing and exporting cement, milk, sugar, rice, animal and vegetable oil, and petroleum extracts were interviewed. Thus, inputs here refer to the raw material used for the different products.

market during 2013-14.[14]Businesses expressed concerns that as international oil prices fall in the coming months, the federal government will not pass on the full effect of the price decline.

- About 58 per cent of firms reported that the insurance cost of trade consignments has significantly risen in the past 12 months. In some cases, the insurance cost was almost one-third of the consignment cost, discouraging smaller traders specifically. These increases in trade costs have made it difficult for exporters to compete in the Afghanistan market with pressures from India and Iran. Most established insurance enterprises in Pakistan are not providing these services for trading with Afghanistan, any Afghan trader wishing to import from Pakistan is also expected to arrange their own transport and logistics services. Absence of an EXIM Bank that can facilitate trade-related guarantees also exacerbates the problems of traders wishing to export high value merchandise.

- About 30 per cent of the firms reported that they want an increased supply of skilled labour (for servicing trade, transport and warehousing sectors). However, 95 per cent of firms has also reported an increase in their wage bills since December 2013. This rising cost of doing business has forced firms to restructure their human resources and reported laying off, 30 per cent of their skilled employees. 85 per cent of the overall layoffs comprised clerical and support staff.[15]

- A better law and order situation is imperative for the firms to flourish as 50 per cent of the firms indicated that they bear the damage costs. The damage costs include theft of goods, missing containers, and damaged containers. The skilled labour also moves out as law and order deteriorates. Security remains a major concern for businesses, particularly those requiring fixed investments from abroad. Exporters consider the law and order of the region to be the most significant hurdle to smooth and efficient trade. Security in general is a hindrance and the trade routes are not considered secure. The threats are not just to the trucks passing across the border, there is also the issue of theft and pilferage.

---

14. For economy-wide impacts of fuel price shocks in Pakistan, see Ahmed and Donoghue (2010).

15. The estimates regarding the unskilled and semi-skilled workers getting unemployed, are weak as many are not registered with the labour market institutions.

- Half of the respondents reported that the APTTA has led to an increase in informal trade and smuggling.[16] Pakistani businessmen are of the view that significant portion of goods imported in Pakistan for onward transmission to Afghanistan get lost in Pakistan and never enter Afghanistan, and those that do, sometimes come back into Pakistan. It is felt that it has severely hampered the domestic and international business in Pakistan and also prospects for enhanced transit and trade relations. There are no evidence based estimates of either the informal trade or smuggling.

- Trolleys and trucks are at times delayed by 2 to 3 days because the clearance system installed at Torkhum is not very organised and systematic. At the time of this study, the customs automated Web-based One Customs or WeBOC facility on the Pakistani side of the borders does not synchronise with the automated facility at the border crossings in Afghanistan.

- Respondents explained the need for the Government of Pakistan to expedite the various promised infrastructure related projects. They explained that if trade with Afghanistan is to be scaled upwards, the road networks that need to be urgently revamped include the Indus Highway (N-55), Regional Cooperation for Development Highway (N-25) connecting Karachi to Chaman via Lakpass, Lakpaas-Taftan (N-40), Sukkur-Quetta (N-65), and Nowshera – Dir – Chitral (N-45) Highway, Gawadar – Hoshab – Khuzdar – Rathodero Motorway (M-8) and Hasan Abdal – Mansehra Expressway. Additionally, if increased trade and transit traffic is to be facilitated across Afghanistan-Pakistan border, a diversification of transport modes is required, particularly in favour of railways. Railways will add to economies of scale for any trading activity in future. The security of cargo is also relatively better in the case of railways.

Despite the lack of infrastructure, the private sector representatives explained that it takes less than 20 hours for transit from Torkhum border to Tajikistan and then other parts of Central Asia. Pakistan already supplies around 60 per cent of the cement used in Tajikistan construction. Pakistan has shown through the signing of the APPTA and

---

16. Informal trade may not be pure smuggling of goods if it comes under extra-legal trading and tolerated in practice by the State even if illegal by law. Our distinction between informal trade and smuggling follows Taneja *et al.* (2004).

extension to Tajikistan the seriousness for expanding regional trade. However, the progress seen on the eastern border has yet to be seen on the western side. For example, the development on the Wagah border with India has been exceptional with five lane crossing points and scanner machines that scan the trucks without opening the containers.

An example of upgrading infrastructure, particularly for transit trade, is the road from Jamrod to Torkhum, from a single road to a dual carriage road with security. While USAID has attempted to fund and implement this, it remains incomplete. Both cash strapped governments may not be able to afford such investments. There is great scope for the private sector in Pakistan to complete or undertake initiatives such as this.

Our discussions with the Ministry of Commerce and Trade Development Authority of Pakistan revealed that the government has recently approved the plan to operate trains twice a week under the APTTA. One of the abandoned projects of rail links between Chaman and Spin Boldak, which was approved in 2004, is now being reconsidered. After re-evaluating the cost of the project, the proposal is under consideration. This rail link was the first phase of the three phase project that will join Pakistan to Central Asia via Spin Boldak – Kandahar – Herat to Turkmenistan. The funding agency is yet to be finalised. Furthermore, on the request of Afghanistan, Pakistan is considering to extend technical support and trainings for capacity building of the staff of the newly established Afghanistan Railway Authority (AFRA).

The business community also felt that Pakistan and Afghanistan both need to diversify the transport infrastructure, thus including not just road linkages, but also rail, seaport infrastructure (from Pakistan) and air connectivity.

- Almost 48 per cent of the survey respondents benefitted from APPTA, despite the fact that many of the respondents said that their businesses were adversely impacted due to the inefficient and opaque practices of customs. Similarly, more than 50 per cent were not satisfied by the examination of goods undertaken by the customs authorities. Only 15 per cent of the firms had been able to file any complaints against APTTA due to the cumbersome grievance redressal mechanisms (entailing high transactions costs). There also appears to be a communication gap between the business community and the relevant authorities, as 80 per cent of the complaints were never addressed by the relevant authorities.

In summary, the followings are the key issues raised by firms engaged in commercial trade with Afghanistan:

• Securing enroute merchandise and also at borders,
• Missing border-related trade infrastructure,
• Inadequate banking facilities,
• Weak marketing of 'Made in Pakistan' in Afghanistan,
• Weak road and rail networks to facilitate any expansion in bilateral trade and transit; and
• Lack of harmonised customs operations at Torkhum and Chaman.

Similarly, the following is the summary of issues raised by firms engaged in transit trade:

• Torkhum terminal for passengers and cargo is still uncompleted due to lack of finances.
• Afghan importers have to bear multiple costs including transport, warehousing, tracker cost, and insurance guarantee cost.
• There is maximum limit of 40 feet containers. The charges are according to the weight. The average charge for a container from Karachi to Peshawar is PKR 110,000 per container. However, for Afghan transit the charges are high varying between PKR 10000 to PKR 20000 per container.
• Multiple containers under one importer are processed all together. In the case of a missing container, the entire shipment is blocked. The traders have the option to either file individual declarations for each container, but as this increases the cost, hence single declaration is filed for a consignment which may have multiple containers.
• Online system (WeBOC) is not yet synchronised with the Afghan system resulting in delays because of requisite clarifications from exporters or their agents. Respondents were also not satisfied with the examination of goods at various stages of transit. Around 80 per cent of the respondents revealed that complaints were not addressed by relevant authorities.
• Pakistan transit goods to Central Asia have 110 per cent insurance costs in violation of APTTA 2010.
• Small and medium scale traders have stopped trading after the dollar regime.[17] As formal money exchange companies at border points are

17. Traders now have to conduct trade in US$.

missing. Pakistan should not apply the same trading rules to Afghanistan that are present for more advanced economies.

• Exporters reported the need for some compensation in the cases where shipments were lost or stolen.[18]

• In a recent announcement, Pakistan Railways informed that it will operate two trains per week from Karachi to Peshawar to facilitate goods under APTTA. However, traders were apprehensive that railways as per the past record may have more uncertain timings than the trucking sector.

Institutional Analysis

As part of this chapter, we also organised group discussions and consultations in Islamabad, Karachi and Peshawar to tap into qualitative knowledge available with various stakeholders for promoting the bilateral economic cooperation. We have particularly taken into account (in this sub-section) interventions by government. There was a general consensus that while there is immense potential for trade with Afghanistan, Pakistan currently lacks a coherent diplomatic and economic foreign policy approach.

Increasing use of technology: For the efficient and smooth flow of trade, border crossing points require modern technology. Pakistan aims to build state-of-the-art border stations at Torkham, Chaman, Wahgah, and Taftan. The Electronic Data Interchange will be developed to provide online real time information of bilateral and transit trade. The issue of registration of Afghan importers is being expedited to resolve issues of partial shipment and undue shipment delays at border crossing points. The issue of multiple tracking devices on Afghan transit freights and requirement of *Jawaznama* (import license issued by the Ministry of Commerce, Afghanistan) by Pakistan is being revisited.

The trader community felt that Pakistani authorities can make an effort to harmonise automated customs processing platforms through appropriate ICT tools and providing technical assistance to the Afghan side, ensuring greater compatibility in systems and procedures. Also, the introduction of · such technology will assist in curbing informal trade and provide incentives for businesses to use the formal channels for their goods and services.

---

18. Currently, in the case of a loss even because of a terrorist activity there is no relief to the owner of shipment. The bonded carrier also does not pay compensation. Earlier Pakistan Railways use to compensate some fraction of the loss. However, Federal Board of Revenue (FBR) had reversed the provision.

Similarly, at the moment there is little monitoring of consignments arriving through the personal baggage, which needs to be taken care of.

Tariff Reforms for Afghanistan and Central Asia: The customs duties levied on imports from Afghanistan are acting as a constraint on improved trade relations. A reduction in tariffs could also prove beneficial especially given the Indian example, where the Indian Government reduced custom duties and taxes by 50 per cent on Afghan origin goods, leading to an increase in bilateral trade. Plastics, rubber, paper and paper board industries are at boom in Afghanistan. However, these sectors face comparatively higher tariffs in Pakistan. The average tariffs on plastics and rubber in Pakistan are 17 per cent and 15.8 per cent, respectively. The same in the case of India are 9.5 and 9.1, respectively.[19]

Outreach Programme: The Government of Pakistan has started to realise the difficulties that are faced by the private sector. In the context of bilateral trade with Afghanistan, the Ministry of Commerce, Federal Board of Revenue and other relevant institutions in Pakistan are working towards the following: customs cooperation agreement for data exchange, resolving issues related to re-exports, expanding trade facilitation available at the trade gates (Torkhum and Chaman), and build an integrated customs and border management facility. While this is being done, an outreach programme by the Ministry of Commerce is important so that the private sector is prepared for these reforms.

Trade in Services: The regulatory regime for the services sector will also need to be revisited. There is a lot of room for service sector exports in Afghanistan. Pakistan's service sector has proven to be effective and has seen high returns in Pakistan. There is scope for Pakistani businesses to use their knowledge and experience to invest and work in the service sector in Afghanistan. Trade Development Authority of Pakistan (TDAP) may take a lead in linking Pakistani service providers to Afghanistan. Trade in services will also require an agreement on treatment of double taxation. This can be done as part of the preferential trade agreement (PTA). A study to quantify the potential of services trade between Afghanistan and Pakistan is also required.

APTTA and Inclusion of Tajikistan: APTTA perhaps provides the greatest promise of cross border trade and forward trade for both

---

19. Refer, Ahmad (2015)

governments. It provides realistic and sustainable steps for increased trade for Pakistan. The stagnation has been a result of lack of political will in the past to take things forward – a trend that exporters are expecting to change given the current relations between Pakistan and Afghanistan. The following are the gaps and areas for improvement:

- Pakistan and Afghanistan have different tariff regimes for the same class of products. Both governments, with the help of technical assistance, should consider some harmonisation of tariff regimes. South Asian Free Trade Agreement (SAFTA) provides a good framework even for bilateral harmonisation. A PTA between both countries could address this point, or at least provide the basis to a solution.

- Pakistan should consider acceding to TIR convention (Convention on International Transport of Goods Under Cover of Transports Internationaux Routiers Carnets, 1975) to simplify guarantee procedures and smoother movement of transit transport across borders.

- In the next round of improvements in APTTA multiple stakeholders should be invited and their recommendations should be considered. The Pakistan Afghanistan Joint Chamber of Commerce and Industry (PAJCCI) is of the view that the consultation process was not thorough in finalisation of the APTTA. Similarly, the business community favours transit facility for Tajikistan, however, they informed that they were not consulted fully before inviting Tajikistan for the January 2015 trilateral meeting in Islamabad.

Making Joint Economic Commission (JEC) Effective: For streamlining the implementation of bilateral economic cooperation reforms it is important to make the JEC more effective and the following are the key recommendations:

- The JEC should meet on a half yearly basis with pre-determined schedule of meetings.

- The JEC should also invite members of Pakistan Business Council, PAJCCI, consumer associations and think tanks in the meetings to discuss outstanding issues faced by civil society stakeholders of both the countries.

- The JEC should become the main forum to review status of large-scale projects that impact both the countries including CASA-1000, TAPI, road and rail networks.

Uncertain Role of Statutory Regulatory Orders (SROs)

Another area of concern highlighted by the respondents is the opaque and cost prohibitive SROs issued by the Federal Board of Revenue (FBR) which are hurting bilateral trade with Afghanistan. The government of Pakistan is now planning to enter into a preferential trade agreement (PTA) with Afghanistan. A draft PTA has already been shared with the Afghan counterparts. This paper while encouraging such steps recommends conducting a detailed analysis of those SROs which are impeding bilateral trade and hurting government's revenues. From key interviews and survey respondents, a number of examples are highlighted below.

For example, wheat is a staple commodity in Afghanistan and important for its food security. The Government of Pakistan under SRO 1185(I)/2007 imposed 35 per cent ad valorem regulatory duty on the export of wheat products. This not only reduced the wheat exports to Afghanistan in value terms (and thereby a disadvantage to Pakistani farmers) but also raised the price of the commodity for Afghan consumers. Even in times of a bumper crop, the Government of Pakistan remains reluctant to relax this duty. Recently, when the Afghan Government wanted to import wheat from India due to a lower price vis-à-vis Pakistan, the latter did not allow transit of Indian wheat in to Afghanistan. This is not only the case with wheat but also several other agricultural items. Another product with high demand in Afghanistan is pulses. The SRO 492(I) 2006 imposes a 35 per cent ad valorem regulatory duty on the export of pulses. Afghanistan has at times demanded removal of such duties citing food security reasons in the country.

Afghanistan also has a fast emerging industrial sector with a boom in the production of several fast moving consumer goods (FMCGs). However, Afghan importers face high duties on the imports of key raw materials used in their production process. An example was given where SRO594(I)/2009 imposes 25 per cent ad valorem regulatory duty on the export of lead, scrap and waste. Similarly, in the case of the textile sector (another fast growing sector in Afghanistan) SRO 323(I)/2010 imposes 15 per cent ad valorem regulatory duty on all types of yarn.

Pakistani exporters also reported that there are some SROs acting as a barrier for new Pakistani exporters to Afghanistan. Under SRO 888(I)/2009 the 'Export Oriented Units and SMEs Enterprise Rules 2008' SMEs are allowed export-related incentives in sales tax and federal excise duty.

However 80 per cent of firm's production for other countries has to be certified by the Engineering Development Board (EDB) for the last 3-years. Respondents believe that such a condition can only be met by large and already established exporters. Mostly, SMEs in Pakistan do not have export capacity. However, several SMEs in Pakistan have prospects to trade with Afghanistan due to proximity. Such firms cannot, however, arrange for the EDB certification as they are just starting to export.

It was also reported that Pakistani exporters had received orders from Afghanistan for winter supplies, which could not go through due to the unfavourable SROs. The SRO1080 (I)/2005 issued after the earthquake in Pakistan (October 2005) requires that exports of blankets, tents and tarpaulins will require approval of Federal and Provincial Disaster Management Authorities. It has been over 9 years since the earthquake and these SROs are still in place and acting as a barrier to seasonal exports to Afghanistan (e.g. in winter season).

The nascent leather industry in Afghanistan has exhibited large growth in several sub-sectors. The SRO 1011(I) 2005 imposes a 20 per cent ad valorem regulatory duty on export of raw and wet-blue hides. Due to the energy shortages in Pakistan, the domestic leather value added sector has not been able to benefit from the increased inventory of such hides. Also making of the exports expensive through regulatory duty has deprived the exporters of hides for catering to the foreign demand.

Importers in Pakistan also reported a lack of knowledge with the customs authorities regarding SRO provisions under the South Asian Association for Regional Cooperation (SAARC) and ECO (Economic Cooperation Organisation of 10 Muslim States). For example, the SRO 558(1)/2004 allows vegetables and fruits to be exempted from customs duties. However, Pakistani officials lacked the knowledge of specific vegetables under SAARC and Afghanistan's status in SAARC. This sometimes leads to unnecessary delays at the border check point and can result in decaying of perishable items. Similarly, 'Olive Oil' is exempted from customs duty for ECO countries but not for Afghanistan. The reason provided was that Afghanistan now comes under SAARC provisions. This will then have to be allowed to other SAARC member countries as well. Importers recommend that such anomalies under the SROs should be carefully checked and Pakistani consumers and exporters should not have to pay the price of such inconsistencies in customs rules.

There is also a dedicated SRO related to firms engaged in tracking and monitoring of cargo. Respondents informed that willing bidders at the time of application are not asked for specific type GSM/GPRS technology to be used. The FBR also has no mechanism for random physical audit whether such technology has been upgraded or not. Some older specifications are also allowed which becomes a key reason of pilferages. This SRO also requires an annual turnover of PKR 350 million to complete registration with FBR. This is a barrier to entry for new and smaller firms who have better technological solutions. The Ministry of Commerce is now keen to scale up railways operations for catering to transit demand. However, under this SRO there is no room for private rail carriers.

Finally, we discuss some SROs which delay the arbitration process in trading with Afghanistan. Under the SRO 888(I)/2004 FBR has a comprehensive list of business persons in the Alternative Dispute Resolution (ADR) committee. But most of these business persons were not found to have current experience of Afghan trade.

The SRO 487(I)/2003 notes the 'Takeover of Imported Goods Rules 2003' which is heavily misused in the case of Afghanistan. The discretion of border authorities is absolute and needs to be matched with exporter's safeguards. Respondents even informed of physical abuse with their clearing agent or representative during the time their merchandise was being inspected. The authorities have little monitoring on consignments arriving through the personal baggage. It was reported that 55,000 people daily pass through the land route at Torkhum (three-quarters without a visa). However, those in formal sector trade are being penalised in the form of visa and merchandise delays.

Preferential Treatment for Afghanistan

The data on the top 5 imports of Pakistan from Afghanistan include vegetables, fruits, raw cotton, carpets, rugs, hides, and skins. If the Government of Pakistan has to embark on a PTA with Afghanistan a key question will be how Pakistan can leverage the PTA for greater access to other markets and deepening the basket of goods that Pakistan utilise through this PTA. Through the survey administered, data collected and key interviews with stakeholders, a number of issues have been highlighted below:

•   A starting point for Pakistan could be to invest in increasing production capacity of these sectors in Afghanistan. For this the Board of Investment will have to allow 'automatic route' investment on both sides and State Bank of Pakistan (SBP) will need to relax rules for transfer of foreign exchange. The Afghan Government will need to reciprocate (an issue which the Ministry of Foreign Affairs can take up with their counterparts).[20]

- The State Bank of Pakistan will need to ease capital repatriation rules for dollar-denominated profits and also improve L/C's processing and rules. There is a reported delay of several months in L/Cs processing if trading via Chaman. These L/Cs carry financial limits and therefore need to be broken into smaller denominations. The businessmen resort to the *Hawala* system and there are no banks near Chaman. Formal sector traders are required to travel back to a main city for banking transactions.

- Afghanistan and Pakistan should incorporate provisions for supply chains under the PTA. This will also require removal of double taxation in services trade between both countries.

- Afghanistan already has LDC status which can be utilised by Pakistani investors willing to enter into value chain arrangements. This will allow Pakistani manufacturers in Afghanistan duty free access to more advanced economies with the added advantage of repatriation of profits back to Pakistan.

To date, there is no study that quantifies potential investment from Pakistan to Afghanistan or the preparedness of Pakistani investors (e.g. in the mining sector) for investing in Afghanistan. Several countries in the region have already started to ensure the presence of their investments in Afghanistan. China has invested US$ 3 billion to develop five million tonne copper deposit near Kabul. Several EU countries have expressed interests in tapping other natural resources. They are also willing to assist Afghanistan in consumer industries. For example, the plastics industry is getting established gradually within Afghanistan resulting in decline of plastics exports from Pakistan.

Pakistan's private sector still finds it difficult to carry out projects inside Afghanistan. This will require an amendment in foreign currency rules (by SBP) and provision of 'automatic-route' investments by Board of Investment in Pakistan.

---

20. This recommendation also applies in the case of other countries with whom Pakistan wishes to pursue investment cooperation. See Ahmed, Suleri, and Adnan (2015).

SBP's information portal on Pakistan's bank branches currently informs us that Bank Al Falah has 2 branches one in Kabul and Herat each. Habib Bank has one branch in Kabul and National Bank has a branch in Kabul and Jalalabad each. However, while the research team was trying to access these branches only Bank Al Falah was found fully operational and the rest of the bank branches could not be accessed or did not have a full portfolio of services at these branches. They also maintain a weak presence on web sources.

The above mentioned measures for value chain linkages will remain critical if Pakistan wishes to increase its potential for trade-led investments in Afghanistan. Furthermore, these measures will have important and favourable implications for improving trade in services with Afghanistan.

Summary and Conclusions
This chapter discusses various issues that require negotiation between Afghan and Pakistani trade officials including: customs clearance process; insurance of transport vehicles, safety of containers and consignments; tracking and monitoring of consignments; role of SROs hurting bilateral trade; credit facility for traders; currency swaps; sluggish progress on port, road and rail projects; high costs of air cargo; and lack of banking channels. In order to strengthen the Afghanistan-Pakistan economic cooperation, this concluding section points towards increased efforts required to strengthen the institutional framework of trade diplomacy.

*   Pakistan has to have a very cogent Afghan policy and this policy must have inputs from its economic, foreign and security advisors. The recent increased and more cordial dialogue between the two countries provides hope for collaboration in the future. Once a cohesive policy has been put in place, Pakistan must announce this policy and follow it accordingly. Of course the cornerstone of this policy should be to improve relations with Afghanistan and to support them in their development and progress.
*   The Ministries of Finance of both the countries, the Planning Commissions, and multilateral institutions should develop a 'first loss' equity fund, particularly for medium-sized entrepreneurs. A good example of such a fund, which can provide the basis of this arrangement, can be extracted from OPICs (Overseas Private Investment Corporation). Similarly, for addressing the issue of lack of insurance facilities while trading with Afghanistan, a proposal to expedite the creation of an EXIM bank should be considered.

- Expediting work on ongoing road and railways projects linking the various cities across the Afghanistan-Pakistan border.
- The civil society and think tanks working on Afghanistan-Pakistan trade cooperation should be strengthened by the governments and development partners. They should independently hold annual Afghanistan-Pakistan trade summits, which may also benefit from the presence of investors and business community of both sides. Supporting Afghan think tanks will also help in building a constituency for Pakistan's view point in Kabul.

  Independent think tanks should be supported to host annual Afghanistan-Pakistan Economic Summit, which can not only bring together the government and business community in a track-II setting but also help in strengthening a community which can undertake longer term work on bilateral cooperation.
- Both Afghanistan and Pakistan will require technical and financial assistance in expediting reforms towards bilateral economic cooperation. Following is a list of initiatives required on urgent basis.
  - The Ministry of Commerce in Pakistan should institutionalise a dedicated Afghanistan desk with research, monitoring and evaluation capabilities. This unit will:
    - coordinate the implementation of decisions undertaken at various government forums; and
    - undertake specific research tasks related to Afghanistan-Pakistan bilateral trade and investment cooperation.
  - Pakistan's Ministry of Commerce in collaboration with the customs officials needs to update current assessments on the missing facilities curtailing cross border transit and commercial trade.
  - Support will also be required for undertaking tariff and tariff-harmonisation reforms.
  - The current project tracking mechanisms within the federal government are weak and stronger support may be required for monitoring the progress of ports, road and rail infrastructure promised in the context of Afghanistan-Pakistan bilateral cooperation.
  - FBR may be supported to undertake a study on identification of specific regulatory, tariff and non-tariff measures which may be reformed in order to formalise the currently growing informal and illegal trade.

- The planned trans-boundary cooperation projects in the Central Asian region should go beyond the currently ongoing work on CASA-1000, TAPI and some road sector projects. A high-powered working group comprising experts from Afghanistan, Pakistan and select Central Asian countries should be facilitated so that an inventory of projects can be planned. Such projects will strengthen economic and political interdependencies in the region.

The elected public representatives from Afghanistan and Pakistan need to fundamentally agree on steps to resolve the trust deficit. The trust deficit is actually not that wide – especially if benefits are emphasised on. The *Pakhtun* areas of Afghanistan have very good ties with the *Pakhtun* areas of Pakistan whether in Balochistan or Khyber Pakhtunkhwa (Hussain, 2000). Another benefit that Pakistanis have at the Chaman border is that the people there are also well versed with the *Dari* language. Trade should leverage these linkages while also addressing the trust deficit. At the moment while India is perceived to be both a better and efficient partner in Afghanistan, there is much scope and potential for trade and business linkages between Afghanistan and Pakistan.

Pakistan has shown its willingness to address the security threats. In June 2014, Pakistan started a major army operation in North Waziristan. Increasing trade is to a very large extent dependent on the success of this operation and the future stability of the security situation. Furthermore, capacity building for the police and other non-military law enforcers is vital. This, however, is a long-term process and to the extent possible lies beyond the gamut of this paper. Of course, as the security situation improves the Pakistani private sector, along with the aid organisations and government authorities will be able to undertake its duties more freely and effectively especially to increase economic activity in conflict zones.[21]

Finally, for creating investment and services trade linkages between both countries, Afghanistan will require support in strengthening the regulatory institutions, particularly those related to competition policy, oil and gas and mining regulatory authorities. Pakistan's recent experience and the evolution of Competition Commission of Pakistan are citied in recent literature as a regulatory success. Pakistan should offer formal support in building such institutions for Afghanistan with possible financial support from development partners.

---

21. See Khan and Ahmed (2014) for role of private sector in conflict zones.

This paper has also pointed some research gaps, which may be addressed in future studies. A list of such studies is as follows:

- A research study is required to look into the enhanced security measures for merchandise trade along Afghanistan-Pakistan border. United Nations Office on Drugs and Crime (UNODC) in Pakistan already has a baseline analysis on this subject which may be updated in the context of cross-border trade and investment activities.

- Till date, there is no study that quantifies potential investment from Pakistan to Afghanistan or the preparedness of Pakistani investors (e.g. in the mining sector) for investing in Afghanistan. This is despite the realisation in Pakistan that the business community would benefit from Afghanistan's LDC status for leveraging export revenues. A value chain analysis of Pakistani SMEs currently trading with Afghanistan is also missing.

- There are no evidence based estimates of either the informal trade or smuggling.

- While Pakistan has undertaken tariff harmonisation exercise with respect to South Asian countries, there is a need to undertake a similar exercise with Central Asian Commerce Ministries. The increased trade diplomacy with Tajikistan and Kyrgyz Republic will also prompt a similar requirement.

- The documented Grievance Redressal Mechanism in Afghanistan-Pakistan Trade and Transit is rarely practiced. It is important to analyse the current challenges before PTA is signed and transit facility is extended to Tajikistan.

- The Commerce Ministries of Pakistan and Tajikistan have agreed to conceptualise in the coming days the Peshawar – Dushanbe Economic Corridor project. It is important at this stage to quantify potential gains from this corridor in trade, cross-border investments and infrastructure cooperation (e.g. in energy and petroleum products).

- As a result of the decline in NATO (North Atlantic Treaty Organisation) transit trade, the corresponding estimates regarding unskilled and semi-skilled workers facing unemployment or underemployment are weak as many are not registered with the labour market institutions. It is important that the Government of Khyber Pakhtunkhwa along with the federal government put in place alternate livelihood schemes to preserve peace, increase the overall economic wellbeing, as well as improve the quality of life.

- A study to quantify the potential of services trade between Afghanistan and Pakistan is also required. Such a study should highlight regulatory issues such as the desired agreement to resolve double taxation.

References

Ahmad, Manzoor (2015). *Boosting Exports for Economic Growth.* Business Recorder (Special Supplement), 27 April.

Ahmed, V., A. Q. Suleri, M. A. Wahab, and A. Javed (2015). Informal Flow of Merchandise from India: The Case of Pakistan in N. Taneja, and S. Pohit (eds.) *India-Pakistan Trade: Strengthening Economic Relations.* Springer India, New Delhi.

Ahmed V., A. Q. Suleri, and M. Adnan (2015). FDI in India: Prospects for Pakistan in N. Taneja, and S. Pohit (eds.) *India-Pakistan Trade - Strengthening Economic Relations.* Springer India, New Delhi.

Ahmed, V. and S. Shabbir (2014). *Afghanistan-Pakistan Trade: Welfare Impact on Balochistan and Khyber Pakhtunkhwa.* Policy Review 2, February. Sustainable Development Policy Institute (SDPI). Available at: http://www.sdpi.org/publications/files/Policy%20Review-FEBRUARY.pdf

Ahmed, V. and C. O'Donoghue (2010). *Global Economic Crisis and Poverty in Pakistan.* International Journal of Microsimulation, Vol. 3, No. 1, pp. 127-129.

Blomberg, S. B., G. D. Hess, and A. Orphanides (2004). *The Macroeconomic Consequences of Terrorism.* Journal of Monetary Economics, Vol. 51, pp. 1007-1032.

Gaibulloev, K. and T. Sandler (2008). *The Impact of Terrorism and Conflicts on Growth in Asia.* Working Paper, School of Economic, Political and Policy Sciences, University of Texas at Dallas.

Hameed, Sadika (2012). *Prospects for Indian-Pakistani Cooperation in Afghanistan. Centre for Strategic and International Studies.* Centre for Strategic and International Studies, Washington D.C.

Hussain, S. Iftikhar (2000). *Some Major Pukhtoon Tribes Along the Pak-Afghan Border.* Arena Study Centre - Russia and Central Asia - University of Peshawar and Hans Seidel Foundation.

Hussain, Sayed Waqar and Alauddin Masood (2008). *The Impact of Afghan Transit Trade on NWFP's Economy, 1999-2000.* Published by Henn Seidal Foundation Germany, Islamabad.

Khan, Riaz Mohammad (2011). *Afghanistan and Pakistan: Conflict, Extremism, and Resistance to Modernity.* Johns Hopkins University Press, Baltimore.

Khan, S. A. and V. Ahmed (2014). *Peaceful Economies: Assessing the Role of the Private Sector in Conflict Prevention in Pakistan.* Stability: International Journal of Security & Development, Vol. 3, No. (1): 24, pp. 1-9, DOI: http://dx.doi.org/10.5334/sta.dv

Muhammad, Nisar (2012). *Agreement for Traffic in Transit among the Governments of the People's Republic of China, the Kyrgyz Republic, the Republic of Kazakhstan and the Islamic Republic of Pakistan.* Presentation at Roundtable on Ways Forward for Corridor-Based Transport Facilitation Arrangements in the CAREC Region held in Beijing, on 2 July 2012.

PAJCCI (2013). *Pak-Afghan Trade: Trend and Issues.* Pakistan Afghanistan Joint Chambers of Commerce and Industry (PAJCCI), December 2013.

PILDAT (2012). *Pak-Afghan Trade.* PILDAT Discussion Paper. Pakistan Institute of Legislative Development and Transparency (PILDAT). Available at: http://www.pildat.org/Publications/publication/FP/Pak-AfghanTrade-DiscussionPaperDec2011.pdf

Taneja, N., M.Sarvananthan, B.K. Karmacharya, and S.Pohit(2004).*India's Informal Trade with Sri Lanka and Nepal: An Estimation.*South Asia Economic Journal, Vol. 5, No. 1. pp. 27-54

World Bank (2014). *Afghanistan Economic Update.* April. The World Bank.

EIGHT

RECENT DEVELOPMENTS IN NEPAL'S TRADE LOGISTICS: IMPLICATION FOR SOUTH ASIA REGIONAL COOPERATION

Pushpa Raj Rajkarnikar

Introduction

Located between two big neighbours – India and China – Nepal is a landlocked country. It has been following liberal trade policy since last three decades. It has expressed its commitment to global and regional integration through different international or regional organisations. Nepal is a member of the WTO, SAARC and BIMSTEC. Also, it has bilateral trade agreements and transit agreements with India, Bangladesh, China and some other countries.

Nepal's total trade was accounted for 43.2 per cent of GDP in 2014. Thus, Nepal's trade dependency ratio, defined as percentage of total merchandise trade to Gross Domestic Product (GDP), is close to that of Bangladesh, India and Sri Lanka. Among SAARC countries, Nepal's trade dependency ratio is less than only Bhutan and Maldives. On the other, Nepal's export to GDP ratio is lowest among all SAARC countries except Afghanistan; it was just 4 per cent in fiscal year 2014-15. Among many other reasons, inadequate and inefficient logistics services have been considered as a major constraint to realise the export potentials of Nepal.

Intra-regional merchandise trade is one of the most important indicators of the depth of regional economic integration. However, trade among SAARC countries remains at just 5 per cent of their total trade, while regional trade among ASEAN countries is 25 per cent and 45 per cent among ASEAN+3 countries. Intra-regional trade is less than 2 per cent of SAARC'S GDP, while it is more than 20 per cent in case of ASEAN. Trade among countries of the region is constrained by a number of factors including weak trade logistics. Intra-regional trade cost for South Asia is greater than inter-regional trade cost (De, 2014). Logistics inefficiencies are a primary source of trade cost (Arvis *et al.*, 2014).

Nepal's trade with SAARC countries accounted for 65 per cent of its total trade in the fiscal year 2014-15. However, share of India in it is as high as 98.8 per cent. Nepal's trade with other SAARC countries is in fact negligible, which is only 0.8 per cent of total trade. This shows that Nepal is much integrated with India, but not with the region as such. Enhancement of regional connectivity would help Nepal's wider integration in South Asia.

Trade Logistics

Trade logistics is one of the most important elements of connectivity development. Trade logistics is broadly defined as transportation, storage and handling facilities required for moving goods from origin to destination in course of trading across the border. Logistics services are required behind and beyond border including transit country. Logistics services form the basis for trade efficiency. Without efficient logistic support, a country or region may not gain competitive strength. Thus, it is an essential element required for providing conducive environment for doing business. Hence, adequate and effective delivery of logistics services is critical for facilitating trade. However, according to the Logistics Performance Index (LPI) 2014, prepared by the World Bank, performance level of the South Asian countries is not encouraging. All of them rank below 50 among 160 countries. Among the South Asian countries, India has been occupying the highest position over the years from 2007 to 2014. However, its position has gone down from 39th rank in 2007 to 54th rank in 2014. Table 1 shows that not only India, but all the South Asian countries except Nepal, Sri Lanka and Maldives have seen a fall in their ranks.

Table 1: LPI Index Scores of South Asian Countries

(Rank)

Country	2007	2010	2012	2014
India	39	47	46	54
Pakistan	68	110	71	72
Bangladesh	87	79	–	108
Sri Lanka	92	137	81	89
Bhutan	128	128	107	143
Nepal	130	147	151	105
Afghanistan	150	143	135	158
Maldives	–	125	104	82
Total members (average)	150	155	154	160

Source: The World Bank (2014)

Current Status of Trade Logistics in Nepal

Though overall LPI rank of Nepal has risen from 130 in 2007 to 105 in 2014, it is still far below than India, Pakistan, Sri Lanka and Maldives. The average of overall LPI scores of landlocked and coastal countries, for the period 2007 to 2014, shows that the coastal countries score better than their landlocked peers at similar incomes. Such a difference is highest in South Asia (Arvis *et al.*, 2014). Among the landlocked countries of South Asia, Nepal is in better position than rest two countries – Afghanistan and Bhutan – in terms of LPI scores.

Transport

Being a landlocked and mountainous country, Nepal heavily depends on road transport for trade. The total length of road network by mid. March 2015 reached 26,935 km with 11,349 km black topped, 6,192 km graveled, and 9,394 km earthen (fair weather) road[1]. However, most of the roads are narrow and in poor condition, limiting the speed of vehicles. These roads were built only to serve national priorities without any consideration of cross-border issues. The Government of Nepal initiated to construct a fast track road linking Kathmandu, the capital town, and Birgunj, the main trade outlet. This 76 km long expressway substantially reduces time, distance and cost of moving goods, and, hence, has a very positive impact on Nepal's trading across border. However, the progress is very slow. The track has not opened completely.

The large scale earthquake (7.8 magnitude) that struck Nepal on 25 April 2015 and subsequent aftershocks have damaged several roads including 110 km long Araniko Highway, the most important trade route to China. This route to China is not yet open, and the inland trade between Nepal and China has almost ceased.

The number of vehicles is increasing in the country. By the first eight months of the fiscal year 2014-15, the number of vehicles in the country has reached to 1,925,434. However, transport service is costly and inefficient due to syndication by transport service providers. Syndication has been prevailing for long and the government policies and institutions are weak and unable to combat it.

As roads are narrow and warehouse facilities are inadequate, traffic congestion is frequent in border customs. Mr. Ganesh Lath, former Chairman

1.   Refer, Economic Survey of Nepal, 2014-15.

of Birgunj Industry and Commerce Association, reported in *Karobar Daily* on 19 February 2016 that it takes three days to move a cargo from Raxaul, the adjoining border town of Nepal in Birgunj, while it takes only two-days from Kolkata, the sea port of India, to reach Raxaul. This may be little exaggeration, but it is true that there is a severe problem of congestion. Problem of traffic congestion exists also in different sections of other major roads like Prithivi Highway, Tribhuvan Highway, Narayanghat Muglin Road, Araniko highway, etc. due to narrow width or poor condition of roads.

Nepal has only two short rail links, one from Janakpur (Nepal) to Jayanagar (India) and other from Birgunj (Nepal) to Raxaul (India). The Janakpur – Jayanagar 42 km rail link is the oldest one and is narrow gauge both for goods and passengers trains. This rail line is dilapidated. The 5.4 km rail line from Birgunj Inland Container Depot (ICD) to Raxaul (India) is for goods traffic only. The freight services on this rail line started from July 2004 under the Rail Services Agreement signed between Nepal and India in 2004. This is a broad gauge line. This line has made possible to link Nepal with major cities and sea ports of India. This has also avoided transshipment of cargo on the border. The condition of this rail line is good and it has been operating smoothly. Currently, it is being operated along Birgunj – Kolkata and Haldia ports corridor. This is the most significant corridor for Nepal, handling over 95 per cent of rail traffic to and from Nepal.

Air services play an important role in international trade particularly for landlocked country like Nepal. The high value and perishable commodities are traded through air routes. However, trade through air routes accounts only for about 15 per cent of the total trade of Nepal. Nepal has only one international airport, which is congested and lacks modern amenities. The Government of Nepal has initiated construction of a second international airport years back, but the progress is very slow. It is still in initial stage. Nepal has bilateral air services agreement with 36 countries, but only 26 international airlines are providing regular air services to and from Nepal.

Domestic air transport too has a significant place in the transportations of goods to and from the hinterland and remote areas of the country. Currently, there are 50 domestic airports in the country, but only 32 are in operation. About 17 airlines are providing domestic air services in the country.

Warehousing

Warehousing is an integral part of trade logistics. It is required at customs, ICDs and ports. It may be in the form of covered sheds, parking lots and godowns, etc. The need of warehousing facility depends on the clearance procedure. Longer clearance procedure requires more warehousing facility. Similarly, form of ware housing depends on mode of transport and nature of goods to be traded.

There are altogether 30 main customs offices all over the country including one at Tribhuvan International Airport. However, in terms of value of trade, only seven customs offices are considered as major ones. Birgunj customs office alone accounts for 70 per cent of total trade. It has three godowns – one for exports and two for imports. In addition, there is a parking space for trucks at Birgunj customs area. The parking space is, however, very inadequate compared to its demand. Because of space limitation in the parking area for the export traffic, vehicles are parked on the road.

There are four ICDs in Nepal – one is rail based and three are road based. These ICDs have proper warehousing facilities. The Tribhuvan International Airport customs office in Kathmandu has a modern cargo complex of 10,200 square meters. The full capacity of this terminal is 24,000 tonnes of exports and 12,000 tonnes of imports. This warehousing space is reportedly adequate, but needs to be improved in terms of equipment and other facilities. There is also a cold storage for export of perishable products.

Customs

In order to make customs services more effective and efficient, the Government of Nepal has been continuously advancing the process of customs reform since 2003, when the first set of reforms was launched. In the fourth phase of reforms, it introduced a four-year Customs Reform and Modernisation Strategies and Action Plan (CRMSAP) 2013-2017. The first guiding principle of this document is to reduce trading cost.

There are altogether 30 main customs offices and 143 sub-customs offices across the country. Nepal has implemented new Customs Act 2007 and rules, which have included many provisions in line with the Revised Kyoto Convention (RKC), through it is yet to accede it. Draft legislation for accession to the Revised Kyoto Convention (RKC) is in the process of getting approval from the parliament.

Nepal has started the process of customs automation in 1996 by introducing ASYCUDA (Automated System of Customs Data). For this purpose, a Single Administrative Document (SAD) was also introduced. To facilitate customs declaration and clearance of cargo, broker module and risk-based selectivity module were also introduced. Nepal Customs is thus moving towards digitalised customs services. It has now upgraded its software to ASYCUDA world in some customs offices.

The Department of Customs has introduced selectivity module to expedite cargo clearance and also established Post Clearance Audit (PCA) office and Intelligence Section to minimise risks. Thus, there have been remarkable legal, technological and administrative reforms in customs procedures of Nepal. The customs component of LPI also shows continuous improvement since 2007. In 2014, the score reached to 2.31 as against 1.83 in 2007. Yet, the score is still below than that of India, Pakistan, Sri Lanka and Maldives, and there are problems of simplification and harmonisation of customs procedures. Logistics services are still inadequate. Reform process is required to be continued to bring up Nepal Customs procedures to international standard.

Integrated Check Posts

Integrated Check Post (ICP) is a mechanism to facilitate trade across the border with harmonised and simplified customs clearance procedure and modern facilities in land customs at the border. Nepal and India have agreed in 2006 through a memorandum of understanding (MoU) to establish ICPs at four main border points between them. These border points include Birgunj (Nepal)/Raxaul (India), Biratnagar (Nepal)/Jogbani (India), Bhairahawa (Nepal)/Sunauli (India) and Nepalgunj (Nepal)/Rupaidiha (India). According to the MoU, these ICPs are to be built by India, whereas only land has to be provided by Nepal on Nepal side. However, the progress is very slow in this regard. Even after ten years, no ICP has come into operation in any of the four border points. There have been some works at Birgunj/Raxaul and Biratnagar/Jogbani border points. However, the work has not even started at Bhairahawa/Sunauli and Nepalgunj/Rupaidiha border points.

Cargo Handling (Freight Forwarding)

Freight forwarders and customs agents or brokers play an important role in international cargo movement. Freight forwarders take charge of goods from exporter/importer and issue Bill of Lading on-behalf of shipping companies; prepare all necessary documents for the movement of cargoes. Customs agents or brokers take responsibility of getting clearance of goods from customs on behalf of importer/exporter. There are about 100 freight forwarders and 500 customs agents working in Nepal. They are all licensed by the Department of Customs. Efficient handling of cargoes requires not only efficient customs administration but also efficient customs agents as well as advanced equipment. But, in most of the customs houses of Nepal, required equipment are either not adequate or are out of order. This has made handling of goods difficult and unsafe.

Trade Logistics in Transit

Birgunj (Nepal)–Raxaul–Kolkata/Haldia (India) road corridor is the transit corridor that is used by Nepal to trade with the world. This 1047 km long corridor has some physical and non-physical barriers. Nepalese trucks are allowed to operate on designated transit routes in India. However, they need entry permit for every trip to India with a validity of three months. Also, impositions of bonds or undertaking at Kolkata discourage Nepalese truck owners from taking their trucks to Kolkata/Haldia. Nepalese transit cargoes are required to be insured against deflection in India at high bond prices fixed by the Indian Customs. On the other hand, Indian trucks are allowed anywhere into Nepal, but are given a limit of 72 hours to return to India. The Birgunj–Kolkata/Haldia rail corridor is yet another important transit corridor. The distance between Birgunj and Kolkata is 704 km and between Birgunj and Haldia is 832 km. This railway service came into operation in 2004 under the Rail Service Agreement signed between Nepal and India.

Most landlocked countries depend on more than one transit country to gain access to port facilities. This provides a competitive element in ensuring that transit costs of imports and exports are not unreasonably burdened. But, Nepal is dependent only on India for its transit trade. Kolkata and Haldia are the two designated ports to Nepal under Kolkata Port Trust. These are the only ports of entry and exit of Nepalese transit cargoes. As these ports are feeder ports linked to Singapore and Colombo, Nepalese Cargoes are required to transship at these ports. Due to this, cost and time for Nepalese import and exports have increased. Further, there are problems of congestion, lack of handling equipment, shortage of storage facilities, etc.

Bangladesh has designated Chittagong and Mongla ports for Nepal's transit trade. India has agreed to provide Kakarvitta–Fulbari (Phulbari)–Banglabandha route for the passage of exports and imports with and through Bangladesh. Nepal has signed an agreement with Bangladesh to use these ports. This agreement provides alternative access to Bangladesh seaports. However, use of these ports is not significant as there are different problems, including transshipment of cargo on Bangladesh border. Nepalese trucks are not allowed to enter into Bangladesh. There is no permanent customs office at Phulbari border post in India. Indian customs officers are normally informed two hours in advance of cargo arrival and are summoned from Phulbari Customs Station, which is 2.5 km from the border checkpost. Also at Banglabandh checkpost, Bangladeshi customs officers are to be summoned from Panchagarh, which is 50 km away for clearing of cargoes. Trucks cannot move freely at any time of the day in the Indian section of this corridor. They must be escorted by the Indian security as a convoy at a time mutually agreed between the parties concerned. On the top of these problems, road condition in the Indian section of this corridor is poor.

This road is a part of 10 road corridors identified by SAARC Regional Multi-modal Transport Study (SRMTS) by a team, led by Dr. Rahmatullah. Improvement of this road will benefit not only Nepal but also Bangladesh and India. However, mere upgradation or improvement in physical connectivity may not be enough for seamless movement of goods across borders. Regulatory support is essential. In this context, Bangladesh, Bhutan, India and Nepal (BBIN), a sub-grouping of four SAARC nations, have signed a Motor Vehicle Agreement (MVA) in June 2015, and also ratified in 2016. With the implementation of this MVA, vehicles of Nepal will reach Bangladesh through India without any hassle.

Recent Development

During Nepal's Prime Minister K.P. Sharma Oli's recent visit to India in February 2016, letters were exchanged between two countries on:

- Simplification of transit between Nepal and Bangladesh through Kakarvitta – Banglabandha Corridor;
- Operationalisation of Vishakhapatnam Port – Amendment in treaty of transit;
- Rail transit to/from Vishakhapatnam – Amendment in Rail Service Agreement; and

- Rail transit facility through Singabad for Nepal's trade with and through Bangladesh

As discussed above, there are a number of non-physical barriers in moving goods along the Kakarvitta – Banglabandha corridor. Hence, simplification of transit in this corridor is very important for improving trade logistics for Nepal's trade with and through Bangladesh.

In view of limitations at ports of Kakarvitta/Haldia, Nepal has approached India to provide it with additional port in Vishakhapatnam for its transit traffic. Exchange of letters for operationalisation of this port by amending existing treaty of transit and Rail Service Agreement between two countries is a remarkable achievement of the visit of the Nepal's Prime Minister. It will have a long-term impact. However, access to this port will depend on physical and non-physical quality of the route designated. The port can be accessed by both motor and rail routes. Birgunj – Raxaul – Katihar – Singabad – Rohanpur – Khulana – Mongla is a regional rail corridor identified by SRMTS. Although there are several physical and non-physical barriers, operationalisation of this rail link will benefit Nepal, Bangladesh and also India. Bangladesh and India had already agreed in 2010 through a joint communiqué that Rohanpur – Singabad – Katihar – Raxaul – Birgunj broad gauge rail link would be available for Nepal's third country trade through Mongla port and, also, for bilateral trade between Bangladesh and Nepal. However, in this regard letters were exchanged between India and Nepal only during Nepal's Prime Minister's visit to India.

Nepal's Prime Minister K.P Sharma Oli also visited China in March 2016. During his visit, an agreement on transit trade was signed between the two countries. This agreement bears high value for Nepal. This will end Nepal's sole dependency on India for transit of goods to and from third countries. Of two neighbouring countries – India and China – Nepal has been using transit facilities of India because of topographical difficulties to reach China. However, in recent years, China has done tremendous development in infrastructure. Roads and railways are coming to the border of Nepal. Nepal needs to develop roads to China border to take advantage of this agreement. Although sea ports in China are far from the Nepal – China border, transit of goods may be feasible due to logistics efficiency, in terms of cost and time, in China. Thus, this is a landmark achievement.

Regional Implication

Upgradation of Kakarvitta – Bangladesh road corridor will contribute to enhance regional trade of Nepal, India, Bangladesh and to some extent that of Bhutan. Similarly, Motor vehicle Agreement (MVA) among BBIN countries will also help in increasing trade among these countries. Among SAARC countries, India is not only big and economically strong but is also centrally located. Other countries may take advantage of logistics development in India. Similarly, India and China may take advantage of easy access to each other's market and beyond using Nepal – China connectivity. It is much important in view of China's effort to revive the ancient Silk Road. Nepal and China have also agreed to conduct a joint feasibility study on free trade agreement between two countries. This shows their willingness to move towards free trade arrangement.

Conclusions

Nepal's trade sector is weak with continuous and widening trade deficit. Though improving, trade logistics are inadequate and inefficient in the country. Also, there are problems in transit. Recently, Nepal has entered into some landmark agreements with India and China, which will have long-term impact on strengthening trade logistics required to support Nepal's foreign trade. However, Nepal's implementation capacity is very low, and also there are instances of bilateral agreements not being implemented or delayed for long. If these agreements are implemented, they will enhance connectivity among BBIN countries and market integration between not only Nepal and China but also between SAARC countries and China. But, the agreements need to be supported by adequate and efficient logistics services. As infrastructure and other trade logistics demand huge fund, large and economically strong countries like India and China, and financial institutions like the Asian Development Bank (ADB) and newly established the Asian Infrastructure Investment Bank (AIIB), should support in implementing trade logistics projects of regional importance.

References

Arvis, J.F., D. Saslavsky, L. Ojala, B. Shepherd, C. Busch and A. Raj (2014). *Connecting to Compete: Trade Logistics in the Global Economy*. The World Bank, Washington D.C.

ADB and UESCAP (2014). *Trade Process Analysis Report for Sub-regional Co-operation in South Asia*. Asian Development Bank (ADB) and the United Nations Economic and Social Commission for Asia and the Pacific (UNESCAP), Manila and Bangkok

De, Prabir and Kavita Iyengar (eds) (2014). *Developing Economic Corridors in South Asia*. Manila: Asian Development Bank (ADB).

De, Prabir (2014). *Improving Trade and Transport Facilitation and Transit in South Asia*. Paper Presented in Regional Conference on Deepening Economic Cooperation in South Asia: Expectations from the 18th SAARC Summit, 2-24 November, Kathmandu, Organised by SAWTEE, Kathmandu.

Kelegama, Saman, R. Adhikari, P. Sharma, and P. Kharel (2012). *Regional Economic Integration: Challenges for South Asia during turbulent times*. South Asia Watch on Trade, Economics and Environment (SAWTEE), Kathmandu; and South Asia Centre for Policy Studies (SACEPS), Kathmandu.

Ministry of Finance, Government of Nepal (2015). Economic Survey 2014-2015: Ministry of Finance, Government of Nepal, Kathmandu.

Rajkarnikar, P.R. (2010). *Adequacy and Effectiveness of Logistic Services in Nepal, Implication for Export Performance*. ARTNeT Working Paper Series, No. 79, April, Bangkok.

SAARC Secretariat (2006). *SAARC Regional Multimodal Transport Study (SRMTS)*, Kathmandu

NINE

TRANSIT THROUGH BANGLADESH: PROSPECTS AND CHALLENGES

Mohammad Yunus

Introduction

Despite the fact that South Asia has been one of the fastest growing economic regions in the world, surface transport system remains fragmented due to various historical, political, and economic reasons. Transport cost is an extremely significant determinant of country's competitiveness in today's competitive world. Therefore, the importance of an efficient and integrated transit[1] system cannot be overemphasized.

Bangladesh enjoys a unique geographical location in South Asia. Bangladesh has two sea ports, namely, Chittagong and Mongla, the services of which the country can provide to the landlocked countries of South Asia and the entire region. Further, as Bangladesh is about to develop two deep sea ports at Matharbari, Cox's Bazar, and Payra, Patuakhali, the competitive edge of Chittagong and Mongla ports vis-à-vis other regional ports will increase manifold. Together with Matharbari, Payra, Chittagong, and Mongla ports, Bangladesh is undoubtedly placed to be a transit hub of the region.

Currently, trade in South Asia faces escalated transport costs due to lack of direct transit corridors. These shortcomings make it both difficult and inefficient for increased trade and investment in the region. For instance, domestic trade of the North Eastern Region of India (NER) with the rest India as well as NER's international trade has to detour through the 'chicken neck'[2], a distance about 1500 km on average.

---

1. Transit, connectivity and transshipment are often used interchangeably. However, these are distinct concepts. While connectivity is a necessary prerequisite for transit as it is for trade, transshipment is neither necessary nor sufficient for transit or trade to take place.

2. The narrow strip of Indian Territory at the border of the states of West Bengal and Assam is popularly known as the 'chicken neck'. On either sides of the chicken neck lie Bangladesh, and Bhutan/Nepal.

The shipment of Assam tea to Europe travels 1400 km to reach Kolkata Port through the 'chicken neck' as there is no agreement at present for India to use the traditional route through Chittagong Port, which reduces the travel distance by about half. Similarly, international shipments from Agartala, capital of Tripur province of India, are required to travel about 1645 km to reach Kolkata Port through the 'chicken neck', while Chittagong Port is only 400 km away from Agartala. The distance will come down to approximately 700 km if a southern corridor for the NER of India from Chittagong port is adopted. Similarly, Bhutan and Nepal may also benefit from accessing Mongla Port in Bangladesh for their international trade.

It is crucial for Bangladesh to realise that the proposed transit service has no market outside the region. Similarly, Bhutan, China, India, and Nepal need to recognise that no country other than Bangladesh can provide these services. In the absence of WTO transit rules, the strategic interaction between Bangladesh and these countries is akin to bilateral monopoly, and, hence, counties can bilaterally settle on charges and fees related to transit.[3] However, the *freedom of transit* stipulates that transit traffic is not subject to any unnecessary delays or restrictions and is exempt from customs duties and all transit duties or other charges[4]. Of course, Bangladesh and India can impose 'reasonable' charges commensurate with administrative expenses entailed by transit or with the costs of services rendered. Even if WTO regulations are dispensed with, it can be theoretically established that the countries in the region will gain more with cooperative game than with the non-cooperative game which is currently at work. In fact, Bangladesh, Bhutan, China, India, and Nepal all stand to gain substantially from cooperation in transit services. While Bangladesh's gain would be direct in the sense of increased foreign exchange earnings, those for Bhutan, China, India, and Nepal would be indirect in the form of savings in distance, costs and time.

Once Bangladesh allows transit, Bhutan, China, India, Nepal, and Myanmar are expected to benefit from lower transport costs due to (i) shorter and direct transit corridors through Bangladesh (and India), and (ii) reduced travel time, mostly due to shorter transit corridors. In turn, Bangladesh would benefit from earnings based on charges and fees in concordance with the relevant rules and regulations of the WTO.

---

3. Refer, Article V, GATT, 1994

4. Refer, Article V (paragraph 2), GATT, 1994

A decision in favour of or against transit raises serious questions of economics, politics and the regional development strategy. Against this backdrop this chapter discusses the prospects and challenges of Bangladesh to be a gateway for transit for the NER of India, the Southern Chinese provinces, particularly Yunnan as well as Bhutan and Nepal. Myanmar can also increase its economic ties with India through Bangladesh.

Rest of the chapter is organized as follows. Section 2 points out the major predicaments along the possible transit corridors. Section 3 highlights a few major initiatives that the regional governments have taken into considerations but are yet to be meaningfully implemented. Section 4 analyses the proposed corridors and compares their competitive edges in terms of reduced distance, travel time and costs per tonne. Section 5 estimates the total volume of freight traffic that would be generated from Bhutan, Yunnan of China, NER of India, and Nepal and the potential levels of diversion through Bangladesh. Sections 6 to 8 shed light on what Bangladesh needs to spend on the development of state-of-the-art infrastructures and facilities, the charges and fees can collect, and ensuing viability of each of the corridors. Section 9 flags some issues that are likely to crop up once proposed transit becomes operational. Finally, Section 10 makes a few concluding remarks and suggests some measures to make the transit system meaningful.

Major Predicaments in Road, Rail, and Waterways

For assessing Bangladesh's gains from transit, 14 different corridors consisting of 8 road corridors, 5 rail corridors and 1 water corridor are analysed. All of them may be selected for potential transit services between Bangladesh and Bhutan, China, India, Nepal, and Myanmar. The analysis hinges upon two major aspects of transit. First, an analysis of the opportunity arising from the potential use of Chittagong and Mongla ports by Bhutan, China, Nepal, and the NER of India. Second, using Bangladesh's surface and water transportation as a corridor from Kolkata to pass through the NER of India and then to Myanmar and to China. As smooth connectivity is a necessary precondition for successful implementation of transit, it is important at first to understand the current obstacles in the regional transit system. To that end the current problems in a few of the roads, rail routes, and waterways were discussed separately for illustrative purpose only.

Roads

Nearly 70 per cent of overland trade between Bangladesh and India passes through Benapole-Petrapole border point. However, the only road connecting Petrapole to Kolkata is merely 5.5 meter wide and highly congested. Trucks cannot move across the border and all freight traffic needs to be transshipped at the border point, resulting in further congestion and delay in time and cost implications. There are no direct truck movements across the borders with the NER. Freight consignments are transshipped at the borders such as at Benapole - Petrapole. India allows the use of the Banglabandha - Phulbari corridor only for bilateral trade between Bangladesh and Nepal. Similarly, Burimari - Chengrabandha corridor is allowed for bilateral trade between Bangladesh and Bhutan. Although the road segments in Bangladesh, Bhutan and Nepal are fairly maintained, the corresponding road segments along these two corridors within India are poorly maintained, if not neglected.

Railways

Freight trains of Indian Railway (IR) travel to the border stations of Bangladesh and the locomotive of the Bangladesh Railway (BR) pull the IR wagons into the country for transshipment to take place. The BR wagons also do not cross the Indian border as Bangladeshi locomotives are unable to haul air-braked freight wagons used by the IR, and is restricted to BCX wagons (covered, vacuum braked eight-wheeler wagons). Holding capacity of loops, yards and terminals are inadequate on the Bangladesh side even at the current low volume of traffic (SAARC Secretariat, 2006). The present load restriction over Jamuna Bridge prohibits movement of fully loaded broad gauge wagons across the bridge,[5] although a dual gauge railway network now exists up to Dhaka. Thus, transshipment between broad gauge / meter gauge (BG/MG) trains could take place at the inland container depot (ICD) in Dhaka until a second one at Dhirashram, Gazipur becomes operational in the next few years.

Inland Water Transport

Inland waterways provide a potentially lower cost alternative for transporting low-value cargo in the region. On 1 November 1972, a Protocol on Inland Water Transit and Trade was signed between Bangladesh and

---

5. Recently, it appears that ISO containers on low platform BLCA/BLCB flat cars having a floor height of 1009 mm can be allowed over the Bridge without any load restrictions.

India in accordance with the Article V of the Trade Agreement, 1972 for a period of five years. This agreement has since been regularly updated. The protocol provided for a uniform documentation for vessels, arrangements for settlement, clearance and remittance, uniform toll charges of vessels, etc. Despite low costs and the absence of cross-border transshipment requirements, inland water transport (IWT) corridors are at a competitive disadvantage because of insufficient navigational aids, rapid siltation, low speeds, and physical constraints such as poor warehouse facilities and narrow access roads to the ports of call (Thapliyal, 1999).

Transit Initiatives
The countries made several attempts both in miniature and grandeur scale to forge regional cooperation where transit is an inseparable component. But, the copious number of regional groupings, organisations, fora and sub-fora, initiatives, projects and treaties is difficult to follow or visualise influence. These fora are overlapping at times, and having competing mandates. Since there is no supranational institution or single leading country, these fora are likely to succeed in spawning transparent dialogue processes, facilitating cooperative solutions to regional issues such as transit. Even though political commitment has ushered into a new era following these initiatives, the implications of the expressed willingness of the policymakers till date are not in place. It is thus imperative to shed light on the major initiatives before Bangladesh commits to any bilateral and multilateral transit agreement.

BIMSTEC
The Bay of Bengal Initiative for Multi-Sectoral Technical and Economic Cooperation (BIMSTEC) was established in 1997 with Bangladesh, Bhutan, India, Myanmar, Nepal, Sri Lanka and Thailand as members. BIMSTEC emphasises on connectivity by road, rail, air, including digital connectivity and electricity corridors throughout the region. Trade liberalisation and free movement of people, goods and services are at the heart of such connectivity. The BIMSTEC region has a huge amount of untapped natural, water and human resources. BIMSTEC has 14 priority sectors covering all areas of cooperation, where a member country takes lead of one such priority sector. Seven priority sectors of cooperation were identified in 1998 and the rest 7 were identified in 2005.

Kunming Initiative

The Kunming Initiative, originally a Track II sub-regional organisation that includes Bangladesh, China, India and Myanmar (BCIM), was born out of the attempts to link the development plans of the Southwestern Chinese province of Yunnan with India's North Eastern Region (NER) under the Look East Policy. To revive landlocked areas that once straddled the Southern Silk Route and used to see throngs of merchants, the Track II Kunming Initiative, signed on 17 August 1999, innovates in several regards. The proposed BCIM region covers Bangladesh, Myanmar, Yunnan province of China, West Bengal and NER of India, which has an area of approximately 1.65 million square km. The corridor, known as K2K, stretches from Kunming to Kolkata (Kunming-Ruili-Bhamo-Lashio-Mandalay-Tamu-Imphal-Sylhet-Dhaka-Kolkata) over 2,800 km. In February 2013, members of BCIM organised a car rally to assess the road situation to be used for transit. The 3,000 km journey followed from Kolkata through to Jessore to Dhaka to Sylhet to Silchar to Imphal to Kalay to Mandalay to Ruili to Tengchong to Erhai Lake to Dali to Kunming. In December 2013, the four nations drew up a long discussed plan, emphasising the need to quickly improve physical connectivity in the region. This marked the formal endorsement on the BCIM-EC by the four nations, whereby it was agreed that the corridor will run from Kunming to Kolkata, linking Mandalay in Myanmar as well as Dhaka and Chittagong in Bangladesh.

Thus, Bangladesh is motivated to work on both East-West and North-South corridors. On East-West corridor, a large portion of Bangladesh's trade with India is carried out through the land ports. If these corridors are used efficiently and are channeled properly with China, there is great opportunity to reduce the current transportation costs. The North-South corridor is envisaged to connect the BCIM hinterland with Chittagong, Mongla ports and the proposed Sonadia deep sea port. These corridors open up immense economic opportunities for Bangladesh and the other countries.

SAARC

The 12th SAARC Summit in 2004 called for strengthening transport, transit and communications links across South Asia. Accordingly, the SAARC Secretariat commissioned a comprehensive study in 2006 (SAARC Secretariat, 2006). The study identified several existing and potential transport corridors to serve as regional gateways and listed major physical, non-physical and institutional constraints hindering the efficient movement of freight and passengers among the SAARC member countries. Many of the recommendations of the SAARC

Regional Multimodal Transport Study (SAARC Secretariat, 2006) were approved at the 2007 SAARC Summit. Whether SAARC will at all take off has been a polemic issue due to continual hostility between India and Pakistan.

Bangladesh-India Joint Communiqué

In January 2010, Bangladesh and India signed a historic 'Joint Communiqué'. The communiqué touched upon bilateral, regional, and international issues. However, several articles are of particular interest from the perspective of transit. Some them include: (i) designation of Ashuganj (Bangladesh) and Shilghat (India) as new ports of call and transshipment from Ashuganj to Tripura by road transport (Article 22); (ii) allowing use of Mongla and Chittagong sea ports for movement of goods to and from India through road and rail (Article 23);[6] (iii) construction of Akhaura-Agartala rail link (Article 24); (iv) making Rohanpur-Singabad broad gauge railway link available for transit to Nepal and converting Radhikapur-Birol railway line into broad gauge to give railway transit link to Bhutan (Article 25); (v) Operationalising land customs stations at Sabroom-Ramgarh and Demagiri-Thegamukh by putting in place necessary infrastructure and issue necessary notifications (Article 35); (vi) provision of bilateral trade to be carried in containers through rail and water transit corridors (Article 32); (vii) allowing Bhutan and Nepal to use Banglabandha-Phulbari corridor (Article 37); and (vii) announcement of a line of credit of US$ 1 billion by India to Bangladesh for railway infrastructure, supply of BG locomotives and passenger coaches, rehabilitation of Saidpur workshop, procurement of buses including articulate buses, and dredging projects (Article 38).

In 2015, Indian Prime Minister visited Bangladesh. Prime Minister Narendra Modi has announced a fresh line of credit of US$ 2 billion to Bangladesh. Both the countries signed 22 agreements, including on cooperation in maritime safety and to curb human trafficking and fake Indian currency. India and Bangladesh have agreed to set-up two Special Economic Zones (SEZs) in Bangladesh. India and Bangladesh exchanged the documents related to the Land Boundary Agreement (LBA), which has paved the way for exchange of territories to settle the 41-year-old border dispute. Under the Agreement, 111 border enclaves have been transferred to Bangladesh in exchange for 51 that become part of India.

---

6. Bangladesh also conveyed intention to give Bhutan and Nepal access to Chittagong and Mongla ports.

Analysis of Corridors

It is utmost important for Bangladesh first to quantify the costs and benefits of the alternative corridors through Bangladesh for transit among the six countries. There are two separate dimensions of the corridors under consideration: first, the possible corridors from Kolkata via Bangladesh to the NER of India, and second, the possible corridors from Chittagong and Mongla ports to Bhutan, China via NER of India and Nepal. The analysis of corridors is limited to Bangladesh territory on the assumption that the best possible options of corridors would be used beyond Bangladesh. This assumption does not make any difference to the present analysis as the main focus is to underscore the costs and benefits of the possible corridors vis-à-vis the existing corridors starting from Kolkata to the NER of India through Bangladesh.

For transit among the six countries, the GATT rules stipulate freedom of transit through the territory of each contracting party, via the corridors most convenient for international transit, for traffic in transit to/or from the territory of other contracting parties[7]. Even though SAARC Regional Multimodal Transport Study (SAARC Secretariat, 2006) has identified and reviewed a large numbers of corridors in the whole South Asia region, a set of 14 corridors can be identified and assessed for their financial viability considering the availability of road, rail, and waterway networks in Bangladesh, Bhutan, China, India, Myanmar, and Nepal. In addition, this subset of corridors is considered from the view point of geographical proximity, availability of direct transport links that are cost effective, convenient, and entail less travel time.

The three nodal points in the NER considered are Guwahati in the North, Silchar in the East, and Agartala in the Southeast.[8,9] Transit corridors through these nodal points will cater to the following traffic:

---

7.   Refer, Article V, Paragraph 2, GATT, 1994

8.   Gundom-Taungbro corridor could not be analysed due to some practical difficulties even though the corridor was mentioned in the Bangladesh proposal of BCIM Initiative. Even though Bangladesh proposed to construct the 43-meter long bridge with two lanes over the river with its own resources under the "Bangladesh-Myanmar friendship Road Link Project" and to build 20 km road from Taungbro to Bawli Bazar inside Myanmar at a cost of US$ 25 million with its own resources and to help construct another 120 km road from Bawli Bazar to Kyautaw in Myanmar at an estimated cost of US$ 116 million with assistance from foreign donors and international monetary organszations back in 2005, little progress has been made so far.

9.   Sabroom-Ramgarh and Demagiri-Thegamukh corridors could not be analysed due to some practical difficulties even though these corridors were mentioned in the Joint Communiqué.

- transit corridor from Guwahati nodal point will cater to traffic originating from/destined to Shillong and eastern parts of Meghalaya through Dawki/Tamabil;
- transit corridor from Silchar nodal point will cater to traffic originating from/destined to whole of Manipur, Mizoram, and Nagaland as well as southern parts of Assam, and parts of Yunnan province of China through Sutarkandi; and
- transit corridor from Agartala nodal point will cater to traffic originating from/destined to Tripura and parts of Yunnan.

Only road transport would be available from the first nodal point; both road and rail transports would be available from the second nodal point; and road, rail, and IWT transport would be available from the third nodal point. For inter-state traffic, transport corridors through road and rail will traverse Bangladesh to reach West Bengal part of India through Benapole and Darshana, respectively, whereas IWT corridor will traverse Bangladesh through Mongla to reach Kolkata port.

In addition, three more nodal points considered for Bhutan and Nepal traffic are Phuentsholing, Birgunj and Kathmandu. Transit corridors through these nodal points will cater to the following traffic:
- transit corridor from Kathmandu nodal point through Banglabandha will cater to road traffic originating from/destined to Nepal as well as the northern districts of West Bengal such as Darjeeling, Jalpaiguri, and Cooch Behar;
- transit corridor from Birgunj nodal point through Rohanpur will cater to rail traffic originating from/destined to Nepal; and
- transit corridor from Phuentsholing nodal point through Burimari will cater to road traffic originating from/destined to Bhutan as well as north-western districts of Assam such as Kokrajhar and Dhuburi.

While transit corridors through all three nodal points will cater to international traffic of these countries, the origin of imports or destination of exports from all three nodal points irrespective of the mode of transport (road or rail) would be Mongla port.

Competing and Existing Corridors

In cognizance of the GATT Article V and the review of the transit corridors identified by Yunus (2013), a total 14 corridors have been identified to assess their suitability to serve as cost-effective and efficient transit corridors through Bangladesh. Table 1 and Maps 1-3 in Appendix show the possible alternative corridors of roads, railways and waterways starting from Kolkata, Chittagong and Mongla ports and ending in three different parts of NER as well as Bhutan and Nepal. In case of BCIM-EC, RD-2 and RL-3 are of high importance as both of them end at Silchar. Even though the segment of the corridor that has been discussed for the NER cover the route Silchar-Imphal-Kalay-Mandalay-Ruili-Tengchong-Erhai Lake-Dali-Kunming, the present analysis will shed light also on the other corridors that are ending at Agartala and Guwahati on the assumption that with further development of BCIM-EC, there would be feasible options to connect Agartala and Guwahati to Imphal, so that the options to connect Kunming with these alternatives corridors remain open.

Table 1: Delineation of Competing Transit Corridors

Road Transit Corridors
RD-1: Guwahati–Dawki/Tamabil–Mawa–Bhanga–Narail–Jessore–Benapole/Petrapole–Kolkata
RD-2: Silchar–Sutarkandi–Mawa–Bhanga–Narail–Jessore–Benapole/Petrapole–Kolkata
RD-3: Agartala–Akhaura–Mawa–Bhanga–Narail–Jessore–Benapole/Petrapole–Kolkata
RD-4: Guwahati–Dawki/Tamabil–Chittagong Port
RD-5: Silchar–Sutarkandi–Chittagong Port
RD-6: Agartala–Agartala/Akhaura–Chittagong Port
RD-7: Kathmandu–Kakarvita–Phulbari/Banglabandha–Mongla Port
RD-8: Thimphu–Phuentsholing/Jaigaon–Chengrabandha/Burimari–Mongla Port
Rail Transit Corridors
RL-1: Silchar–Mahishashan/Shahbazpur–Dhaka–Mawa–Bhanga–Darshana/Gede–Kolkata
RL-2: Agartala–Agartala/Akhaura–Dhaka–Mawa–Bhanga–Darshana/Gede–Kolkata
RL-3: Silchar–Mahishashan/Shahbazpur–Chittagong Port
RL-4: Agartala–Agartala/Akhaura–Chittagong Port
RL-5: Birgunj–Katihar–Rohanpur–Khulna–(by road) Mongla Port
Inland Water Transport-cum-Road Transit Corridor
IWT: Kolkata–Namkhana/Raimongal–Mongla–Narayanganj–Ashuganj–(by road) Agartala

Diversion of freight traffic from the existing corridors to new corridors depends on comparative advantages with respect to distance, transport costs per unit, and travel time. While advantages on all three fronts make corridor a strongest contender to the existing corridor for full diversion, any disadvantage in any of the factors, especially the last two, make it a weaker contender.

Transit traffic usually starts and ends at nodes and travels through links. For smooth movement of traffic through a corridor both nodes and links need to perform efficiently. Any delay at either of these two would increase transport costs per unit or delay in travel time even if the distance across two corridors were the same. An attempt has, therefore, been made to analyse thoroughly each transit corridor with a view to identifying inefficient nodes and links where additional investment in infrastructure and facilitation measures is necessary for improvement.

Table 2: Comparison between Competing and Existing Corridors

Corridors	Distance (km)		Time (Hours)		Costs (US$/Tonne)	
	Competing	Existing	Competing	Existing	Competing	Existing
Road Transit Corridors						
RD-1	822 (66)	1081	48.5	76	34.59	24.86
RD-2	688 (77)	1284	35.8	147	26.51	38.52
RD-3	471 (79)	1680	31.5	75	23.84	42.00
RD-4	630 (70)	1081	201.0	272.8	35.13	39.17
RD-5	493 (86)	1284	189.3	196.8	22.03	46.57
RD-6	253 (97)	1680	182	271.8	15.24	50.05
RD-7	1314 (51)	1323	156	249.8	83.10	121.45
RD-8	880 (68)	1039	133	238.8	25.25	27.79
Rail Transit Corridors						
RL-1	692 (74)	1496	37.9	43	23.80	47.87
RL-2	477 (73)	1680	29.1	75	19.26	54.00
RL-3	429 (87)	1496	178.5	271.8	14.02	62.05
RL-4	213 (95)	1680	189.3	239.8	18.48	56.13
RL-5	905(41)	704	137	249.8	31.12	27.76
Inland Water Transport-cum-Road Transit Corridor						
IWT	937 (71)	1680	150	75	25.61	50.08

Notes: (i) Figures in the parentheses indicate percentage of the length of corridor within Bangladesh.
(ii) Existing corridors are through the 'chicken neck'.
Source: Adapted from Yunus (2013).

In order to get precise idea about the comparative advantages (disadvantages) of the competing corridors vis-à-vis existing corridors with regard to distance, travel time and costs the details are adapted from Yunus (2013). It may be noted that road transport vehicles would need to travel on average 700 km along the transit corridors (see Table 2). At present, transport vehicles are constrained to detour more than 1000 km in the region. The minimum distance was found along RD-6 only 253 km. Around 50 per cent of the road segment of the maximum distance falls within Bangladesh, and almost the entire corridor RD-6 is within Bangladesh. Availing transit facility along this corridor would save about 85 per cent of the detouring distance. In contrast, along the maximum distanced corridor, there is hardly any saving in terms of distance. Thus, almost all of the transit corridors enjoy comparative advantage in terms of distance traveled.

The situation with rail transit is almost similar except for one corridor. Transit trains would need to travel about 500 km if Bangladesh allows transit facilities to China, and India. The minimum distance of travel is offered by RL-4 is 213 km. About 70 per cent of the distance falls within Bangladesh. At present, freight trains along the existing corridors are constrained to travel more than 1000 km. Thus, transit facilities would allow China, and India to cut down more than 50 to 85 per cent of their travel distance. Unless, there is high congestion at Kolkata port, this disadvantage in distance is more than compensated by reduced travel time, and transport costs. It is less likely that Nepalese international freight carried by train would find it more profitable. The lone IWT-cum-road corridor was also found to be advantageous in terms of distance traveled.

China, and India as well as Bhutan and Nepal obtain sizeable savings in travel time when the new transit corridors are used. Table 2 provides a consolidated position of total travel time along the competing vis-à-vis the existing corridors as well as the extent of savings in actual time if transit traffic moves along road, rail, and IWT transit corridors through Bangladesh.

It may be noted that there would be substantial savings in travel time along all road transit corridors except RD-5. The savings in travel time range between as high as 111 hours for RD-2 to as low as 8 hours for RD-5. These reductions imply that the extent of savings in travel time ranges between 75 per cent and less than 5 per cent. Thus, seven of the eight road transit corridors enjoy significant advantage in terms of reduced travel, whereas RD-5 enjoys very little advantage in terms of reduced travel time even it has sizeable advantage in terms of reduced distance (Table 2).

All of the rail transit corridors are advantageous in terms of reduced travel time vis-à-vis existing ones. The travel time ranges between 30 hours (RL-2) and 189 hours (RL-4) along the competing transit corridors. The status of this corridor with regard to diversion potential would depend on the comparative transport costs and charges. The lone IWT transit corridor is in disadvantageous situation in respect to time.

The most overriding factor in deciding diversion of freight traffic is comparative transport costs. Even if there are significant advantages in terms of the other two factors, any disadvantage in cost will soon erode advantages in the other two factors. Table 2 presents the total transports costs and charges along the competing vis-à-vis the existing corridors.

Of the eight road transit corridors, seven competing corridors enjoy advantage over the respective existing corridors. Transport costs and charges along these eight corridors were estimated between US$ 15 and US$ 35 per tonne. In contrast, traders at present are billed between US$ 25 and US$ 50 per tonne along the existing corridors. Consequently, the extent of savings ranges between US$ 12 and US$ 35 per tonne i.e., a reduction of 30 to 70 per cent of the existing transport costs and charges. However, transport corridor, RD-1, is at a disadvantage when compared with the existing corridor (US$ 35 along the competing corridor vis-à-vis US$ 25 along the existing corridor). Even though it enjoys significant advantages in terms of both distance and travel time, it loses in terms of transport costs and charges.

Similarly, of the five rail transit corridors, four competing corridors enjoy advantages over the respective existing corridors. Transport costs and charges along these four corridors range between US$ 14 and US$ 24 per tonne. In contrast, at present traders are constrained to spend US$ 50 to US$ 60 per tonne along the existing corridors. Consequently, the extent of savings ranges between US$ 24 and US$ 48 per tonne. In other words, traders would save between 50 to 67 per cent of the current transport costs and charges. The lone IWT transit corridor enjoys significant advantage in terms of transport costs and charges, when compared with the existing corridor through rail. Traders would save about US$ 24 per tonne or more than 50 per cent of the current transport costs and charges, if transit through Bangladesh is provided and availed.

In view of the above three factors, traders and freight transporters in 12 out of 14 transit corridors would find it advantageous to divert wholly or partially due to shorter and direct connectivity. RL-5 loses both in terms of distance and transport costs and charges per tonne; RD-1 loses in terms of transport costs and charges per tonne. Hence, these two competing corridors will not be analysed further. Even though the lone waterway corridor, IWT, loses in terms of travel time, it will be analysed further in view of significant advantages in terms of transport costs and charges.

It was reported that the size of the transport subsidy given to the NER was Rs. 9 billion in the late 1990s, and was around 25 per cent of the transport cost (Islam, 2008). If this rate of subsidy is withdrawn, the transport costs of the existing corridors as listed in Table 2 are likely to increase by 25 per cent.

Volume of Freight Traffic and Diversion Potential

The potential diversion of freight traffic along each of the 12 transit corridors identified critically hinges on the current movement of the volume of such traffic. The Government of India publishes annual inter-state movement of freight volumes by air, rail, and water.[10] Both inward and outward movement of volumes of inter-state freight traffic was estimated for the NER of India based on this publication for years 2006 to 2008. The data for the latest year was taken as base volume for the inter-state freight movement by *rail only*.[11] Assam, Nagaland, and Tripura appear to have utilised bulk of the rail services for inward and outward movements of freight traffic. In contrast, movement of freight traffic to and from other NER states (such as Manipur, Meghalaya, and Mizoram) was found to be marginal in comparison. Finally, Arunachal Pradesh was not considered as one of the sources of diversion of freight traffic on the ground of tenuous proximity factor.[12]

As the NER states are landlocked and the air freight facilities are under-developed, a conservative assumption is made that 30 per cent of the inter-state freight is carried by rail and the remainder is carried by road. This apportionment roughly corresponds to the Indian average of 28:72.[13] Absence of data on inter-modal share of freight traffic for the NER states

---

10. Refer, Director General of Commercial Intelligence and Statistics (2008)

11. Movements by air and water were ignored for practical reason.

12. As (i) Arunachal Pradesh, on the other side of Assam, is the farthest of all the NER states from Bangladesh, and (ii) as only partial diversion from Assam would be assumed, no diversion of freight traffic was assumed from this state.

13. Although it is arguable that there is low volume of rail freight traffic in the in NER due to poor rail network, one may note that Assam has good rail connectivity and the state accounts for over 80 per cent of the total freight traffic. Thus, the assumption may be justified in view of the dominance of Assam.

has necessitated making this simplifying assumption even though it may introduce certain degree of bias in the estimates of road and rail freight.

Data for the movement of international and domestic containers by rail is available in aggregate form.[14] As a result, in the first stage, it is assumed that movements of container freight traffic are proportional to the size of the economies of the NER states in order to decompose the aggregate data. In the second stage, the decomposed data has been used to calibrate data on the movement of international and domestic freight containers by road using the assumed shares for rail and road, i.e. 30:70.

The results of the traffic scenario analysis are presented in Table 3. The decomposition results reveal that about 38.54 million tonnes of cargo has been moved between NER states and the rest of India, where Assam alone accounts for about 34.33 million tonnes. The distant second is Nagaland with 2.32 million tonnes of cargo. In addition to cargo freight traffic, about 18,000 TEUs are moved between the NER states and the rest of India. In addition to cargo freight traffic, the Kolkata Port Trust (KoPT) has handled about 52,000 TEUs for the NER states and Nepal.

Table 3: Movement of Total Freight Traffic of Bhutan, Nepal,
NER of India and Yunnan of China

States/ Provinces Countries	International		Domestic		Total (in TEU)		
	TEU	Tonne	TEU	Tonne	International	Domestic	All
Arunachal Pradesh	701	88477	817	184515	6599	13118	19717
Assam	12267	1394662	10007	34330941	105245	2298737	2403982
Manipur	1034	130577	1205	272313	9739	19359	29099
Meghalaya	1524	192450	1776	401346	14354	28533	42887
Mizoram	651	82180	759	247199	6130	17238	23368
Nagaland	1768	201008	1442	2317791	15169	155962	171130
Tripura	2328	264671	1899	788516	19973	54467	74440
Total India	20273	2354025	17906	38542621	177208	2587414	2764622
Bhutan	-	58000	-	-	3867	-	3867
Nepal	31765	858000	-	-	88965	-	88965
Yunnan, China	123558	3029862	-	-	376047	-	376047
Grand Total	175,596	6299887	17906	38542621	646087	2587414	3233501

Sources: (i) Adapted from Yunus (2013) and (ii) extrapolation for 2008 based on UNESCAP (1995).

14.. Data from records of the ICDs at Amingaon, Assam were obtained by courtesy of CONCOR, India.

Compared to inter-state movement of freight traffic, the movement of international cargo and container traffic is relatively small. The Kolkata port has handled about 2.35 million tonnes of cargo for the NER states. Not surprisingly, Assam alone accounts for 12,267 TEUs. Following UNESCAP (1995), it is estimated that Yunnan province of China has handled 4.51 million metric tonne of international freight in 2010. Of these 4.51 million metric tonnes, 3.02 million tonnes are break bulk cargo and the rest 1.48 million tonnes are containers.

Table 4 presents results of the potential traffic diversion analysis. Based on the factors mentioned above, it is assumed that 45 per cent of freight traffic from Assam and 50 per cent of freight traffic from Meghalaya would be potentially diverted. This partial diversion would occur from Southeastern part of Assam and Eastern part of Meghalaya. An analysis of the road, railway, inland waterways links of the NER states with Bangladesh indicates that for states of Manipur, Mizoram, Nagaland, and Tripura, there is potential for complete diversion. There would be no diversion of road traffic to and from Meghalaya to Kolkata region through Bangladesh due to cost disadvantages.

Similar geographic factors apply to Bhutan and Nepal. It was assumed that 50 per cent of freight traffic from and to Nepal could be potentially diverted,[15] while, for Bhutan, complete diversion through Bangladesh is possible. The partial diversion of the Nepalese traffic is due to cost disadvantage of competing rail corridor through Birgunj-Rohanpur-Mongla vis-à-vis Birgunj-Rauxal-Kolkata. Analysis shows that cost per tonne along the competing Birgunj-Rohanpur-Mongla would be marginally higher, compared to existing corridor through Birgunj-Rauxal-Kolkata. As a result, Nepal's international traffic by rail will not get diverted to Mongla Port.

15.. In addition to the Nepalese international freight traffic, Banglabandha-Mongla road transit would attract small diversion of West Bengal international freight originates or destined to districts bordering Assam.

Table 4: Potential Diversion of Freight Traffic from Bhutan, Nepal, NER of India, and Yunnan of China

States/ Provinces Countries	International		Domestic		Total (in TEU)		
	TEU	Tonne	TEU	Tonne	International	Domestic	All
Arunachal	-	-	-	-	-	-	-
Assam	5520	627598	4503	13045758	47360	874221	921581
Manipur	1034	130577	1205	272313	9739	19359	29099
Meghalaya	762	96225	-	-	7177	-	7177
Mizoram	651	82180	759	247199	6130	17238	23368
Nagaland	1768	201008	1442	2317791	15169	155962	171130
Tripura	2328	264671	1899	788516	19973	54467	74440
West Bengal	13543	-	-	-	13543	-	13543
Total India	25606	1402259	9808	16671577	119091	1121247	1240338
Bhutan	-	58000	-	-	3867	-	3867
Nepal	15883	429000	-	-	44483	-	44483
Yunnan, China	61779	1514931	-	-	188023	-	188023
Grand Total	103268	3404190	9808	16671577	355464	1121247	1476711

Source: Author's calculation based on the assumptions cited in the text.

Similar partial diversion is likely to take place from Yunnan province of China. It was reported by UNESCAP (1995) that 43 per cent of Yunnan's trade volume originated or destined for Myanmar in 1995. As China fostered a closer tie with Myanmar over the years it would not be unreasonable to assume that Myanmar's share has gone up to 50 per cent by 2010. It may be noted that India's share in total trade of China is about 2 per cent. However, it may introduce downward bias if the same share is applied to Yunnan's international trade vis-à-vis India as the latter's close proximity with the province will allow to trade more with it. As such it has been assumed that 10 per cent of Yunnan's international freight volume or about 460,000 metric tonnes would originate from or destined to India. The rest 1.85 million metric tonnes is likely to be diverted through Bangladesh using Hong Kong and Fangcheng in Guangxi as its ports for international freights. While the distances between Kunming and Hong Kong and Kunming and Fangcheng are about 2,400 km and 1,000 km, respectively, Hong Kong is far away, and Fangcheng is rather small sea port, indicating a possibility of diversion.

The estimates of potentially diverted traffic volumes (TEUs and tonnes) are presented in Table 4. It has been found that about 16.67 million tonnes of NER inter-state cargo freight traffic would be potentially diverted through Bangladesh. Of this amount, about 13.05 million tonnes would be potentially diverted from the state of Assam only. The distant second worth 2.32 million tonnes would be potentially diverted from Nagaland. In addition to the above cargo traffic, about 9800 TEUs of NER inter-state containers would be potentially diverted through Bangladesh. As in the case of cargo, the contribution of Assam is significant in terms of the number of containers originated or destined.

Compared to inter-state freight traffic, only 2.91 million tonnes of international cargo would be diverted through Bangladesh. Of this amount, Yunnan would account for 1.51 million metric tonnes and Assam would account for 0.63 million tonnes. In addition, 74,000 TEUs would also be diverted through the country. Of this amount, about 62,000 TEUs would be diverted from Yunnan and the rest from the NER of India.

Table 5: Potential Diversion of Traffic through Different Transit Corridors

Corridors	Diversion to and from	Volume (TEU)
Road Transit Corridors		
RD-1	Meghalaya 100%	-
RD-2	Assam, Manipur, Mizoram, and Nagaland 15%, Yunnan 0.5%	163497
RD-3	Tripura 20%, Yunnan 1.0%	14762
RD-4	Meghalaya 100%	7177
RD-5	Assam, Manipur, Mizoram, and Nagaland 20%, Yunnan 5.0%	34638
RD-6	Tripura 20%, Yunnan 10%	41640
RD-7	West Bengal 5% and Nepal 50%	45719
RD-8	Assam 10% and Bhutan 100%	8689
Rail Transit Corridors		
RL-1	Assam, Manipur, Mizoram, and Nagaland 70%, Yunnan 3.0%	765495
RL-2	Tripura 80% Yunnan 4.0%	73604
RL-3	Assam 70% and Manipur, Mizoram, and Nagaland 80% Yunnan 10%	81614
RL-4	Tripura 80% Yunnan 15%	72545
RL-5	Nepal 50%	-
IWT-cum-Road Transit Corridor		
IWT	Assam, Manipur, Mizoram, and Nagaland 15%, Yunnan 1.5%	167258
Total		1476638

Source: Author's calculation based on the assumptions cited in the text.

The possible diversion of freight traffic by transit corridors is presented in Table 5. Owing to the existing level of capacity utilisations of road rail and IWT transport services, it is assumed that bulk of the transit freight would be handled by rail transport alone. Accordingly, it has been assumed that 70 per cent of the inter-state freight traffic to and from the NER states of India would be carried by rail and the rest would be equally shared by road and IWT. About 80 per cent of the international freight traffic of these states would be carried by rail and the rest by road. The ratios would apply in the case of the 20 per cent of Yunnan's half of international freight (which is 10 per cent of the total).

After arriving at the diversion of freight traffic at the base year, the future diversion of freight traffic is estimated at 8 per cent per annum. However, it has also been documented that small-scale industries have not been viable and there is widespread industrial sickness (Sachdeva, 2006; Misra, 1991). However, relative stability in the NER states in recent years does not corroborate the concern. Further, the growth rates of state GDP in the NER are not far behind that of other states in India (Padeco, 2014).

Costs of Infrastructures and Facilitation Measures to Bangladesh

Once Bangladesh opens up its borders for transportation of freights, it will incur costs for building new infrastructures and facilities and up gradation of existing ones to handle the increased flow of traffic.[16] These capital costs would entail operations and maintenance (O&M) costs. Since the volume of transit traffic passing through the various transit corridors is a fraction of Bangladesh national traffic, apportioned capital and O&M costs proportional to the total traffic volume are attributed to transit traffic.[17] Further, double counting of capital and O&M costs for overlapping portions of the transit corridors have been avoided by dividing the apportioned capital and O&M costs of the overlapped sections in proportion to the transit traffic found at the bifurcation before or after the overlapping sections.

Some basic physical facilities have to be developed at transit points and a 'one-stop-window' type clearance facilities need to be set-up to

16. Similar investments need to be made on the Bhutan, Indian, Myanmar, Nepal and Chinese sides. Since this study focuses particularly on Bangladesh, estimates of such costs are ignored for the sake of brevity.

17. Where infrastructure development is already planned by the Government of Bangladesh as part of its national development plan, the entire cost is not taken but a part of such capital cost is taken into account in the current analysis.

verify transit traffic and seal the containers/covered vans. At the exit point, the same authority should then allow transit traffic to pass through with minimum formalities. Installation and maintenance of such facilities will definitely entail capital and O&M costs on the transit providing countries, namely, Bangladesh and India. Such costs are estimated for Bangladesh here.

Table 6: Capital Costs for the Road Transit Corridors

(US$ million)

Corridors	Road Segments	Chittagong Port	Mongla Port	Land Port	Total
RD-2	32.65	0.00	0.00	7.27	39.92
RD-3	6.57	0.00	0.00	6.02	12.58
RD-4	10.75	9.47	0.00	3.93	24.15
RD-5	20.43	17.92	0.00	0.33	38.68
RD-6	5.63	5.27	0.00	2.11	13.02
RD-7	23.97	0.00	151.59	3.93	179.49
RD-8	4.06	0.00	13.17	3.93	21.16
Apportioned	104.06	32.67	164.76	27.52	329.01
Total	1543.90	326.57	396.83	27.51	2294.80

Note: Costs of the overlapping segments are prorated by the shares of overlapping corridors
Source: Adapted from Yunus (2013)

Bangladesh needs to invest in road, rail, and port infrastructure and border-crossing facilities to avail the benefits from diverted traffic from Bhutan, Nepal, NER and Yunnan province of China. Table 6 illustrates the capital costs for the road sector. A total of US$ 2.3 billion investment is needed in road, ports and land port infrastructures. Of this, about US$ 128 million is prorated for transit facilities at different components of the transit corridors.[18] Of this amount, about US$ 76 million is needed to rehabilitate critical segments of roads along the five transit corridors. About US$ 33 million is needed to improve efficiency of Chittagong Port, and US$ 20 million is needed for improvements at Tamabil, Akhaura, Sutarkandi, and Benapole land customs ports/stations (Yunus, 2013).

It is assumed that capital costs are incurred over five years. In addition, the country needs US$ 13 million each year to maintain the road over a

18. RD-1 (Tamabil-Benapole) was not included in the benefits-costs analysis as the competing corridor was found disadvantageous compared to the existing one. Hence, the corridor was excluded in the assignment of costs.

period of 20 years. A 10 per cent O&M cost is assumed for roads to take into account of the growth of freight traffic in future that is expected to increase wear and tear of infrastructures and facilities along the corridors. For rail and IWT, the usual 5 of capital costs are assumed. It may be noted that all of these costs are apportioned between domestic traffic and diverted traffic, where applicable. Only full costs are attributed to diverted traffic, where new facilities are required to be created exclusively for the diverted traffic. Further, costs of Chittagong port are apportioned based on domestic and diverted freight traffic in the first stage, and between road and rail based on the relative volumes carried by each of the modes in the second stage (Yunus, 2013).

Table 7: Capital Costs for the Rail Transit Corridors

(US$ million)

Corridors	Rail Segments	Chittagong Port	Mongla Port	Land Port	Total
RL-1	1269.18	0.00	0.00	0.00	1269.18
RL-2	78.82	0.00	0.00	0.00	78.82
RL-3	149.86	79.87	0.00	0.00	229.73
RL-4	39.92	20.35	0.00	0.00	60.28
Apportioned	1537.79	100.22	0.00	0.00	1638.02
Total	2740.15	326.57	0.00	0.00	3066.71

Note: Costs of the overlapping segments are prorated by the shares of overlapping corridors.
Source: Adapted from Yunus (2013).

Bangladesh would need to spend about US$ 2.7 billion over five years for development of infrastructures along the rail transit corridors (see Table 7). Of this amount, about US$ 1.5 billion will be required for the transit freight traffic along four corridors. In addition, US$ 100 million is prorated to transit traffic for the improvement of efficiency of the Chittagong Port. The country would need to spend US$ 82 million as O&M costs each year over the 20-year period in order to avail of the benefits of diverted traffic from the NER of India and Yunnan of China. The high costs apportioned to rail sector were due to higher volume of freight to be carried by the rail service during the period under consideration. For this to materialize, the rail sector needs to procure locomotives, flat cars, wagons, brake vans, etc. for BG and MG tracks in order to carry the diverted freight traffic.

Table 8: Capital Costs for the IWT cum Road Transit Corridor

(US$ million)

Name of the Project	Total	Apportioned
Dredging and Hydraulic Survey	35.69	35.69
Raimongal-Mongla Section of the Corridor	9.89	9.89
Hot Spots near Bhabanir Char and between Mongla and Ghasiakhali	25.79	25.79
Installation of Night Navigational Equipments	1.10	1.10
Construction of Transshipment Facilities at Ashuganj Port of Call	14.46	14.46
Akhaura Land Port	3.93	3.93
Total of the Corridor	55.18	55.18

Source: Adapted from Yunus (2013).

The only IWT (Raimongal-Ashuganj) corridor needs hydraulic survey and dredging in the Raimongal-Mongla section and at several hot spots near Bhabanir Char and between Mongla and Ghasiakhali. Further, the corridor needs installation of equipment for night time navigability. Therefore, Ashuganj has to be developed as full-fledged river port with modern transshipment facilities to handle transit cargo. All these activities would require about US$ 51 million investment plus addition US$ 4 million for the Akhaura land port (Table 8). These activities will take about five years to complete. Since the O&M costs for typical IWT corridors are minimal given constant flow of water, a 5 per cent O&M cost is assumed in this case, suggesting about US$ 5 million will be needed annually for operations and maintenance (Yunus, 2013).

The project specific investment costs in roads, railways and waterways are presented in the Annexure[19]. It contains the priority projects and the future investment costs, which are needed to implement an efficient transit through Bangladesh. As these costs are estimated at 2010 in terms of Bangladeshi Taka, the relevant amount would have to be adjusted upward to take into account of the domestic inflation. As the benefits are estimated for 2014, the dollarized prorated amounts were adjusted upward at the rate of 5 per cent per annum in the benefits-costs analysis (Table 9).

---

19. Due to limitation of space, we are forced to remove the annexure. The same will be available to interested author on request.

Economic Benefits to Bangladesh

Charges that Bangladesh Can Impose Under WTO Rules

The freedom of transit stipulates that transit traffic is not subject to any unnecessary delays or restrictions and is exempt from customs duties and all transit duties or other charges (Article V, Paragraph 2, GATT, 1994). However, Bangladesh can impose 'reasonable' charges commensurate with administrative expenses entailed by transit or with the costs of services rendered. Bangladesh should be compensated for the costs of facilities and infrastructures to be created and maintained for the purpose of transit only. Thus, transit charges for road, rail, and waterway may be applied following Newbery (1988).

As a result, when international traffic to and from Bhutan, China, NER of India, and Nepal have access to Chittagong and Mongla ports, and the inter-state freight to and from the NER can traverse Bangladesh for through movement, Bangladesh will have the following sources of earnings. First, transports charges earned by road transporters, water transport operators, and Bangladesh Railway. Second, port charges (except customs and related charges imposed on exports and imports) earned by Chittagong Port Authority (CPA) and Mongla Port Authority (MPA). Third, charges for transit facilitation measured at the land ports/ land customs stations. Fourth, toll charges for major bridges such as Jamuna Bridge or Padma Bridge (once constructed and opened), and ferry crossings. Fifth, transit charges for (a) infrastructure damage costs (road, rail, waterways, ports, and border crossings), (b) congestion costs (road), (c) accident externalities (road), and (d) environmental pollution (road and waterways).

Transit vehicles would impose numerous types of costs on the road, rail and IWT infrastructures in Bangladesh. Some of these costs include damage to infrastructures, congestions, accident externalities, and environmental pollution costs.[20] Besides, there would be costs for administrative and institutional management, security of the transit goods, customs services, etc. For sub-regional transit, a national committee formed by the Government of Bangladesh suggests charging transiting vehicles at the minimum rate of 8.96 cents a tonne per km for road transit, 3.84 cents for railway and 3.20 cents for waterways (Yunus, 2013). These base estimates have been derived

---

20. See, for example, Newbery (1988) for the road sector

from best practices around the world.[21] These rates are used in the present analysis.

The development of transit would result in manifold benefits. The benefits can be quantified and categorised into three types in Bangladesh: (i) freight charges from transport services provided within the territory, (ii) charges from the port(s) services provided, and (iii) charges "reasonable, having regard to the conditions of the traffic" (GATT Article V) for allowing transit across the territory. These three sources constitute the total benefits from the development of transit corridors.

It may be noted that roads and other transport infrastructures deteriorate with the passage of time under the influence of weathering and other environmental factors, in combination with the effects of traffic. Based on the weather and traffic conditions Newbery (1988) assumed 20 years of road life. This time is applied for all three modes transport in this exercise.

The 'charges' would focus on identifying the additional costs (road damage, congestion, accidental externalities, and environmental pollution costs) and establishing an appropriate allocation of capital and O&M costs as a result of the additional transit traffic on the transport networks of Bangladesh that meets the WTO and GATT principle of non-discrimination.

In estimating benefits from transport charges, it is assumed that each country would retain the benefits of transport charges for the segment of the corridor that belongs to it. For example, if a truck carries a load of cargo from Kolkata to Agartala, Bangladesh earns benefits of transport charges from Benapole to Akhaura and India earns benefits of transport charges from Kolkata to Petrapole and again from Akhaura to Agartala. The assumption is applied to all transit corridors and transport modes. In estimating the charges from ports, it is assumed that Bangladesh would apply non-discriminatory charges on transit containers/cargoes.

It was assumed that the road transit corridors would carry 15 per cent of the diverted traffic and the IWT corridor handles the same fraction of freight traffic as the road transit corridors together. The rest of the diverted freight traffic, 70 per cent of the total diverted freight traffic, would be handled by the rail transit corridors through Bangladesh.

---

21. See, Transport Cost Literature Review, available at www.vtpi.org

The above benefits have been calculated under 8 per cent growth of diverted freight traffic. It is assumed that the respective transit corridors would carry 10 per cent of the potentially diverted freight traffic during each of the fourth and fifth years, and would increase to their full potentials from the sixth year onward. The low levels of transit freight during the first five years are assigned in view of the structural bottlenecks of the facilities under development even with the utmost sincerity on the part of Bangladesh. The gross annual benefit during the first five years would be around US$ 98 million. When all the planned infrastructure facilities are fully implemented, the gross benefit will reach more than US$ 2 billion.

Benefits vis-à-vis Costs to Bangladesh

The rate of return or net benefit depends on how much would be gained compared with the costs as discussed above, particularly the cost to the national economy. In order to assess the net benefits to the economy of Bangladesh, initially all of the road, rail, and IWT transit corridors are analysed separately. In the second stage, all road and rail transit corridors are taken together as All Road and All Rail transit corridors. At the third stage, the aggregate benefits-costs analysis is carried out by combining all three types of transit corridors together.

The results of the above analysis by transit corridors as well as groups and aggregates are presented in Table 9. It may be noted that all the five road transit corridors considered are economically viable in the sense that the internal rates of return (IRRs) are above the opportunity costs of capital (12 per cent).[22] Similarly, all of the four rail transit corridors are economically viable. The IRRs for these transit corridors are well above the threshold level used by the Government of Bangladesh. The Government may develop any of the rail transit corridors on a priority basis. However, from the viewpoint of the net worth, it is rational for the Government to develop these transit corridors following the ranks listed in the last column of Table 9. Finally, the lone IWT corridor is also economically viable as the IRR is well above the threshold level.

---

22. The 12 per cent rate is usually applied in discounting publicly funded projects in Bangladesh.

Table 9: Results of Benefits-Costs Analysis

Corridors	Criteria	Estimates	Ranking
Road Transit Corridors			
RD-2	IRR (%)	115.44	1
	BCR	40.20	
	NPV (US$ million)	1780.68	
RD-3	IRR (%)	59.68	5
	BCR	9.18	
	NPV (US$ million)	117.14	
RD-4	IRR (%)	29.00	7
	BCR	2.61	
	NPV (US$ million)	44.15	
RD-5	IRR (%)	54.79	3
	BCR	7.75	
	NPV (US$ million)	296.95	
RD-6	IRR (%)	83.02	4
	BCR	18.52	
	NPV (US$ million)	259.52	
RD-7	IRR (%)	33.87	2
	BCR	3.30	
	NPV (US$ million)	470.08	
RD-8	IRR (%)	41.57	6
	BCR	4.65	
	NPV (US$ million)	87.85	
Rail Transit Corridors			
RL-1	IRR (%)	41.80	1
	BCR	5.05	
	NPV (US$ million)	4856.19	
RL-2	IRR (%)	44.88	2
	BCR	5.65	
	NPV (US$ million)	346.61	
RL-3	IRR (%)	27.87	3
	BCR	2.56	
	NPV (US$ million)	339.54	
RL-4	IRR (%)	48.49	4
	BCR	5.74	
	NPV (US$ million)	270.20	
Transit Corridors by Modes			
All Road	IRR (%)	59.64	2
	BCR	9.16	
	NPV (US$ million)	3056.38	

All Rail	IRR (%)	40.59	1
	BCR	4.76	
	NPV (US$ million)	5812.53	
IWT	IRR (%)	102.76	3
	BCR	36.30	
	NPV (US$ million)	1437.42	
All Transit corridors	IRR (%)	47.45	
	BCR	6.25	
	NPV (US$ million)	10306.34	

In case of financial resource constraint, the Government may consider the sequential development of the three types of transit corridors. As all road transit corridors and all rail transit corridors taken together are economically viable, the Government may consider the net present values (NPVs) of the three modes. From this perspective, rail transit corridors should be developed first, followed by the road transit corridors and the lone IWT corridor in that order.

If there is no resource constraint, the Government may consider developing all the transit corridors simultaneously. From that perspective, aggregate benefit-cost analysis is also conducted. The results presented at the last panel of Table 9 shows that providing transit to neighbouring countries and regions is an economically viable option for Bangladesh. The IRR of the aggregate analysis at 50.61 per cent is well above the threshold level (12 per cent) used by the Government of Bangladesh in assessing viability. The benefit-cost ratio (BCR) is 7.10, which is well above unity. Finally, the NPV is US$ 10.57 billion, which indicates that the investments are worth making.

Other Transit Related Issues

Border Processes: As mentioned earlier, the competing transit corridors enjoy comparative advantage over the existing ones in terms of both reduced costs and travel time under the assumptions that the customs stations and land ports will be efficient, speedy and perform at low cost. These assumptions will only be valid, if there are pre-registration of trucking companies, vehicles and drivers such that border processes are limited to checking. Such pre-registration needs to be accompanied by proof of agreed insurance. Vehicles are to be checked for compliance with the Bangladesh 10-ton axle-loading limit. Besides, vehicle loads are to be sealed and unsealed at entry and exit by Bangladeshi customs with tamper proof seals. Finally, bonds are to be lodged to be forfeited, if seals are not intact—the level of the bond to be calculated on a punitive basis to discourage arbitrage with normal import duties.

Subsidy in Fuel: Due to existence of implicit and explicit subsidy, diesel fuel is cheaper in Bangladesh than India. This price differential will encourage arbitrage by road and IWT transit drivers—these vehicles will enter Bangladesh empty and leave full. Such activities, albeit rational on the part of the drivers, will result in the leakage of subsidy to India. As the fuel subsidy will be enjoyed by only those transit vehicles that will refuel in Bangladeshi petrol stations, this will have to remain outside the purview of the 'transit charge' and will have to be collected separately at the sales points. Besides, several recommendations have been made for improvement of the situation at the borders, which include pilot introduction of reciprocal cross-border movement of trucks of both countries such as allowing Indian trucks travel to designated cities in Bangladesh and vice versa; coordination of time for custom inspection, etc. Specific measures suggested include customs positioning; improved law and order measures; standardized sales tax procedures; compatibility of working days and hours; insurance and banking services, etc. (Padeco, 2009).

Conclusions and Way Forward

The foregoing analysis reveals that there is high potential for diversion of sizeable volume of traffic from the NER of India as well as the Yunnan province of China through Bangladesh. Inter-state cargo and containers destined for Kolkata region, originating from NER states of India, namely, Nagaland, Mizoram, Manipur, Tripura, eastern part of Meghalaya, eastern part of Assam, and Yunnan province of China will find it highly cost effective and convenient to get transit through Bangladesh — should such transit facilities are on offer. The savings would involve significant reduction in distance (between 24 and 72 per cent for road, between 44 and 72 per cent for rail), travel time (between 58 and 36 per cent for road, between 12 and 61 per cent for rail). In addition, transport costs would range between 9 and 77 per cent depending on the transit corridor being used. The extent of savings could range between US$ 4 and US$ 48 per tonne of transit traffic. Similarly, containers and cargo to and from the NER of India to Kolkata port will also find it attractive in terms of reduced distance, travel time and transport costs per tonne to use Chittagong port for their export and import traffic.

If the Government of Bangladesh manages the transit corridors and services directly, it can impose various types of user charges in exchange of both capital and maintenance costs. At least four such charges may be identified such as damage costs, congestion costs, accident externalities, and environmental pollution.

An assessment of Bangladesh transport system revealed that in order to carry such a large volume of transit and international traffic, considerable investment would be needed. As part of its national development plan, for enhancing capacity and modernisation of its transport system, Bangladesh has already identified a number of major projects — rail, road, IWT and port development projects. Apportioned costs are duly accounted for in the capital cost estimates for cost-benefit analysis. However, implementation of these development projects is likely to take around 3 to 5 years, which have been reflected in the analysis. During the interim period, Bangladesh should be able to provide limited transit facility to China and India by arranging one or two container trains, and a few loads of road transit for high value and perishable goods. For this purpose, immediate investment shall have to be made to rehabilitate some of the crucial road links, as well as a container transshipment facility at Akhaura rail yard, and Ashuganj river port.

Due to structural weakness of Bangladesh's road transport network, only 10-tonne axle load trucks should be allowed and this should be strictly enforced. The high value and perishable commodities can be accommodated through road transit corridors, across Bangladesh using transshipment facilities.

Alternatively, a sub-regional initiative should be mooted to float a joint venture trucking company, with shareholders in Bangladesh, Bhutan, Nepal, China, India, and Myanmar. The company may own medium-sized, multi-axle truck-trailers and covered vans, registered in all member countries to facilitate movement of transit traffic across Bangladesh.

To address the structural weaknesses of Bangladesh road network, the ultimate solution would be to go for construction of high standard expressways (toll roads), through private sector investment, along the national highways, using the existing right of ways, with provision for service lanes on both sides of the expressway, which could be made available for use free of charge.

To derive the anticipated benefits, Bangladesh would be required to invest in various projects along the identified transit corridors for facilitating seamless movement of transit traffic. As there are sizable direct benefits, the country should release about US$ 1.8 billion for projects to be implemented along the transit corridors and put enough financial resources for the proper maintenance of the facilities thus created, if the Government of Bangladesh decides to manage these infrastructures and facilities.

Bangladesh would earn about US$ 98 million annually during first five years, when facilities are being created along the identified transit corridors under user charge approach. Once the infrastructure projects and facilities are completed, the country would earn more than US$ 2 billion annually from the sixth year onwards. From 11th year of the discounted period, the annual earnings would reach US$ 3 billion and would ultimately end up at US$ 5.9 billion. This stream of benefits, albeit partial, would more than justify the investment amounts mentioned.

The results of the aggregate benefit-cost analysis with 8 per cent growth of the diverted freight traffic show that provisioning transit services is an economically viable option for Bangladesh. The IRR of the aggregate analysis is 50.61 per cent, the benefit-cost ratio is 7:10 and the NPV is US$ 10.57 billion. The sensitivity analyses show that the estimates are robust to cost escalation, but susceptible to reduced flow of transit freight traffic than that forecasted.

Further, lack of disaggregate and up-to-date data required for a detailed benefit-cost analysis has necessitated making several simplified assumptions. Hence, the results have to be treated with caution and a much more detailed analysis is required for formulating policies. The study is not a substitute for a full-fledged feasibility exercise that will be required at the time projects are taken up. It is evident that Bangladesh can serve as an efficient gateway for transit for the NER of India and Yunnan province of China.

The transit corridors entailing numerous infrastructure development activities will bring dynamic benefits to the region in business and trade. The dynamic benefits can be classified under three main categories:

- *Trade Efficiencies*: Once the transit corridors are at work, private investors would reorient their business models as the investments become more competitive. Exporting goods becomes a commercially viable option and allows for linking up with regional supply chains.
- *Network Externalities*: Once the transit corridors are integrated with the network of region, there is substantive potential for positive non-

linear network externalities as new corridors from other regions begins to benefit from the existing transit corridors.

- *Leveraging Private Investment*: The initial public investments in rehabilitating the transit corridors will leverage private investment in ancillary activities such as storage facilities and other logistics development, feeder transport connecting points, etc., that previously would not have been lucrative. Transit will allow for increased business opportunities, more business travel, and increased employment opportunities in the region for the unemployed youth and the landless labor.

Finally, Bangladesh should negotiate regional and subregional agreements. In this regard, a rigorous comparative assessment is warranted to determine which option accrues more benefits to the country. Besides, Bangladesh needs to seriously formulate options to be put on the negotiation tables with the partner countries that can be convincingly traded against provision of transit facilities.

References

Director General of Commercial Intelligence and Statistics (2008). *Inter-State Movements/ Flows of Goods by Rail, River and Air*, Kolkata

Islam, S. (2008). Bangladesh-China-Northeast India: Opportunities and Anxieties. *ISAS Insights*, No.36, September 2008, National University of Singapore.

Maciariello, J. A. (1975). Dynamic Benefit Cost Analysis: Policy Evaluation in a Dynamic Urban Simulation Model. *Socio-Economic Planning Sciences*, 9(3-4), June, pp.147-168.

Misra, U. (ed) (1991). *Nation Building and Development in North East India.* Guwahati: Purbanchal Prakashan.

Murshid, K. A. S. (2011). Transit and Transshipment: Strategic Considerations for Bangladesh and India. *Economic and Political Weekly*, 46(17), pp. 43-51.

Newbery, D. M. (1988). Road User Charges in Britain. *Economic Journal*, 98(390), pp. 161-176.

PADECO. (2009). *Preparing the South Asia Subregional Economic Cooperation Transport Logistics and Trade Facilitation Project*. RETA 6435-REG. *Draft Inception Report*.

Sachdeva, G. (2006). India's Northeast: Rejuvenating a Conflict Ridden Economy. SATP at www.satp.org/satporgtp/publication/faultlines/volume6/Fault6-GSach-F.htm, accessed on 25 June 2013.

SAARC Secretariat (2006). *SAARC Regional Multimodal Transport Study*. Kathmandu: SAARC Secretariat.

Thapliyal, S. (1999). India–Bangladesh Transportation Links: A Move for Closer Co-operation. *Strategic Analysis*, Vol. XXII, March.

Transport Cost Literature Review at www.vtpi.org, accessed on 25 June 2013.

UNESCAP (1995). Trans-Asian Railway Route Requirements: Development of the Trans-Asian Railway in the Indo-China and ASEAN Subregion, Section 3, Volume 3, Bangkok.

Yunus, M. (2013). Economic Gains from Developing Functional Transit Facilities in Bangladesh. Paper presented at the UN ESCAP's ARTNeT Conference, Macao, China.

Map 1: Road Transit Corridors

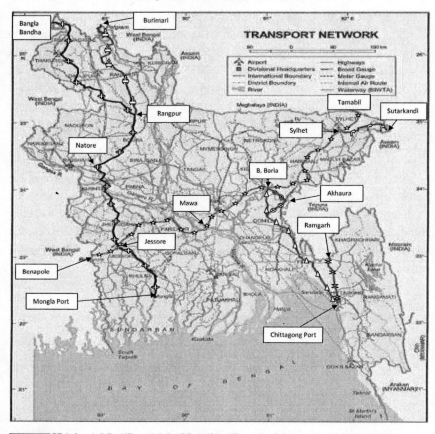

RD-1: Guwahati–Dawki/Tamabil–Sylhet–B.Baria–Mawa–Bhanga–Narail–Jessore–Benapole/Petrapole–Kolkata

RD-2: Shilchar–Sutrakandi–Sylhet–B.Baria–Mawa–Bhanga–Narail–Jessore–Benapole/Petrapole–Kolkata

RD-3: Agartala–Akhaura–B. Baria–Mawa–Bhanga–Narail–Jessore–Benapole/Petrapole–Kolkata

RD-4: Guwahati–Dawki/Tamabil–Sylhet–B. Baria–Chittagong Port

RD-5: Shilchar–Sutrakandi–Sylhet–B. Baria–Chittagong Port

RD-6: Agartala–Akhaura–Chittagong Port

RD-7: Kathmandu–Kakarvita–Phulbari/Bangalbandha–Rangpur–Natore–Mongla Port

RD-8: Thimpu–Phuentsholing/Jaigaon–Chengrabandha/Burimari–Rangpur–Natore–Mongla Port

RD-9: Sabroom–Ramgarh–Heako–Fatickchari–Chittagong Port

Map 2: Rail Transit Corridors

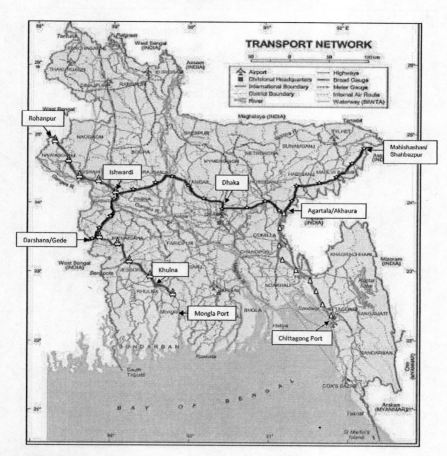

RL-1: Shilchar–Mahishashan/Shahbazpur–Akhaura–Dhaka–Ishwardi–Darshana/Gede–Kolkata.

RL-2: Agartala–Agartala/Akhaura–Dhaka–Ishwardi–Darshana/Gede–Kolkata.

RL-3: Shilchar–Mahishashan/Shahbazpur–Akhaura–Chittagong port.

RL-4: Agartala–Agartala/Akhaura–Chittagong Port.

RL-5: Birganj–Ishwardi–Darshana–Khulna–(by road) Mongla Port.

Map 3: IWT Corridors

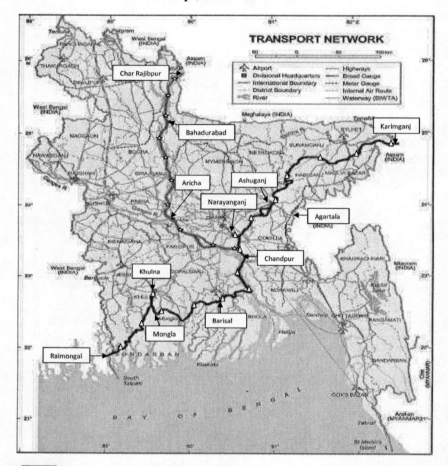

IWT-1: Raimongal-Mongla-Chandpur-Narayanganj-Ashuganj-(by road) Agartala/Ashuganj-Karimganj.

IWT-2: Namkahana/Raimongal-Mongla-Chandpur-Aricha-Char Rajibpur.

TEN

IMPLICATIONS OF PAKISTAN'S TRADE NORMALISATION WITH INDIA

Indra Nath Mukherji and Subrata Kumar Behera

Introduction

Prior to the partition of the Indian sub-continent in 1947, the economies of newly emerging countries were complimentary in nature, just as the different parts of the same economy usually are. The sub-continent was developed as one economic and political unit. India depended on Pakistan for her raw jute, raw cotton, food grains, and a few other raw materials. Pakistan, on the other, being deficient in industrial base, had to source coal, textiles, sugar, matches, jute manufactures, iron and steel, and some other manufactured goods from India.

On 15 August 1947, Indian sub-continent was divided and two separate states of India and Pakistan came into being. Envisioning that the inter-Dominion boundary line would create economic hardships to both the countries, it was considered necessary to maintain the *status quo* in the matter of trade relations. The Stand-still Agreement was an interim measure for the continuation of the pre-partition economic and commercial relations till 29 February 1948 (Government of India, 1949). It aimed at removal of all types of impediments on the movement of goods, people and capital along the frontier of the two countries during the specified interim period.

The Committee No. VII on Economic Relations (Trade) came into being "to examine matters regarding all trade and movement between the territories of the successor governments" (Government of India, 1949). The two governments were not permitted, among other measures, to change existing customs tariffs, excise duties, cesses, or transit levies on goods passing across the territory of the other (Government of India, 1949).

Till 1965, India-Pakistan trade was governed by "positive list" approach under which only those products specified by each country in its positive list were allowed to export by the other. The products not thus listed were not permitted to trade. With the outbreak of hostilities between the two countries in 1965, formal trade between them during the period 1966 to1974 was suspended.

In accordance with the Shimla Agreement of 1972, a Protocol on Resumption of Trade was signed by India and Pakistan on 23 January 1975, which had recommended that the trade would be conducted based on the Most Favoured Nation (MFN) basis (Government of India, 1975). India has accorded MFN status to Pakistan in 1996 in conformity with its general approach. However, Pakistan continued with the positive list strategy, i.e. allowing only selected items for import from India, and is yet to offer MFN to India.

The Composite Dialogue between India and Pakistan from 2004 to 2008 addressed all outstanding bilateral issues including trade. It completed four rounds and the fifth round was in progress, when it was paused in the wake of Mumbai terrorist attack in November 2008.

After a gap of nearly two years, the Composite Dialogue process was renewed as a result of the meeting of Indian Prime Minister Dr Manmohan Singh and Pakistan Prime Minister Mr Gilani, who mandated the two countries' Foreign Ministers and Foreign Secretaries to hold discussions on the modalities to pave the way for a comprehensive and sustained dialogue on all issues of mutual interest and concern in April 2010 in Thimpu, Bhutan on the side-lines of the 16th SAARC Summit. The meeting of Indian External Affairs Minister Mr. S.M. Krishna and Pakistan Foreign Minister Mr. H.R. Khar in New Delhi on 27 July 2011 marked the culmination of the first round of the resumed dialogue.

During the 5th Round of Talks on Commercial and Economic Cooperation (RTCEC), it was decided to establish designated Working Group to address both tariff and non-tariff barriers (NTBs) (Government of India, 2011a). Further, a Joint Technical Group for promotion of trade and travel was to meet in June 2011 and thereafter every month to ensure adherence to the October 2011 timeline on both sides for a new Integrated Check Post (ICP).

It was also decided to formalise an arrangement in the form of a Customs Liaison Border Committee, which would meet at least once in every two months to resolve any operational issues at the field level.

For harmonisation of customs procedures, facilitation of trade consignments, exchange of trade data, both sides agreed that a Sub-Group on Customs Cooperation would meet in New Delhi before 15 June 2011. It was agreed that Pakistan would draft customs cooperation agreement within a month (May 2011).

The Joint Statement at the end of the 6th RTCEC stated that the move to full normalisation of trade relations would be sequenced. In the first stage, Pakistan will adopt a "negative list" in place of the current positive list.[1] The consultation process on devising this negative list was almost complete (Government of India, 2011b). It stated:

> "A small negative list shall be finalized and ratified by February 2012. Thereafter, all items other than those on the negative list shall be phased out. The timing for this phasing out will be announced in February 2012 at the time the List is notified and it is expected that the phasing out will be completed before the end of 2012."

Following the visit of Indian Commerce Minister Mr Anand Sharma to Pakistan in February 2012, Pakistan notified its negative list on 20 March 2012 (Government of Pakistan, 2012). Thereafter, both sides agreed to move towards preferential trading arrangement under the SAFTA process.

The 7th RTCEC reiterated that the roadmap for liberalised trade drawn in earlier Ministerial meetings would be "scrupulously" adhered to (Government of India, 2012).

Both sides developed a long-term plan of trade liberalisation. It was noted that Pakistan then had 936 tariff lines at 6-digit under its SAFTA "sensitive list"[2], as against 614 tariff lines at 6-digit of India. It was agreed that after Pakistan has notified its removal of all restrictions on trade through Wagah-Attari trade route, India would bring down its SAFTA sensitive list by 30 per cent before December 2012 keeping in view Pakistan's export interests (Government of India, 2012).

Following Pakistan's transitions fully to MFN status offer to India by December 2012, India would thereafter bring down its SAFTA sensitive list to 100 tariff lines by April 2013. As India notifies the reduced sensitive list, Pakistan, after seeking approval of the Cabinet, will also notify its dates of

---

1. Under "negative list" approach, all products are importable, barring those under the negative list.

2. "Sensitive list" under SAFTA are those products that are not eligible for tariff preference, but are importable on MFN basis.

transition to bring down its SAFTA sensitive list to a maximum of 100 tariff lines within the next five years (2017). Before the end of year 2020, except for this small number of tariff lines under respective SAFTA sensitive lists, the peak tariff rate for all other tariff lines would not be more than 5 per cent (Government of India, 2012).

Official level trade talks have stalled since the 7th RTCEC, which was held in September 2012. The possibility of resumption of official level talks brightened following the meeting between Indian Union Minister of Commerce and Industry Mr. Anand Sharma and Mr. Shahbaz Sharif, Chief Minister of Punjab Province of Pakistan, who was accompanied by Pakistan's Minister of State for Commerce, Textile and Privatisation Mr. Khurram Dastgir Khan, High Commissioner of Pakistan to India Mr. Salman Bashir, and Pakistani businessman Mr. Mian Muhammad Mansha along with other senior officials from Pakistan on 12 December 2013.[3] Mr. Sharma conveyed to the Pakistan side that India stands committed to the roadmap for bilateral trade normalisation as was worked out in September 2012 meeting between Commerce Secretaries of India and Pakistan.

During the Commerce Secretary-level talks on 20-21 September 2012 in Islamabad, a roadmap was established to move forward towards full normalisation of bilateral trade. However, in the absence of the first step of the roadmap, viz. Pakistan permitting all importable items through Wagah-Attari land route (as against current only 137), the roadmap remained unimplemented.

In their meeting in New Delhi on 18 January 2014, Commerce Ministers of India and Pakistan reaffirmed the commitment to expedite establishment of normal trading relations and to provide Non-Discriminatory Market Access (NDMA), on a reciprocal basis. They decided to intensify and accelerate the process of trade normalisation, liberalisation and facilitation and to implement the agreed measures before the end of February 2014. Implementation of these steps, *inter alia*, removal of 'Negative list' and removal of restrictions on the number of importable items via Wagah land route by the Government of Pakistan is awaited (Government of India, 2014).

Following the background of this study, Section 2 of this chapter examines the data and methodology of the study. Section 3 presents the recent trend in India-Pakistan trade. Section 4 examines the implications

3. See, 'Anand Sharma Meets Shahbaz Sharif' Press Information Bureau, Government of India, Ministry of Commerce and Industry at: http://pib.nic.in/newsite/PrintRelease.aspx?relid=101745

of trade normalisation by Pakistan on India's market access in the former's market. Some anomalies in Pakistan's negative list approach to its bilateral and SAFTA trade with India are examined in Section 5. Section 6 examines Pakistan's apprehensions in its bilateral trade with India. Section 7 discusses the ground reality in relation to Pakistan's apprehensions. Section 8 examines WTO implications of India-Pakistan trade. Concluding observations are presented in Section 9.

Data and Methodology

UNCOMTRADE data has been used in this study, sourced from the World Bank's World Integrated Trade Solution (WITS) online database. The data available in this database is at 6-digit under the Harmonised Commodity Description and Coding System (HS) of trade classification.[4] However, various trade related notifications issued by the governments of India and Pakistan are at the 8-digit HS level. Therefore, for the purpose of analysis, all the 8-digit HS level products were converted to 6-digit HS level product by ignoring the last two digits. Hence, the number of products at 6-digit HS level is less than the number of 8-digit HS level products for any notification by the respective governments. Therefore, calculations are based on this aggregated level product lists and is indicative of the trade pattern. To examine the implications of trade normalisation by Pakistan, the data has been considered for 2015, the latest available year at the time of writing this paper.[5] However, 2011 data has been used to examine some anomalies in Pakistan's trade with India. For examining overall bilateral trade between India and Pakistan, the data covering the period 2011 to 2015 has been used. Unless otherwise stated, the number of products mentioned in this study refers to HS 6-digit level of classification.

India's trade with Pakistan, which was earlier based on a positive list of 1,932 products, at 8-digit classification was replaced by a negative list approach vide a notification S.R.O. No. 280 (I) /2012 dated 20 March 2012 under which all products became importable from India barring 1,209 items under 8-digit HS classification. For the purpose of comparison, it is necessary

---

4. The Harmonised Commodity Description and Coding System (HS) of tariff nomenclature is an internationally standardised system of names and numbers for classifying traded products developed and maintained by the World Customs Organization (WCO) (formerly the Customs Co-operation Council), an independent intergovernmental organisation with over 170 member countries based in Brussels, Belgium.

5. The paper was submitted in July 2016.

to aggregate all 8-digit products to their 6-digit equivalents. Translated to 6-digit HS classification, this comes to 788 products, of which Pakistan did not import 99 products, while India did not have supply capability in 2 products, thereby making an effective negative list of 689 products (see detailed analysis in Table 1).

This paper uses the concept of Additional Market Access Frontier (AMAF) to assess the additional market access potential on the identified products. It gives the possibility of AMAF across all products under most favourable competitive conditions after netting the existing exports of the supplier country, the supply being set by the country's world exports (see Appendix 1 for definition and note).

Trends in India-Pakistan Trade

Figure 1 presents the trends in India-Pakistan bilateral trade. It is observed that India's export to Pakistan has increased from a mere US$ 0.16 billion in 2001 to US$ 1.96 billion in 2015, after reaching a peak of US$ 2.17 billion in 2014. By contrast, India's import in the same period has increased from US$ 0.07 billion in 2001 to US$ 0.46 billion in 2015 with a peak of US$ 0.53 billion in 2014. Consequently, India's trade surplus with Pakistan increased from US$ 0.09 billion in 2011 to US$ 1.50 billion in 2015.

Figure 1: Trends in India's Trade with Pakistan

(US$ billion)

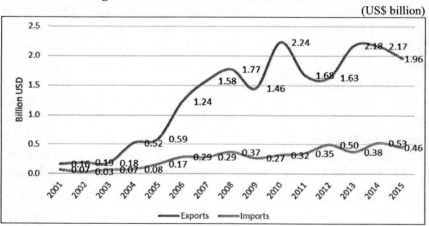

Source: Authors' calculation based on WITS

Implications of Trade Normalisation

India-Pakistan bilateral trade shows that India has exported 4,537 products, valued at US$ 262.1 billion, to the world, of which only US$ 2 billion was exported to Pakistan in 2015. In the same year, Pakistan imported 4,207 products, valued at US$ 43.9 billion, from the world.

Our negative list products analysis indicates that Pakistan's effective negative list for ban on India's exports to the former consists of 687 products at 6-digit HS classification. Products worth US$ 67 million were exported to India even though listed in the negative list category.

India's AMAF on all products in Pakistan's negative list amounts to US$ 5.8 billion. An analysis of positive list products has been done at two levels: (i) all matched world exports and world imports products of India and Pakistan, respectively, without any bilateral exports from India to Pakistan (positive list I), and (ii) all such globally matched products but including existing exports from India to Pakistan (positive list II). In other words, Pakistan has already liberalised its trade with India in its positive list to India. Full normalisation would imply just a small step forward.

In the former case (positive list I), India's AMAF is US$ 4.5 billion, while in the latter case (positive list II), India's AMAF is US$ 14.6 billion. As against a combined value of US$ 19.1 billion, India's AMAF on its negative list products is only US$ 5.8 billion. This comes to only 23 per cent of total AMAF of US$ 24.9 billion to India on its full trade normalisation. Figure 2 illustrates this clearly.

Table 1: Normalisation of Trade with Pakistan and Implications for India (2015)

Sl. No.	Description	No of Products (HS 6-digit)	Trade Value (US$ billion)	AMAF (US$ billion)
		Overall trade		
1	India exports to World	4,537	262.1	
2	Pakistan imports from World	4,207	43.9	
3	India exports to Pakistan	1,560	2	
		Negative list analysis		
4	Pakistan's negative list for India: 8-digit HS	1,209		
5	Pakistan's negative list for India converted to HS 6-digit	788		

6	Out of 788 products in negative list, Pakistan did not import	99		
7	Effective Negative List for India at HS 6-digit (sl.no.5 less 6)	689		
8	Out of 689 products, India does not have supply capability in	2		
9	Feasible Negative List for India (sl. No 7 less 8)/Additional market available to India under Negative List□	687	0.06	5.8
Positive list analysis				
10	Matched products of India exports to world (but not to Pakistan) and Pakistan imports from world in Positive list I	2,133	0	4.5
11	Actual exports from India to Pakistan (Positive list II)□	1,325	1.8	14.6
12	Total AMAF available for India in Positive list items (sl. no. 10+11)	NA	NA	19.1

Note: 'In Sl. No. 9 the AMAF is for 674 products as 13 of these have data anomaly. In Sl. No. 11 the AMAF is for 1187 products since 138 of them have data anomaly. This arises when India's bilateral exports to Pakistan exceed the latter's world imports from its reporting data.
Source: Authors' estimation based on WITS database.

Figure 2: India's AMAF on Positive List I, Positive list II and Negative list

(US$ billion)

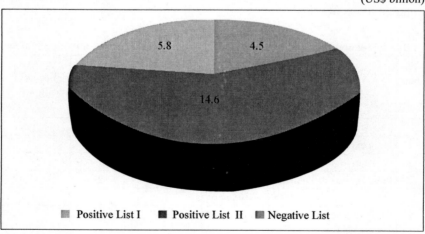

Source: Authors own

Some Anomalies in Negative List Approach to Bilateral Trade

The perseverance with negative list approach by Pakistan has created some anomalies with Pakistan's SAFTA sensitive list for non-least developed countries (NLDCs) as may be seen in Table 2. To illustrate, some 279 items may be identified in Pakistan's sensitive list for non-LDCs, which are also listed by Pakistan under negative list for India. Of these, 87 products valued at US$ 39.5 million were being exported by India (India reporter). Pakistan reported imports of 67 such products valued at US$ 35.4 million.

Further, Pakistan's negative list had contained 31 products earlier under its positive list for India, but now has been denied access under Pakistan's negative list. Data for 2011 reveals that of these products, India has exported to Pakistan 17 products valued at US$ 17.9 million (India reporter), while Pakistan reported import of 16 products valued at US$ 16 million. This reflects how Pakistan has used its negative list approach to restrict entry of some products from India, hitherto under Pakistan's positive list. Further, there were 279 products in Pakistan's sensitive list that were also in Pakistan's negative list for India. Of these 279 products, India used to export 87 products to Pakistan as per India's reporting, and Pakistan used to import 67 such products as per Pakistan's reporting. Further, 279 products in Pakistan's sensitive list for non-LDCs under SAFTA were also listed in the country's negative list for India. This is likely to create confusion among Indian traders considering accessing the Pakistan market. This is, however, not to deny that overall India's access to Pakistan's market under its negative list approach stands significantly enhanced.

Table 2: Some Anomalies in Negative list Approach to Bilateral Trade (2011)

Sl. No.	Products Classified by Lists	No. of Products (US$ million)
1	Products earlier in positive list but denied access under negative list	31
2	India's exports to Pakistan for products under Sl. No.1 (India reporting)	17 (US$ 17.9)
3	Pakistan's imports from India for products under Sl. No.1 (Pakistan reporting)	16 (US$ 16)
4	Products under Pakistan's sensitive list kept in its negative list for India	279
5	Exports of India to Pakistan in products under sl.no. 4 (India reporting)	87
6	Pakistan imports from India in products under 16 (Pakistan reporting)	67

Source: Based on authors' estimates from United Nations Commodity Trade Statistics accessed from World Integrated Trade Solution (WITS) database in July 2013.

Pakistan's Apprehensions

Pakistan had launched several official as well as ministerial level meetings with Indian counterparts. There had emerged wide constituencies in Pakistan to recognise the need and positive outcome of opening up trade with India. However, the impending Pakistan elections had delayed the process.

After the new government, led by Mr. Nawaz Sharif, was formed in May 2013, expectation of a forward movement towards trade normalisation has emerged. However, the unfortunate incident across the line of control on the India-Pakistan border in January 2013 has proved to be a dampener. Meanwhile, several stakeholders had began to express the view that a level playing ground should first be created before the process of trade normalisation could be attained. Several lobbies were becoming prominent, supporting this apprehension.

The influential farmers lobby has been most vocal in opposing free trade with India. Their contention is that Pakistan's agriculture would suffer from highly subsidised farm imports from India. In November 2012, the president of the Basmati Growers' Association (BGA) warned that BGA members had faced "economic suicide". Further, head of Farmers Association of Pakistan (FAP) threatened to literally block Indian agricultural products from entering Pakistan.

It is contended that the farmers of Pakistan have not been taken on board while taking the decision to grant MFN to India. Such a decision should not have been hastily taken without prior cost-benefit analysis in view of the two countries' respective agricultural subsidies (Basu, 2013a; Bucha, 2012; Hasan, 2012).

Several lobbies have also emerged in the industrial sector. The pharmaceutical industry fears that India's abundance of cheap pharmaceutical intermediate raw materials and large economies of scale will marginalise Pakistani products, whereas the chemical/synthetic fiber sector worries that India will dump its large fiber surplus in Pakistani market (Basu, 2013b)

Pakistan's automotive manufacturers are also apprehensive that Indian auto parts would flood the Pakistani market and disrupt the local industry. An expression of such a concern is that nearly 400 products, out of a total of 1,209 products, in Pakistan's negative list, are contained in this sector.

Deeply embedded in Pakistani businessmen and policymakers is the alleged concern on a plethora of non-tariff barriers imposed by India on Pakistani products. The imposition and application of standards in India is perceived as a major non-tariff barrier by Pakistani exporters. Pakistan has an export interest in textiles and agricultural products, which are also happened to be sectors where import restrictions/standards are more vigorously applied by India. Even though technical barriers to trade (TBTs) and sanitary and phyto-sanitary (SPS) measures are not discriminatory across trading partners, Pakistan's exports have been negatively affected by the NTBs, owing to more stringent application of such regulations.

The Ground Reality

It appears that the ground reality on Pakistan's apprehensions is somewhat more complex. According to Kugelman and Hathaway (2013a), some food producers "actually relish the prospect of acquiring foodstuffs from India because they believe such products will be of higher quality than their own, and hence generate greater profits." Another surprising source of support they cite is Pakistan's textile industry, which is optimistic of capturing a sizeable share of the Indian market. With India opening up to allow private investment from Pakistan, some Pakistani home textile and bed ware manufacturers have already explored joint venture options with Indian partners.

After initial opposition to opening up with India, not only has the harsh opposition from Pakistan's auto industry diminished, on the contrary, business opportunities from trade in auto parts with India is becoming visible. Car assemblers of Pakistan are willing to import parts that are completely knocked down (CKD), but are opposing imports of completely built up units. The imports of major car parts from India at competitive rates could bring down substantially the cost of producing cars. Suzuki and Toyota have affiliates in both the countries, and with trade in auto parts being permitted, these companies can source car components from whichever of their affiliates or their vendors who produce them at cheaper rates. Auto part makers in Pakistan have expressed interest in setting up joint ventures with Indian auto part makers (Kugelman, 2013b).

If the negative list is lifted, a lot of imports from India, if competitive, will simply replace imports from other countries, without impinging on the domestic manufacturers.

To illustrate, parts and accessories of motor vehicles were earlier excluded for imports from India under Pakistan's positive list, and subsequently also when these products were brought under its negative list.

However, it is interesting to observe that Pakistan was less averse in importing these products from third countries. To illustrate, Pakistan had imported US$ 180 million worth parts and accessories of motor vehicles from the world in 2011, where the principal suppliers were Thailand, Japan and China.[6]

Similarly, Pakistan has kept most of the products under electric machinery equipment and parts (HS 85) and vehicles of railway/tramway and rolling stock (HS 87) under its negative list. However, import data for 2011 again reveals that the country imported substantially from the world, particularly from China, Japan and Thailand[7].

By keeping such products in its negative list, Pakistan is giving third countries first opportunity in its markets. This becomes even more apparent in the context of Pakistan's FTA with China. If Pakistani manufacturers can brace up to competition from China (often identified as manufacturing hub of Asia), what prevents them from offering similar market access to India?

An analysis of the NTMs notified against India shows that some of these NTMs did not pose any barrier to entry as they are applicable to both imports as well as domestically manufactured goods, and hence, in accordance with the principle of national treatment. There are also some other measures where India has already initiated corrective action, but the information on such action perhaps has not been made available to other countries (eg. on labelling/customs valuation).

In the 6th RTCEC, held in New Delhi during 14-16 November 2011, a specific slot was allotted to discuss the NTBs perceived by Pakistan in respect of their exports to India. The discussions explained how insistence on specific standards by importers was due to the commercial considerations and not because of any Government requirement (Government of India, 2011b).

An Annexure attached to the 6th Round of India-Pakistan bilateral trade talks clarified all issues raised by the Pakistan side. On the issue of compulsory certification of cement, the Pakistani side was informed that Bureau of Industrial Standards (BIS) was mandated to give license within six months and inspection visit was to be completed within 1-2 months after an application is registered. About 13 licenses were already operational and renewal licenses for two years were being given to all cement manufacturers, who had applied for the same (Government of India, 2011b).

---

6. The data source is UNCOMTRADE data as obtained from WITS online database.
7. Ibid.

As noted earlier, the farm lobby in Pakistan is concerned about the agricultural subsidies that India applies on food, fertilizers, power and irrigation.

Estimates made in a recent study by Hoda and Gulati (2013) show that in recent years non-product specific support has remained below the *de minimis* level of 10 per cent of the total value of agricultural production, except in 2008-09, when it rose on account of unprecedented rise in fertilizer prices.

The authors' calculations for product specific investment and input subsidies show that after making allowance for inflation since 2008, the minimum support price is well below the fixed external reference price. The negative gap between the fixed external reference price and the minimum support price is large enough to allow full adjustment of the product specific investment and input subsidies.

The most obvious apprehensions on the Indian side have been Pakistan's non-compliance of MFN trade relations with India and restricting the passage of goods across the Attari-Wagah border to only 137 products.

Implications of WTO Compliance

At the Ninth Ministerial Conference, held in Bali, Indonesia, from 3 to 7 December 2013, Ministers adopted the "Bali Package", a series of decisions aimed at streamlining trade, allowing developing countries more options for providing food security, boosting least-developed countries' trade and helping development more generally (WTO, 2013a).

The draft Ministerial Declaration on public stockholding for food security purposes states:

"In the interim, until a permanent solution is found, and provided that the conditions set out below are met, Members shall refrain from challenging through the WTO Dispute Settlement Mechanism, compliance of a developing Member with its obligations under Articles 6.3 and 7.2 (b) of the Agreement on Agriculture (AoA) in relation to support provided for traditional staple food crops in pursuance of public stockholding programmes for food security purposes existing as of the date of this Decision, that are consistent with the criteria of paragraph 3, footnote 5, and footnote 5&6 of Annex 2 to the AoA when the developing Member complies with the terms of this Decision (WTO, 2013a)."

Pakistan has so far been a lone member under the G-33 that has been opposing the stand taken by other members, led by India, to remove the ceiling on Aggregate Measurement of Support[8] (AMS) set by 10 per cent of the value of gross agricultural output. They have been arguing that India must bring down its level of subsidies so that Pakistan's farmers may have a level playing ground in meeting the challenge of cheap agricultural imports from India. This has been one of the factors restraining the normalisation of trade with India. Now that the Bali Package allows for public stockholding for food security purposes as an interim measure until a permanent solution is found in the next four years in 2017, Pakistan has no option to challenge India under the WTO Dispute Settlement Mechanism.

It follows that, if threatened, Pakistan can follow a number of other trade defence measures. While removing products in its negative list, it may choose, as a temporary measure, to retain a few agricultural products it feels to be particularly threatened, in its negative list. So far there are very few agricultural products in Pakistan's negative list.

Next, while pruning its sensitive list under SAFTA, Pakistan may decide to retain agricultural products for a longer period.

Finally, Pakistan may decide to apply Tariff Rate Quotas (TRQs) on agricultural products it considers sensitive. The Bali Package provides modalities for administration of TRQs. An understanding on tariff rate quotas (WTO, 2013b) states:

> "Tariff quota administration of scheduled tariff quotas shall be deemed to be an instance of "import licensing" within the meaning of the Uruguay Round Agreement on Import Licensing Procedures and, accordingly, that Agreement shall apply in full, subject to the Agreement on Agriculture and to the following more specific and additional obligations."

Therefore, we need some obligations to ensure that the quotas so assigned do not remain unduly utilised for long periods. Pakistan, thus, has

---

8. The Aggregate Measurement of Support (AMS) is set by the difference between the procurement (administered) price paid to farmers and the external reference price set by the average world price of the crop prevailing between 2006 to 2008. India has been questioning the validity of the external price in relation to the current world prices of food grains.

the option to apply TRQs to ensure a fair balance to protect its farmers, while at the same time not fully denying the advantages of competitive and cheap imports from India.

From the point of view of Pakistan, the most obvious violation is Article 1 of WTO that highlights the core principle of non-discrimination under its MFN treatment.

Conclusions

The delay in normalisation of trade between India and Pakistan has been prolonged for quite some time. This is neither in the interest of Pakistan nor of India. Pakistan is losing by not being able to access cheaper intermediate and capital goods from India, while importing the same at much higher cost from third countries. On the other, India is not only losing its additional market access in Pakistan in respect of products contained in the latter's negative list. However, given that China has preferential access to Pakistan's market on those very products, India is suffering a double whammy by being deprived of first mover advantage that China is exploiting to its economic and strategic advantages.

Further, the set intersection of products in Pakistan's sensitive and negative lists creates an anomalous situation that the Indian traders may find ambiguous and hard to filter.

The study highlights that, under its positive list approach, Pakistan has been already offering high AMAF of US$ 19.1 billion to India, whether or not the matched products were actually being exported to Pakistan by India. In case of normalisation of trade, when ban on negative list products are lifted, India's AMAF would be US$ 5.8 billion, being much less that what India is availing under its positive list with Pakistan. This amounts to no more than 23 per cent of India's total AMAF of US$ 24.9 million, when normalisation of Pakistan's negative list is considered along with its positive list.

This chapter highlights Pakistan's apprehensions of opening up its market through trade normalisation with India. Farmer lobbies draw attention to the high rate of subsidisation of agriculture in India, which would put Pakistani farmers at a disadvantage, when agro products are imported from India. The WTO Ninth Ministerial Declaration at Bali ensures that no country can take India to Dispute Settlement mechanism even if the *de minimis* subsidy on agriculture is breached. Hence, we suggest several trade defense measures, which Pakistan could take to address this problem. Tariff Rate Quotas are also applicable as per modalities set under the Bali Declaration. For industrial products, Pakistan can, if it feels threatened, always apply the Safeguard Mechanism as provided for under SAFTA.

As noted earlier, the most obvious apprehensions on the Indian side have been Pakistan's non-compliance of MFN trade relations with India and restricting the passage of goods across the Attari-Wagah border to only 137 products. Once these conditions had been met, trade liberalisation between the two countries under SAFTA could have proceeded briskly.

This chapter highlights that Pakistan has already opened a large part of its market to India under its positive list approach. Freeing its products out of its negative list will not cause a wide expansion in India's market access. It will merely enable its more competitive products to enter Pakistan's market. Accessing more competitive intermediate goods from the Indian market will only aid Pakistan's industrialisation. However, all will depend how and when Pakistan offers WTO compatible MFN status to India.

Appendix 1

Additional Market Access Frontier (AMAF) for product /sector i is given as:

$(SE_i, MI_i) - ET_i$

When the value is summed over all products/sectors, we have:

$$\sum_{k=i}^{n} MIN(SE_i, MI_i) - ET_i$$

where – SE_i = Supplier's (India's) Global Exports; MI_iMI_i = Market's (Pakistan's) Global Imports; ET_i = Supplier's (India's) Existing Exports to Pakistan Market.

Note: The concept is used to give the upper limit of additional market access frontier (AMAF) of the supplier country's product i, after netting its existing exports to its partner importing country, the supplies being set by the former country's world exports and market access limit set by the latter country's world imports. It must be understood that the term "frontier" is notional since it only sets the upper limit to which the supplying country could substitute its partner country's demand for the product from rest of the world. Actual penetration of the supplying country's rest of the world imports would depend on the its improving competitiveness whether from improved productivity, improved trade facilitation measures, or from availing preferential access from its partner country's market. The concept is nevertheless useful as the supplier country is likely to be more successful when faced with a wider market where its existing share is modest. In such a scenario, even a miniscule increase in market share could substantially increase the value of bilateral trade.

References

Basu, Nayanima (2013a). *Delay in MFN status to India due to agricultural lobby in Pakistan.* Business Standard, 6 February.

Basu, Nayanima (2013b). *Pakistan's pharma sector objects to MFN status to India.* Business Standard, New Delhi, 30 March.

Bucha, Tariq (2012). *MFN to India catastrophic for Pakistan.* The Nation, 09 December.

Business Line Bureau (2013). *India, Pakistan may agree to resume talks on easing trade.* The Hindu Business Line, 13 December, 2013.

Dawn (2013). *Trade with India.* Dawn, 24 December. Available on: http://www.dawn.com/news/1075920/trade-with-india/print

Government of India (1949). *White Paper on Indo-Pakistan Relations: (15 August 1947-31 December 1949).* Government of India (GoI), New Delhi.

Government of India (1975). *Trade Agreement Between the Government of India and the Government of the Islamic Republic of Pakistan.* Islamabad, 23 January. Available on: http://mea.gov.in/Portal/LegalTreatiesDoc/PA75B1660.pdf

Government of India (2011a). *Joint Statement of the 5th Round of Talks on Commercial and Economic Co-operation between Commerce Secretaries of India and Pakistan.* Department of Commerce and Industry, Government of India. Available on: http://commerce.nic.in/trade/JPS27-28Apr2011.pdf

Government of India (2011b). *Joint Statement of the 6th Round of Talks on Commercial and Economic Co-operation between Commerce Secretaries of India and Pakistan.* Department of Commerce and Industry, Government of India. Available on: http://commerce.nic.in/trade/Minutes14-16Nov2011.pdf

Government of India (GoI 2012). *Joint Statement of the 7th Round of Talks on Commercial and Economic Co-operation between Commerce Secretaries of India and Pakistan.* Department of Commerce and Industry, Government of India. Available at: http://commerce.nic.in/trade/Joint_Press_Statement_CS_Pakistan_India_Sept_20_21st_2012.pdf

Government of India (2014). *India-Pakistan Relations.* Ministry of External Affairs, Government of India. Available on: http://www.mea.gov.in/Portal/ForeignRelation/Pakistan_April2014.pdf

Government of Pakistan (2012). *Pakistan's Notification* S.R.O. No. 280 (I) /2012 dated 20th March 2012. Ministry of Commerce and Textile Industry, Government of Pakistan (GoP). Available on: http://www.tdap.gov.pk/pdf/SRO-280-I-2012.pdf

Gulati, Ashok and Anwar-ul-Hoda (2013). *Beware the peace clause.* The Financial Express, 11 November, 2013. Available on: http://www.financialexpress.com/archive/column-beware-the-peace-clause/1193232/

Hasan, Munawar (2012). *Farmers demand level playing field. The News,* 14 December. Available on: http://www.thenews.com.pk/Todays-News-3-148188-Farmers-demand-level-playing-field

Kugelman, Michael and Robert Hathaway (2013a). *Pakistan India Trade: what needs to be done-what does it matter?* Wilson Centre. Available on: http://www.wilsoncentre.org/program/asia-program

Kugelman, Michael (2013b). *What's holding up India-Pakistan trade normalization?* The AFPAK Channel, 16 May. Available on: http://afpak.foreignpolicy.com/posts/2013/04/16/whats_holding_up_india_pakistan_trade_normalization.

World Trade Organisation (2013a). *Public stockholding for food security purposes.* Draft ministerial decision WT/MIN(13)/W/10, 6 December. World Trade Organisation (WTO). Available on: http://wto.org/english/thewto_e/minist_e/mc9_e/tempdocs_e.htm

World Trade Organisation (2013b). *Understanding on tariff rate quota administration provisions of agricultural products,* as defined in article 2 of the agreement on agriculture, Ministerial Decision of 7 December 2013.

World Trade Organisation (2013c). Document: WT/MIN(13)/39,WT/L/914 dt. 11 December 2013. Available at: http://wto.org/english/thewto_e/minist_e/mc9_e/tempdoc s_e.htm

ELEVEN

INDIA AND BANGLADESH CONNECTIVITY WITH MYANMAR

Kavita Iyengar

Introduction

The Indian subcontinent had a strong historical and cultural relationship with Burma (Myanmar) as evinced by the spread of Buddhism and evolution of the Myanmarese (Burmese) script. Burma was part of British India. Although separated in 1938, the ties in modern history were strengthened by thriving trade links and the presence of a large Indian community in Myanmar. After India's independence and partition in 1947, the new international borders hampered the old transport and trades linkages in South Asia, and later the linkages to Myanmar also declined.

Connectivity with Myanmar presents several economic opportunities for the South Asia sub-region. Myanmar is sub-continent's land link to the Southeast and East Asian markets. Thus, road or rail connectivity with Myanmar will lead to greater trade. Myanmar also connects South Asia and Southeast Asia. Direct benefits of connectivity for India include potential access to Myanmar's gas reserves and to a market of 60 million people. Bangladesh is also seeking to strengthen road and rail networks with Myanmar to advance economic opportunities and trade between the two countries. Trade facilitation between the countries also has implications for regional and inter-regional trade, and establishing the land routes offers gains to the landlocked countries of Bhutan and Nepal.

This chapter focuses on the current border trade between India and Myanmar and Bangladesh and Myanmar and the tremendous potential the region has, which can be harnessed with enhanced connectivity. Myanmar's current trading patterns provide the context for the analysis of trade and connectivity potential with its South Asian neighbours.

* The views expressed are those of the authors and do not necessarily reflect the views and policies of the Asian Development Bank (ADB) or its Board of Governors or the governments they represent. Atul Sanganeria's support in data computation is gratefully acknowledged. Usual disclaimers apply.

Myanmar's Trading Patterns

India, China and Thailand have been important export partners of Myanmar. Between 2006 and 2010, the three countries accounted for nearly 75 per cent of Myanmar's cumulated exports. The share of these countries in Myanmar's total exports remained 75 per cent during 2011- 2015. However, the share of China increased from 19 per cent in 2011 to nearly 40 per cent in 2015, while the shares of Thailand and India during the same period decreased from 40 per cent to 27 per cent and 14 per cent to 8 per cent, respectively. Figure 1 shows export shares of Myanmar between 2011 and 2015.

China, Thailand and Singapore accounted for nearly 75 per cent of Myanmar's imports during 2006 to 2010. However, this share fell to around 70 per cent during the period 2011-2015. China's share in Myanmar's imports increased from around 39 per cent in 2011 to 42 per cent in 2015. Thailand's share in Myanmar's import basket fell from 23 per cent to 18 per cent. Other countries such as South Korea, Malaysia, Japan, and India contributed in the range of 4-5 per cent of total exports during 2011 to 2015. Figure 2 shows Myanmar's import shares by origin between 2011 and 2015.

Figure 1: Myanmar's Export Shares by Origin, 2011-2015

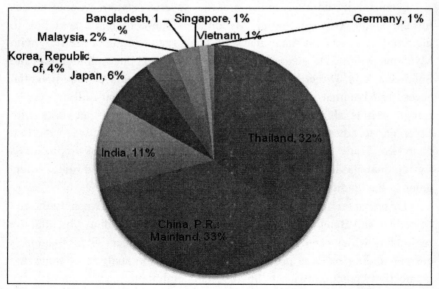

Source: Calculations based on DOTS, IMF

Figure 2: Myanmar's Import Shares by Origin, 2011-2015

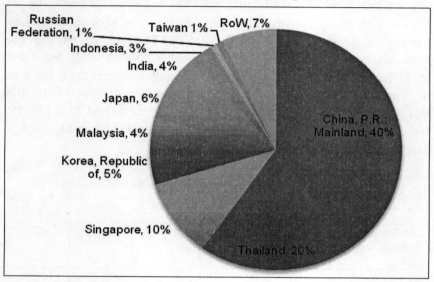

Source: Calculations based on DOTS, IMF

Myanmar's export basket is laden with fuels, food and other primary commodities, including precious stones and gems, which constituted nearly 90 per cent of total exports between 2006 and 2010. However, more than 70 per cent of its imports are manufactured goods (Ferrarini, 2013).

Myanmar's export to Thailand mainly comprises natural gas, wood, fish, copper, whereas exports to China mainly comprises wood, and minerals and metals including ores and concentrates of base metals, pearls and precious or semi-precious stones, natural rubber, etc. Myanmar imports petroleum products, edible products, lime, cement and prefabricated construction material, alcoholic and non-alcoholic beverages from Thailand. The composition of imports from China includes manufactures like motorcycles, fabrics, woven man-made textiles, internal combustion piston engines, iron and steel bars, rods, angles, and shapes.

India-Myanmar Bilateral Trade

Over the past decade, the bilateral trade between India and Myanmar rose from US$ 328 million in 1997-98 to US$ 921.19 in 2006-07 and to US$ 2.18 billion in 2013-14 (Tables 1 and 2). For Myanmar, India is the fifth largest trading partner, third largest export destination, and the seventh largest source of imports. India has had negative trade balance vis-à-vis Myanmar. However, India's significance as Myanmar's trading partner has declined from 2006 to 2015. Of Myanmar's total exports, India accounted for nearly 17 per cent during 2006 to 2010, but it fell to 11 per cent during 2011 to 2015. In comparison, India's share in Myanmar's total imports was only 3.4 per cent during 2006 to 2010, and this increased marginally to 3.7 per cent during the period 2011 to2015. India still stood as the fourth largest trading partner among Myanmar's neighbouring countries.

Table 1: Bilateral Trade Structure between India and Myanmar

(US$ million)

	2008 – 09	2009 – 10	2010 – 11	2011 – 12	2012 – 13
Total Trade of Myanmar with India	1,150.60	1,497.77	1,388.29	1,926.52	1,957.35
Growth (%)		30.17 %	-10.65 %	43.95 %	1.60 %
India's Total Trade	488,991.67	467,124.31	620,905.32	795,283.41	791,137.33
Growth (%)		-4.47 %	32.92 %	28.08 %	- 0.52 %
Share in India's Total Trade (%)	0.24 %	0.32 %	0.22 %	0.24 %	0.25 %
India's Trade Balance	- 118,400.95	- 109,621.45	- 118,632.94	- 183,355.57	- 190,335.97

Source: Ministry of Commerce, Government of India

Agriculture and timber dominate India-Myanmar bilateral trade, which is heavily in Myanmar's favour. As seen in Tables 3 and 4, Myanmar contributed to nearly one-fifth of India's timber imports. Timber and wood products accounted for more than 27 per cent of Myanmar's exports to India (US$ 600 million). Export of wood in log form has been banned since April 2014. Myanmar is the second largest supplier of beans and pulses to India. India's exports to Myanmar include steel and iron products, electrical machinery, pharmaceuticals products, machinery and equipment, mineral oil, rubber products, plastics, etc. Exports of Indian pharmaceuticals grew from US$ 76.09 million in 2011-12 to US$ 94.55 million in 2012-13, but declined to US$ 74.17 in 2013-14.

For India, there is a large potential for bilateral trade, investment and other forms of economic cooperation with Myanmar. Growth in imports from India has outpaced growth in exports to India. The value of imports from India significantly increased from US$ 51.03 million to US$ 94.30 million. The potential areas for trade are pharmaceuticals, agricultural machinery, agrochemicals, electrical goods, iron and steel, pulses and beans, investment in plantations, ICT and IT-related products and services.

Table 2: Trends in India-Myanmar Bilateral Trade

(US$ million)

Year	2009-10	2010-11	2011-12	2012-13	2013-14	2014-15 (Apr-Nov)
India's exports	207.97 (6.17%)	320.62 (54.17%)	545.38 (70.1%)	544.66 (-0.13%)	787.01 (44.5%)	483.81
India's imports	1,289.80 (38.84%)	1,017.67 (-21.1%)	1,381.15 (35.72%)	1,412.69 (2.28%)	1395.67 (-1.20%)	951.78
Total trade	1,497.77 (30.17%)	1,338.29 (-10.65%)	1,870.20 (39.75%)	1,957.35 (1.6%)	2182.68 (11.51)	1135.59

Note: Figures in parentheses indicate variation from previous year.
Source: Directorate General of Foreign Trade (DGFT), Department of Commerce, India.

Table 3: India's Major Imports from Myanmar

(US$ million)

Commodity	2008-09	2009-10	2010-11	2011-12	2012-13	2013-14
Pulses and beans	611.78	851.53	570.82	628.57	552.12	468.68
Wood and articles of wood	311.01	404.95	419.16	388.71	402.28	605.54
Products of animal origin	2.93	6.22	12.32	0.56	1.07	-
Others	2.34	7.19	7.88	14.65	25.72	30.23
Raw hides and skin	-	2.05	4.55	3.41	0.84	
Coffee, tea, mate and spices	0.91	3.07	2.94	1.22	-	
Rice	-	-	-	-	-	18.17
Medical Equipment			-	-	-	40.4

Source: Central Statistical Organisation (CSO), Myanmar.

Table 4: India's Major Exports to Myanmar

(US$ million)

Commodity	2008-09	2009-10	2010-11	2011-12	2012-13	2013-14
Others	94.17	79.85	111.4	110.12	129.86	147.48
Meat and edible meat Offal	-	1.91	71.59	13.31	0.29	-
Pharmaceuticals	49.92	55.98	61.29	76.09	94.55	74.17
Iron and Steel	63.93	43.66	40.21	26.29	59.60	168.91
Sugar and sugar Confectionery	-	0.07	21.27	-	0.09	-
Electrical machinery and equipment	13.62	16.69	16.39	26.81	26.03	58.34
Chemicals and allied products	-	9.81	12.27	5.4	7.20	-
Oil well and Mining Equipment	-	-	-	75.88	0.85	-

Source: CSO, Myanmar.

If trade along border is allowed, even with the current composition, both countries will benefit as the trade volumes go up.

Bangladesh-Myanmar Bilateral Trade

Bilateral trade between Myanmar and Bangladesh stood at US$ 50 million in 2014-15, with a peak of US$ 160 million in 2010-11 (Table 5).

Table 5: Trends in Bangladesh-Myanmar Bilateral Trade

(US$ million)

	2009-10	2010-11	2011-12	2012-13	2013-14	2014-15
Bangladesh's exports	3.73	5.04	8.22	11.6	15.4	15.7
Bangladesh's imports	68.5	155.7	74.6	81.8	71.6	28.8

Source: IMF DOTS

As seen in Tables 6 and 7, Myanmar's exports to Bangladesh comprised marine products, beans and pulses, and kitchen crops, while its imports from Bangladesh include pharmaceuticals, ceramic, cotton fabric, raw jute, kitchenware, and cosmetic.

Table 6: Bangladesh's Exports to Myanmar (2011-12)

Commodity	Value ('000 US$)	Share (%)
Medicaments (incl. veterinary medicaments)	3610	31
Fertilizers (other than those of group 272)	2141	19
Flat-rolled prod., iron, non-alloy steel, coated, clad	2060	18
Flat-rolled prod., iron, non-alloy steel, not coated	1185	10
Flat-rolled products of alloy steel	841	7
Petroleum oils or bituminous minerals > 70 % oil	483	4
Metal containers for storage or transport	359	3
Leather	82	0.7
Textile yarn	81	0.7
Cutlery	79	0.7

Source: UNCTAD statistics.

Table 7: Bangladesh's Imports from Myanmar (2011-12)

Commodity	Value ('000 US$)	Share (%)
Wood in the rough or roughly squared	46216.5	48.5
Rice	45967.3	48.2
Fish, fresh (live or dead), chilled or frozen	1799.7	1.9
Footwear	928.8	1.0
Spices	283.2	0.3
Other inorganic chemicals	57.3	0.1
Ferrous waste, scrape; remelting ingots, iron, steel	50.0	0.1
Crude vegetable materials, n.e.s.	27.6	0.0
Inorganic chemical elements, oxides & halogen salts	25.1	0.0
Miscellaneous manufactured articles, n.e.s.	9.1	0.0

Source: UNCTAD statistics.

Bangladesh and Myanmar share about 271 km of land border, of which around 150 km lie in hilly areas. Both the countries also share maritime border. Despite political issues, the countries have expressed desire to improve the volume of bilateral trade, which stands at less than US$ 100 million. For both countries neighbourhood policy has become a priority and they target to improve connectivity through the Bangladesh-China-India-Myanmar (BCIM) Economic Corridor.

Myanmar's Border Trade

Myanmar shares borders with Bangladesh, India, Lao PDR, China, and Thailand. Myanmar had border trade worth US$ 407 million in the financial year 2002, went up to over than US$ 1 billion in 2006-07, and to US$ 6.8 billion over 2014-15, with US$ 4.2 billion in exports and US$ 2.4 billion in imports. In 2015, trade with China accounted for 87 per cent of Myanmar's border trade, while trade with Thailand was 12 per cent. India accounted for just 0.8 per cent and Bangladesh a mere 0.2 per cent.

The value of documented cross-border exports and imports account for around 10 per cent of total trade of Myanmar, and, hence, cross-border trade is important for the country. In 2009, Myanmar's documented cross-border trade with China and Thailand accounted for 47 and 51 per cent, respectively. Increases in cross-border trade are attributed to Myanmar's bilateral cooperation with neighbouring countries following the 1996 border trade agreement with Thailand, which led to 186 per cent rise in Myanmar's cross-border exports between 1996 and 2007.[1]

India-Myanmar Border Trade

In order to permit trade of locally produced commodities, as per the prevailing customary practices on both sides of the India-Myanmar border, an agreement on border trade between India and Myanmar was signed in January 1994 and operationalised in the following year. The Agreement envisaged border trade through Moreh in Manipur and Zowkhathar in Mizoram, corresponding to Tamu and Rhi in Myanmar, respectively. Forty items[2] are permitted for the border trade between India and Myanmar with 5 per cent duty.

According to the Myanmar Department of Border Trade, the border trade turnover between India and Myanmar has ranged from US$ 10 - 22 million over the past seven years. As is evident, 99.5 per cent of India -

1. http://isdp.eu/content/uploads/publications/2009_set-aung_the- role-of- informal-cross-border-trade.pdf

2. Mustard/Rape Seeds, pulses and beans, fresh vegetables, fruits, garlic, onion, chillies, spices (excluding nut-meg, mace, cloves and cassia), bamboo, minor forest produce (excluding teak), betel nuts and leaves, food items for local consumptions, tobacco, tomato, reed broom, sesame, resin, coriander seeds, bicycle's spare parts, soya bean, roasted sunflower seeds, katha, ginger life-saving drugs, fertilizers, cotton fabrics, insecticides, stainless steel utensils, menthol, agarbatti, spices, cosmetics, leather footwear, paints and varnishes, sugar and salt, mosquito coils, bulbs, blades, x-ray paper and photo paper, imitation jewellery.

Myanmar trade takes place through seaports and the land trade is meagre and insignificant. Apparently, there are no serious legal impediments for normal trade to take place through the land customs stations (LCS) across the land borders. Almost all trade takes place in head loads only, following the barter mechanism.

Presently, Moreh is the only LCS through which formal trade across land route from India to Myanmar takes place. The other LCSs are open, but only traditional exchange takes place. Bilateral trade for the last 19 years across the land borders are given in Table 8.

Table 8: India's Border Trade with Myanmar

(Rs. million)

Year	Import Value	Import Duty	Export value	Export Duty/ Cess/Etc.	Total
1995 – 96	53.90	4.60	104.50	0.52	158.40
1996 – 97	167.00	13.76	297.90	2.26	464.90
1997 – 98	371.90	31.20	251.60	2.67	623.50
1998 – 99	37.40	3.78	48.80	0.45	86.20
1999 – 00	65.20	0.00	33.10	0.00	98.30
2000 – 01	124.10	0.00	56.80	0.00	180.90
2001 – 02	81.30	0.00	12.90	0.00	94.20
2002 – 03	119.00	0.00	38.40	0.00	157.40
2003 – 04	88.50	0.00	94.50	0.00	183.00
2004 – 05	53.80	0.00	64.90	0.00	118.70
2005 – 06	52.12	2.98	38.67	23700.00	90.78
2006 – 07	26.96	2.65	48.22	31600.00	75.18
2007 – 08	134.67	12.73	30.90	0.19	165.57
2008 – 09	7.61	0.71	16.06	0.00	23.67
2009 – 10	83.15	7.78	21.50	0.00	104.66
2010 – 11	38.02	3.66	2.60	0.00	40.62
2011 – 12	13.66	1.26	14.97	0.00	28.63
2012 – 13	205.54	19.09	278.50	0.00	484.04
2013 – 14	29.52	1.49	70.67	0.00	100.19

Source: Author's own

From Table 8 and Figure 3 we can see that in 2012-13, India's total bilateral trade with Myanmar stood at US$ 1.96 billion, of which trade through the LCSs represented a meagre US$ 8 million or just 0.48 per cent of the total. In three years 1996-97, 1997-98 and 2012-13, the trade volumes were relatively good. Otherwise, the trade has been very low, averaging just US$ 1.64 million.

Figure 3: Trends in India's Border Trade with Myanmar
(US$ million)

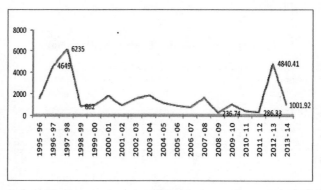

Source: Commissioner of Customs, North Eastern Region, Shillong, 2014.

The commodity-wise break-up of India's border trade with Myanmar is given in Tables 9 and 10. The major exports to Myanmar include cotton yarn, auto parts, soya bean meal and pharmaceuticals while the major imports from Myanmar are betel nut, dried ginger, green mung beans, black matpe, turmeric roots, resin and medicinal herbs.

Table 9: India's Major Border Imports from Myanmar
(US$ million)

Commodity	2008-09	2009-10	2010-11	2011-12	2012-13	2013-14
Pulses and beans	611.78	851.53	570.82	628.57	552.12	468.68
Wood and articles of wood	311.01	404.95	419.16	388.71	402.28	605.54
Products of animal origin	2.93	6.22	12.32	0.56	1.07	-
Others	2.34	7.19	7.88	14.65	25.72	30.23
Raw hides and skin	-	2.05	4.55	3.41	0.84	

Coffee, tea, mate and spices	0.91	3.07	2.94	1.22	-	
Rice	-	-	-	-	-	18.17
Medical equipment			-	-	-	40.44

Source: CSO, Myanmar.

Table 10: India's Major Border Exports to Myanmar

(US$ million)

Commodity	2008-09	2009-10	2010-11	2011-12	2012-13	2013-14
Others	94.17	79.85	111.4	110.12	129.86	147.48
Meat and edible meat offal		1.91	71.59	13.31	0.29	
Pharmaceuticals	49.92	55.98	61.29	76.09	94.55	74.17
Iron and steel	63.93	43.66	40.21	26.29	59.60	168.91
Sugar and sugar confectionery		0.07	21.27		0.09	
Electrical machinery and equipment	13.62	16.69	16.39	26.81	26.03	58.34
Chemicals and allied products		9.81	12.27	5.4	7.20	
Oil well and mining equipment				75.88	0.85	

Source: CSO, Myanmar.

Surface trade is likely to become more significant as construction advances on the India-Myanmar-Thailand Trilateral Highway that runs 1,360 km from Moreh via Mandalay to Mae Sot, Thailand. Currently, most of the border trade takes place through Moreh. The main commodity imported is betel nut and main export item is cumin seeds. More banks are opening branches in Moreh, a town of only around 15,000 people, and prompting plans to upgrade the frontier crossing. However, a recent change in the Reserve Bank of India's customs regulations in December 2015 forbids the traditional practice of barter trade. The central bank's attempt to formalise cross-border trade does not seem to have taken account of the undeveloped banking network in Myanmar or the difficulty of securing compliance from informal traders there.

The restrictive border trade agreement and lack of infrastructure are cited as the main impediments to border trade.

Bangladesh-Myanmar Border Trade

The signing of the border trade agreement in 1994 and the inauguration of Teknaf-Maungdaw trade in 1995 marked the beginning of the recent revival of Bangladesh-Myanmar border trade. In 2003, the agreement to cooperate in road and water transportation was signed, which was a significant development.[3] Despite challenges on strategic issues, both Myanmar and Bangladesh have been trying to improve bilateral ties through regional and sub-regional fora, such as BIMSTEC, BCIM, etc. Although, the potential for cooperation between Bangladesh and Myanmar are significant, the focus has been on border trade.

The bilateral trade dropped by almost half in the main trade centres of Sittwe and Maungdawin 2014-2015 mainly due to a sharp drop in fishery products and the general instability caused by the Rakhine-Rohingya conflict. The Sittwe-Bangladesh border trade which stood at US$ 15.336 million in 2011-12 went down to US$ 7.250 million in 2012-13 to US$ 4.33 million in 2014-15. The imports through Maungdaw also fell from US$ 7.831 million in 2011-12 to US$ 5.385 million in 2012-12 and exports from US$ 0.692 million to US$ 0.531 million, respectively. The Maungdaw hub processed a trade volume of US$ 3.62 million in 2014-15, marking a drop of US$ 1.72 million compared to the previous year.

Currently, five companies trade across the Bangladeshi border via Maungdaw border trade center. The main exports from Myanmar are fish products, prawns, slippers and cosmetics, while most frequent imports include cement, water pots and water distillation machines. Tariffs were lifted on 152 different products in March 2013, but trade figures did not show improvement.[4]

Connectivity at the Borders

The growth of border trade depends on political and security situation in the border area as well as the transport infrastructure and the institutional and regulatory arrangements that facilitate the movement of goods and services. The legalisation and regularisation of cross-border trade in Myanmar drastically increased its trade with its neighbours. It was estimated in 2009 that half of Myanmar's exports, including natural gas

---

3. In March 2003, three agreements, namely, Coastal Shipping, Trade Account and Joint Business Council, were concluded.

4. Ibid

pipelines to Thailand, are through the land route, while 30 per cent of the imports are cross-border.

An ERIA study demonstrates how investment in multimodal transport connectivity – in road, rail, air, and waterways, opens up a new dynamism in regional production networks, which would boost trade and investment, and economic activity, thus deepening regional cooperation and integration. Figure 4 shows the various proposed and ongoing connectivity projects involving India and Southeast Asia. It is clear that Bangladesh and Myanmar are central to these activities. ADB's study on the East Coast Economic Corridor has been initiated and once there is connectivity between the corridors of the sub-region, Myanmar's centrality is key to the success of their cross-border functioning.

Figure 4: South-Southeast Asia Connectivity

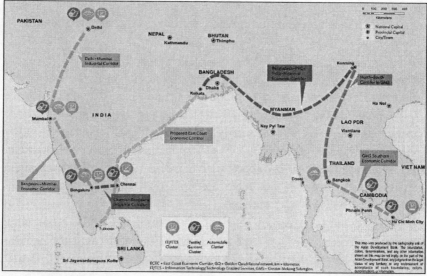

Source: Scaling New Heights: Vizag-Chennai Industrial Corridor, India's First Coastal Corridor, Asian Development Bank, 2016.

India-Myanmar Connectivity

From India, the best connection to Myanmar is through Moreh, which is directly connected to Mandalay, Myanmar's commercial hub. One of the most apparent constraints on the growth of the trade is the poor state of infrastructure, starting with road connectivity and telecommunication to facilities at border transit points and banking and other financial networks. The state of infrastructure and connectivity influence the transit and transaction costs of trade, whereas the improved connectivity and good infrastructure lower transit and transaction costs and facilitate trade.

Road

The India-Myanmar Friendship Road, which links Moreh with Kalewa in Myanmar, is in need of repairs. India has agreed to upgrade 71 bridges between Kalewa and Yargi, while Myanmar said it would upgrade the road from Yargi to Monywa and other road segments. The countries have agreed to repair and upgrade the entire stretch from Moreh to Mae Sot in Thailand by 2018. They have also agreed to launch a bus service between Imphal and Mandalay but concerns exist regarding customs and other modalities. The largest project is the US$ 120 million Kaladan Multimodal Transport Project, involving the upgradation of Sittwe port and dredging the Kaladan river to allow boat access from Sittwe to connect to Mizoram, has been slow.

Border Infrastructure

These overland crossings are among the most inefficient in the world, and little effort has been made to improve their conditions. Roy and Banerjee (2010) pointed out that basic infrastructure and logistics required for international trade are almost totally absent at all customs stations at the border. For instance, where food items form the bulk of exchange and trade, there is neither food testing laboratories nor cold storage. Warehouses and weighbridges are absent and there are no transit sheds or transhipment platforms for loading and unloading of goods. Electricity is erratic and power cuts could last over a week. Traders usually make do with portable generators. Due to the poor logistics, most of the trade across the Indo-Myanmar border takes place in head-loads (traditional exchange or informal trade) and on foot.

Regulatory Issues

A three-tier system of trade was introduced for cross-border trade at Moreh:
- Tier 1: Locally produced items that were traditionally exchanged between the indigenous people residing within 40 km on either side of the border to be traded under simplified documents up to a maximum value of US$ 1000.

- Tier 2: Barter Trade of 22 agreed upon exchangeable items up to a maximum value of US$ 20,000. The items that can be traded under this category are locally produced commodities consisting of agricultural and minor forest products.
- Tier 3: Normal or Regular Trade under the Letter of Credit System as per Export/Import Policy guidelines.

Institutional factors, especially those relating to trade facilitation, need to be addressed in order to improve Indo-Myanmar border trade. Several studies on border trade (Bezbaruah, 2007, Bhagowati and Das, 2015) argue that the volume of informal trade at the India-Myanmar border exceeds formal trade by several times and comprises third country products from China or the Far East. Although the value of border trade (according to official statistics) accounts for only 7 per cent of Myanmar's total trade value, the actual value of border trade is likely to be much higher due to the value of undocumented trade that flows through borders. If undocumented trade were to be included in official statistics, the value of border trade would have accounted for around 25 per cent of Myanmar's total value of trade in 2006.[5] However, the Foreign Trade Law of Myanmar that provides for transit trade, under which goods can be imported to Myanmar for final delivery in a third country, results in an artificially lowered price of the goods for the buyers in the final destination. The unusually low price of third country products imported to India from Myanmar in informal border trade can be partly ascribed to this factor. It works as an unfair competition for domestic producers in the destination country and the Myanmar Government also loses in terms of customs revenue.

The main reason cited for high informal trade is not evasion, but cumbersome process of trade at the border points. The barter trade system requires balancing exports by imports to be completed within a period of six months (Indian Institute of Foreign Trade, 1998), which hinders free flow of trade. Any delay in supply of imports makes it difficult for traders to complete the balancing obligations within stipulated period. Further, the narrow range of items identified for formal border trade is also a restriction. While both countries may have general negative lists for imports and exports, the scope of border trade needs to be extended to cover all items

---

5.   Refer, Aung (2009)

on which trading is permissible as per the existing rules for external trade of the countries. Stakeholder consultations by CII emphasize the need for addressing institutional factors such as dual Currency Exchange Rate System of Myanmar, which causes a discrepancy and diversion of trade to informal channels; lack of involvement of banks and other financial institutions which are causes for weak trading system.

From the Myanmar side, reasons cited are: to avoid lengthy licensing process; to import products without having earnings from exports; and to import/export products that are restricted on a temporary or permanent basis. Studies show that there is strong demand in Myanmar for Indian products such as bicycles and its parts, life-saving drugs, fertilizers, insecticides, cotton fabric including *lungis* (a sarong-like garment wrapped around the waist), stainless steel utensils, menthol, agarbati and perfumes, spices, chemicals, cosmetics, textiles, and motor cycles. This indicates that border trade can be enhanced significantly by inclusion of manufactured goods of Indian origin. There is also a need to have proper financial institutions between the borders so that the normal trade takes place through banking process. At the same time, there is a strong requirement for bringing the three-tier trade system within a proper regulatory framework (Singh, 2007).

Rail

The process of rail connectivity between India and Myanmar could significantly improve the trade between the two countries. Rail-link projects like the Jiribam-Imphal-Moreh line in the Indian state of Manipur and the Tamu-Kalay-Segyi line in Myanmar, as well as rehabilitation of Myanmar's existing Segyi-Chaungu-Myohaung line would greatly boost connectivity. According to the state-run company, Rail India Technical and Economic Services Ltd. that conducted a feasibility study of the proposed freight corridor, the Jiribam-Imphal-Moreh rail link is estimated to cost US$ 649 million, the Tamu-Kalay-Segyi link in Myanmar US$ 296 million, and the cost of refurbishing the Segyi-Chaungu-Myohaung line has been pegged at US$ 62.5 million. This rail links would ultimately join the New Delhi-Hanoi rail link. The objective is to link Manipur with India's main railway corridor and to upgrade and repair railway networks in Myanmar. India is planning New Delhi-Hanoi Rail Link with two possible routes. The first route will connect Hanoi via Myanmar, Thailand and Cambodia; while the second route would lean towards Bangkok via

Ye and a newly constructed portion of Ye and Dawei in Myanmar, and then connect to Hanoi through Thailand and Laos. The project announced in 2004 is yet to be completed. The 110-km Jiribam-Tupul-Imphal project on the Indian side was supposed to be completed by 2016. It has now been revised to 2018.

Waterways

The North East Region has about 3,839 km of navigable river routes. There are seven operational port locations in the state for import and export to the Kolkata and Haldia ports. There is an inland container depot (ICD) at Amingaon, 10 km from Guwahati, Assam, operated by the Container Corporation of India Ltd. (CONCOR). Waterway between Mizoram and the port of Sittwe is under construction and this could lead to enhanced trade opportunities within the country.

Bangladesh-Myanmar Connectivity[6]

There is need of enhanced infrastructure and administrative process to encourage trade not only across Teknaf and Maungdaw, but also through coastal shipping and other channels.

An Agreement on Direct Road Link between Bangladesh and Myanmar was signed in 2007 in Dhaka. According to the Agreement, Bangladesh is to finance construction of approximately 23 km of the road between Taungbro and Bawlibazar in Myanmar including bridges and culverts. Bangladesh submitted another proposal to the Myanmar authority to consider Teknaf-Maungdaw-Sittwelink road as the alternative route on the plain land across the coast of Bay of Bengal.

Bangladesh government is also interested in setting up a rail link between Kunming city in Yunnan province and Chittagong via Myanmar. Furthermore, Bangladesh has shown its recent renewed interest in the proposed Trans-Asian Railway (TAR). Once materialised, it will link Bangladesh, among others, with six East Asian countries such as Myanmar, Thailand, Laos, Cambodia, Malaysia and Singapore. As part of TAR agreement that Bangladesh signed in 2007, a 130-km-railway-track is to be laid from Dohazari of Bangladesh to Gundum in the Arakan state of Myanmar via Ramu in Cox's Bazaar.

---

6.   Refer, Morshed (2006).

Besides infrastructure improvements along the border, trade facilitation measures required to improve trade include establishing a working banking system in Myanmar, possible easing of visas for Bangladeshi businessmen and exchange rate adjustments as needed. Since the maritime boundary between Myanmar and Bangladesh has not been delimited, it has inhibited the offshore exploration of gas.

The Prospects for Increased Economic Cooperation[7]

Overland cross-border trade between the Indian sub-continent and Myanmar and beyond can transform economic growth for the BIMSTEC partners. It will also bridge the countries of South Asia via the Northeastern region of India and Myanmar with the ASEAN countries. International trade across this land border can supplement and expand the size of markets on either side attracting business interests to the rich and pristine natural resources of the region. Once developed, it can enable seamless transport of goods from manufacturer to markets or, raw material to manufacturers, across the region. The Bangladesh-India-Myanmar border region is rich in natural resources, with high incidence of poverty and poor infrastructure and logistics.

India-Myanmar Cooperation

Since the launch of the 'Look East' policy in 1991, the Government of India took several steps towards India-Myanmar cooperation. These include support for bilateral development projects, in particular the cross-border projects, which comprised of training, provision of expert knowledge, line of credits and grant-in-aid. Infrastructure projects include Kaladan Multimodal Transit Transport Project, Trilateral Highway, Rhi–Tiddim road, Renovation of Thanbayakan Refinery; Setting up of an IT University in Myanmar, Advance Center for Agricultural Research and Education, Yezin, upgradation of Yangon Children Hospital and Sittwe General Hospital. Business projects include the setting up of Tata Motors Heavy Truck Assembly Plant, Industrial Training centers at Pakokku and Myingyan, Tamanthi and Shwezayi Hydropower projects. Using the augmented gravity model, De (2014) estimated the trade potential between India and Myanmar can go up to US$ 11.56 billion by 2018.

---

7.   This section summarises the discussions from http://www.indianchamber.org/border-trade/

Prospects for Northeast India

Food Security: The immediate impact of removing trade restrictions and introducing systems for transit trade is expected to be on the increase in trade volumes between the Northeastern India and Myanmar. The two regions have all most similar economic structures with agriculture being dominant economic activity. However, Northeast India is still dependent on food supplies, including most of the rice and pulses requirements, from other parts of India. The supplies are unstable due to road conditions, especially during monsoons, and high transport costs. Myanmar has traditionally been a surplus producer and exporter of these two commodity groups. Northeast India can also provide markets for other agricultural products of Myanmar such as onions, which now comes from such distant states as Maharashtra. Market expansion will be an incentive for farmers in Myanmar to adopt better technology and expand production. A supply of staple food items will allow farmers in Northeast India to concentrate on production of high value horticultural and other commercial crops for which the region possesses suitable agro-climatic conditions. This will boost farm income on both sides of the border.

Agriculture and Forest Products: Myanmar continues to export forest products like timber and timber-based items. Northeast India had rich forest resources, but unsustainable commercial and industrial exploitation to such an extent that in 1998 the Supreme Court of India banned the felling of timber in the region. A possible new supply line from Myanmar, subject to sustainable growth within the country, can revive the forest-based industries in the region, which have virtually closed down.

Manufactured Goods: De and Majumdar (2014) found that trade between Northeast India and Bangladesh involving cement, ready-made garments, processed food, bicycles, and plastic products has been steadily growing, facilitated by regional and bilateral trade agreements. While Bangladesh buys cotton yarn from India, the Northeast region of the country buys readymade garments from Bangladesh. Increasing evidence of vertical (or, horizontal) production networks is emerging between the two countries and they could undertake policy measures to facilitate gains from production networks, possibly through improvements in logistics services. Though current levels of trade are extremely low, besides agricultural and forest products, De and Majumdar (2014) suggested production networks between the Northeast region of India and Myanmar are possible in pharmaceuticals and preparations, rubber products, refined petroleum products, other non-metallic mineral products, cement, and textile and textile articles.

Services: An area of potential trade between Myanmar and Northeast India is trade in services such as health care, hospitality and tourism, which through backward linkage can generate trade in transport, communication and related services. Over the last few years facilities for advanced medical treatment have come up in the region. Most of the facilities are concentrated in Guwahati, and freer movement of people across the border could open these facilities for residents of Myanmar.

Trade in Minerals: Myanmar has rich mineral deposits. Granite produced in Myanmar can find a market in Northeast India, where residential construction is booming. At present, heavy and bulky stones like marble and granite for construction are brought from Rajasthan. Myanmar is also known for production of precious stone such as jade and ruby and transit through the northeast opens a large market in India.

Energy: Natural gas in Myanmar's coastal areas can find a large market with the growing demand for energy in India. Laying pipelines in the sea is much more expensive and the land route through the Northeast via Tripura pipeline would be a viable option. The imported and domestic natural gas can be used for thermal power generation and other industrial uses. The Northeast India is currently dependent on hydel power, which is inadequate for its electricity requirement. Punj Lloyd Ltd. is executing a part of Myanmar-China Oil Pipeline and Myanmar-China Gas Pipeline projects along with South East Asia Crude Oil Pipeline Company Ltd and South East of Asia Gas Pipeline Company since May 2011 with an estimated total investment of US$ 475 million.

The Northeastern region of India has come to acquire a significant capacity for refining crude oil. The four refineries of the region, all located in Assam, together have a refining capacity of about seven million tonnes of crude annually. In the event of all the four refineries operating near capacity, the region will have a substantial exportable surplus of refinery products. Exporting these surpluses to neighbouring countries can be a viable proposition.

Foreign Direct Investment: Manufactured items such as bicycles, motor parts, fertilizers, medicines and food products like Moltova and Horlicks are seen to have a market across the border in Myanmar. The liberalisation of border trade will allow Indian manufacturers to explore markets in Myanmar more extensively. Chinese production centres set up near and across the Myanmar borders have allowed successful penetration of Chinese goods into the Myanmarese markets. The attractive package of fiscal and other concessions for new industrial establishments under the North-East Industrial and Investment Promotion Policy 2007 of the Government of India provides economic incentive for Indian manufacturers to set up production bases in the Northeast. This will provide a fillip for industrialisation of the region and also allow access to the Myanmar market.

With Myanmar opening up for investment, Indian businesses increased activities in the region and significant developments have been made in the energy and infrastructure sectors. Tata Motors Limited transferred truck assembly technology to Magwayin in association with Myanmar Automobile and Diesel Industries Limited (MADI). The plant deals with highly flexible chassis and frame assembly line along with a cab manufacturing, painting and trimming activities with a capacity to deliver 1000 vehicles per year. In 2013, Tata Motors opened its first sales, service and spares showroom in Yangon. TVS Motors launched its two-wheeler dealership in Mandalay. Sonalika Tractors, New Holland Tractors, Escorts and their farm implements from India have good presence in Myanmar. Other Indian companies such as Birla Corporation, Parry Agro Industries, Amalgamated Tea Plantations Ltd., Oberoi Group, ITC Hotels, Bharti Airtel, Kirloskar Pumps, and Asian Oilfield Services India, Royal Solar, GMR, JK Paper and Cement, have shown considerable interest in investing in Myanmar.[8] Large projects from foreign investors in the sectors of power, petroleum and infrastructure are crucial to maintaining Myanmar's economic growth. Most of India's investments have been in the oil and gas sector and the country has approved investment of US$ 508.46 million in all. India is currently the fourth largest source of foreign investment in Myanmar, well behind China, which invested an estimated US$ 13 billion in 2011.

Prospects for Bangladesh-Myanmar Relations[9]

The tri-nations direct road link connecting Bangladesh, Myanmar and China is an extension of the highway from Cox's Bazar to Bawli Bazar up to Kunming of China and will contribute significantly to enhance the economic activities among the three countries. The Trans-Asian Railway

8.   http://www.indiaembassyyangon.net/
9.   This section draws from http://www.globalsecurity.org/military/world/bangladesh/forrel-mm.htm

and the East-West Economic Corridor (EWEC) will promote Bangladesh's economic interests in ASEAN and beyond.

A unique case of Bangladesh–Myanmar cooperation at practical grass-roots level is the microcredit project replicated by the Grameen Trust in the Delta Zone of Myanmar. The Grameen Trust is an affiliate of the Grameen Bank that pioneered a banking system of collateral-free loans to poor families. The Grameen Bank replication project in Myanmar has been an outstanding success, bringing together 13,000 families within its loan network with an excellent record of recovery. It is estimated that the success of the project owes much to the matriarchal pattern of Myanmar society, since the Grameen Bank itself is heavily oriented to women. The project, which is sponsored by the UNDP, is run by six Bangladesh staff members of Grameen.

Myanmar has vast potential for hydroelectric power production. A private company has shown interest to set up a hydroelectric power plant in Rakhine State with a production capacity of 500 MW and export electricity to Bangladesh.

Conclusions

The economic changes taking place in Myanmar present an unprecedented opportunity. Multimodal transport is crucial for Mekong-India connectivity. Northeast India, Bangladesh, and Myanmar are surrounded by the fastest growing areas in the world, namely, ASEAN, India, and China. Building more physical infrastructure to establish connectivity will boost trade and growth. The lack of roads, ports and railways is a major obstacle (Osius and Mohan, 2013) and land linkages, connecting India's northeast, Bangladesh, and Myanmar, is of strategic and economic importance, and presents vast opportunities for economic growth and cooperation.

References

Asian Development Bank (2012). Draft Report on Indo-Myanmar Border Trade. Unpublished Paper, D.D. Ingty, Manila.

Aung, Winston Set (2009). *The Role of Informal Cross-border Trade in Myanmar*. Asia Paper, September. Stockholm-Nacka, Sweden: Institute for Security and Development.

Bezbaruah, M.P. (2007). India Myanmar Border Trade,*Dialogue*, Vol.9, No.1, July-September.

Bhagowati, Surajit Kumar and Rishi Bhargav Das (2015). *Opportunities of Border Trade in North East India: With Special Reference to Indo-Myanmar Border Trade*. Available at: https://www.academia.edu/10829239/OPPORTUNITIES_OF_BORDER_TRADE_IN_NORTH_EAST_INDIA_WITH_SPECIAL_REFERENCE_TO_INDO-MYANMAR_BORDER_TRADE

Indian Embassy (2016) Bilateral Economic and Commercial Relations. Available at: http://www.indiaembassyyangon.net/index.php?option=com_content& view=article&id=60&Itemid=189&lang=en

Indian Chamber of Commerce (2016) Border Trade. Indian Chamber of Commerce. Available at: http://www.indianchamber.org/border-trade/

Myanmar News (2015) Border trade with Bangladesh Declines, 1 May 2015. Available at: http://www.elevenmyanmar.com/business/border-trade-bangladesh-declines

Myanmar Times (2015) Border Trade Tops $2.4 billion, *Myanmar Times,3 September 2015. Available at:*http://www.mmtimes.com/index.php/business/16294-border-trade-tops-2-4-billion-official.html

Chatterji, Rakhahari, Anasua Basu Ray Chaudhury and Pratnashree Basu (2015). *India-Myanmar Connectivity: Possibilities and Challenges.* Proximity to Connectivity: India and Its Eastern and Southeastern Neighbours, Part 2. Kolkata: Observer Research Foundation.

De, Prabir (2014). India's Emerging Connectivity with Southeast Asia: Progress and Prospects, ADBI *Working Paper Series No. 507.*Tokyo: Asian Development Bank Institute.

De, Prabir and ManabMajumdar (2014) *Developing Cross-Border Production Networks between North Eastern Region of India, Bangladesh and Myanmar: A Preliminary Assessment,* New Delhi: Research and Information System for Developing Countries.

Ferrarini, Benno (2013). Myanmar's Trade and its Potential.ADB *Economics Working Paper Series No. 325,* Manila: Asian Development Bank.

Morshed, Kaiser (2006). Bangladesh–Burma Relations *in Challenges to Democratization in Burma: Perspectives on Multilateral and Bilateral Responses.* Stockholm: International Institute for Democracy and Electoral Assistance.

Osius, Ted and C. Raja Mohan (2013).*Enhancing India-ASEAN Connectivity.* Centre for Stretegic and International Studies. Plymouth: Rowman and Littlefield.

Price, Gareth (2013). India's Policy towards Burma. *Asia ASP 2013/02,* London: Chatham House.

Ryan M. Rodrigues (2016), Indian rule change cuts off Myanmar border trade, Available at: http://asia.nikkei.com/politics-economy/international-relations/indian-rule-change-cuts-off-myanmar-border-trade?page=2

Roy, Jayanta and Pritam Banerjee (2010). Connecting South Asia: The Centrality of Trade Facilitation for Regional Economic Integration in Sadiq Ahmed, Saman Kelegama and Ejaz Ghani (eds.) *Promoting Economic Cooperation in South Asia: Beyond SAFTA.* World Bank and Policy Research Institute of Bangladesh, Washington, D.C.

Seshadri, V. S. (2014).*Transforming Connectivity Corridors between India and Myanmar into Development Corridors,* New Delhi: Research and Information System for Developing Countries.

Singh, Thiyam Bharat (2007). *A Study on Indo-Myanmar Border Trade,* mimeo. Available at: http://www.dgciskol.nic.in/vaanijya0907/B%20Vaanijya%20Article.pdf

Singh, Uday Bhanu (2009), Myanmar's Relations With Bangladesh Since 1988, 15 May, Fellows' Seminar. Available at: http://www.idsa.in/event/myanmar-bangladeshrelation_ubsingh_150509

REFRAMING SOUTH ASIAN COOPERATION WITH THE 2030 AGENDA: BENCHMARKING THE SDGS AND A NEW ROLE FOR SAARC

Debapriya Bhattacharya and Umme Shefa Rezbana

Introduction

Member states of the United Nations (UN) formally adopted *Transforming Our World: The 2030 Agenda for Sustainable Development* in September 2015 following a long process of global consultations and inter-governmental negotiations (UN, 2015a, 2015b). The agenda consists of 17 Sustainable Development Goals (SDGs) with 169 targets and a 2030 deadline and integrates the three dimensions of sustainable development – the economic, social and environmental. The agenda officially came into effect on 1 January 2016 and a set of 230 global indicators proposed by the Inter-agency and Expert Group on SDG Indicators was then agreed in March by the UN Statistical Commission (UN, 2016c). Moving forward, 193 countries from across the world have started implementing the 2030 Agenda.

The SDGs build on the Millennium Development Goals (MDGs) that were adopted in 2000 as part of the Millennium Declaration and expired in 2015. Experts on the SDGs have underscored that they would go much further than their predecessors. The SDGs are much more integrated in nature, while the MDGs were addressed in isolation. The inclusiveness and transformative vision of the SDGs also differentiate them. Notably, the new goals are universal – they call for action by all countries irrespective of their economic status (UN, 2016b). Moreover, they try to address some important issues that were ignored by the MDGs. For example, the MDGs were criticised for not clearly covering peace and governance issues, while the SDGs include peace as a cross-cutting issue and SDG 16 "Promote peaceful and inclusive societies for sustainable development, provide access to justice for all and build effective, accountable and inclusive institutions at all levels" is dedicated to promote peace (Saferworld, 2016). Other issues, such as human rights principles and standards, the prevention of conflict, violence, insecurity and their interlinked challenges, and the availability of quality and disaggregated data for review and follow-up, also received more attention in the SDGs.

Learning from the Millennium Development Goals (MDGs) experiences, the role of regional organisations in implementing the SDGs is being prioritised. For instance, UN regional commissions have been tasked with assisting governments to integrate the three dimensions of sustainable development into national plans and policies, providing them with technical support and facilitating follow-up and review in an effective manner. Notably, the UN Statistical Commission pointed out that the agreed set of 230 global indicators is intended for the global review of and follow-up on the SDGs and may not necessarily apply to all national contexts. It also mentioned that sub-national, national and regional indicators for monitoring will be developed and national reviews will be voluntary and country-led (IISD, 2016).

Since South Asia has 23.7 per cent of the global population (World Bank, 2016) and 37 per cent of the world's poor (UNESCAP, 2015a), meeting global targets on ending poverty and sharing prosperity is not possible without development in the region. South Asia's importance to achieving the SDGs is, therefore, critical. According to the UNESCAP, the 2030 Agenda is especially relevant for South Asian countries – Afghanistan, Bangladesh, Bhutan, India, the Maldives, Nepal, Pakistan and Sri Lanka (UNESCAP, 2015a). These countries managed to achieve some MDG targets, such as eliminating poverty, realising gender equality in primary education, reducing tuberculosis (TB), and increasing forest cover and protected areas, but achievements varied both across goals and targets as well as across and within countries (UNESCAP, 2015a). In addition to poverty, unemployment, social exclusion and infrastructure gaps, almost all countries face major governance failures (Rahman, 2004). The Worldwide Governance Indicators provided by the World Bank illustrate the state of poor governance in South Asia (see, World Bank, 2015c). Such poor governance erodes governments' capacities to address the basic needs of their populations – especially the poor and disadvantaged segments – and threats to regional peace and security, inter-state conflicts, and cross-country migration and refugee flows. However, SDG 16 on governance, peace and security can open a new vista for the region.

Concerns have been raised about how the 2030 Agenda will be implemented and monitored at the country and regional levels. Governments have been focussing on how to tailor the global goals to national contexts for their successful implementation and tracking progress. Measuring progress on the SDGs, especially soft goal areas such as SDG 16, will require an unprecedented amount of quality and disaggregated data (UN, 2016c). Special emphasis has been given to strong commitments from all stakeholders; national, regional and global leadership and, above all, cooperation. Unfortunately, a regional approach to the MDGs was largely missing in South Asia. Despite being the best established regional inter-governmental organisation, the South Asian Association for Regional Cooperation (SAARC) – consisting of the eight aforementioned South Asian countries; Afghanistan, Bangladesh, Bhutan, India, the Maldives, Nepal, Pakistan, and Sri Lanka – failed to play a vital role in this regard. How South Asian countries will transform themselves and the region as a whole to achieve the SDGs, particularly SDG 16, with a successful regional approach has now become significant.

The objective of this chapter is to revisit the prospects of strengthening regional cooperation and integration for successful implementation of the 2030 Agenda, with special attention to governance, peace and security, in South Asia. Relevant literature related to the 2030 Agenda and regional cooperation and integration in South Asia and around the world was reviewed for this chapter. Country experiences and successful regional cooperation mechanisms, from which South Asian countries can draw lessons, were also explored. Among other things, MDG reports, official documents of the 2030 Agenda and SAARC summit declarations were consulted to make comparisons and benchmark SDGs in the region. Analysis was conducted using data and information collected from various national and international data sources. An earlier draft of the paper was presented as an inaugural keynote at the SDPI's Eighteenth Sustainable Development Conference on 'Securing Peace and Prosperity' held on 7-10 December 2015 in Islamabad and expert · opinions expressed at the session were reviewed during the preparation of the present version of the chapter.

Following this introduction on the current status of the 2030 Agenda and South Asia, the chapter discusses the opportunities that were missed in the MDGs and outlines the need to strengthen regional efforts for implementing the more ambitious SDGs. In the third section, regional aspects of the 2030 Agenda are identified and references to the MDGs and SDGs in SAARC Summit declarations are located. The fourth section deals with benchmarking the SDGs according to the three dimensions of sustainable development. Governance, peace and security issues in South Asia from the perspective of the 2030 Agenda are described in the fifth section. Proposals for the upcoming SAARC Summit are provided in the last section.

Regional Approach to MDG Implementation: Missed Opportunities and MDG Achievements in South Asia

Progress on the MDGs was the fastest in Asia, though hundreds of millions of people remain in extreme poverty and even the countries that were considered high achievers were not on track to achieve some of the non-income goals (Müller, 2006). A sub-region of Asia, South Asia experienced relatively slow progress on the MDGs (Bhattacharya, 2015a). Analysis of South Asia's MDG achievements (Table 1) shows that countries in the region achieved notable success with regards to the targets on poverty reduction, gender equality in primary education, reducing TB, increasing protected areas and access to safe drinking water. Certain South Asian countries also managed to get on track towards achieving the targets on underweight children, HIV prevalence and TB incidence. However, the region as a whole faced challenges in eliminating gender disparity in tertiary education, reducing maternal mortality, increasing the number of births attended by skilled health personnel, achieving antenatal care coverage and providing basic sanitation. In addition, Bangladesh, Nepal, Pakistan and Sri Lanka were found to be off track in terms of land area covered by forest, while Afghanistan, Bangladesh and the Maldives were off track in terms of carbon dioxide (CO_2) emissions. Above all, significant gaps and uneven progress were found across countries in the region (UN, 2015a).

Table 1: South Asian Countries on and off Track for the MDGs

Goals	1		2			3			4		5			6			7				
Indicators	$1.25 per day poverty	Underweight children	Primary enrolment	Reaching last grade	Primary completion	Gender primary	Gender secondary	Gender tertiary	Under-5 mortality	Infant mortality	Maternal mortality	Skilled birth attendance	Antenatal care (≥ 1 visit)	HIV prevalence	TB incidence	TB prevalence	Forest cover	Protected area	CO_2 emissions per GDP	Safe drinking water	Basic sanitation

Legend:

- Early achiever: Already achieved the 2015 target
- On track: Expected to meet the target by 2015
- Off track: Slow, but expected to meet the target after 2015
- Off track: No progress, regressing, stagnating or slipping backwards

Rows (countries): Afghanistan, Bangladesh, Bhutan, India, Maldives, Nepal, Pakistan, Sri Lanka

Source: Adapted from UNESCAP, ADB and UNDP (2015).

Literature shows that there are specific and crosscutting factors that underpin the performance of the MDGs in different countries. For instance, an analysis of India's performance with regard to MDG done by the UNESCAP mentions five key drivers that could improve the MDG achievements for the country. These are: (1) broad-based and employment-creating economic growth; (2) adequate allocation of resources towards the social sectors and basic services; (3) strong design and effective implementation of MDG related programmes; (4) creating basic infrastructure for better access and delivery of MDG related services; and (5) women's empowerment" (UNESCAP, 2015d).

In case of Pakistan, among others, governance and weak institutions, resource security, localisation and ownership for MDGs, lack of coordination, political instability, and natural disasters were identified as reasons behind not achieving the MDGs in the country (Usman, 2015). Criticisms are also found in improvements shown in national averages in regard to MDGs, but the women and girls, people living in rural areas and extreme poverty, disabled person were left behind. MDGs were also criticised for not being inclusive and not concentrating on shared problems in the region as a whole.

The Need to Strengthen Regional Efforts

Addressing ongoing challenges and achieving the SDGs in South Asia need strong regional cooperation and the establishment of a regional monitoring and review mechanism. Certain countries need to progress more or faster and regional efforts are essential for assisting individual countries (Heyzer, 2008). For instance, South Asia has fallen short in reducing the share of people living in hunger. In 2015, the region had the second highest Global Hunger Index score after sub-Saharan Africa (Von Grebmer, *et al.*, 2015). Moreover, South Asia had one of the lowest regional Human Development Index values at 0.607 (UNDP, 2015), with cross-border and internal conflicts remaining the biggest threats to human development. Notably, labour markets in South Asia are characterised by poorly paid and unprotected jobs and informal and agricultural employment (ILO, 2014). MDG experiences indicate that regional cooperation is key to achieving development goals. Achieving food security in the region requires liberalised trade, efficient food markets and adequate investment. Water sharing, the power and energy sectors, watershed management, regional interconnectivity, and regional transportation and storage facilities also need to be improved (Khan, 2013).

In addition to weak regional cooperation, lack of regional monitoring and review mechanisms was one of the fault lines of the MDGs (Bhattacharya, 2015b). The availability of and access to reliable data and information remain major concerns in South Asia (Khan, 2013). Due to insufficient data, development policy-making at the regional level continues to be challenging (UN, 2015a). An effective regional monitoring and review mechanism would facilitate SDGs implementation at both the national and regional levels by informing the development policy-making process, increasing transparency and broadening participation (Bhattacharya, 2015b).

Examples of Successful Regional Mechanisms in Achieving MDGs

Two examples of successful regional mechanisms that helped countries achieve at least some of the MDGs are the New Partnership for Africa's Development (NEPAD) and Organisation of American States (OAS). Established by the Organisation of African Unity, the African Union's predecessor, in 2000, NEPAD is an economic development programme that focusses on: operationalising the African Peer Review Mechanism, a voluntary self-monitoring mechanism of the African Union open to any member state; facilitating and supporting implementation of short-term regional infrastructure programmes as well as food security and agricultural development programmes; preparing coordinated African positions on market access, debt relief and official development assistance reforms; and monitoring and intervening to ensure that the MDGs are met (Sanga, 2011). NEPAD has a long list of successes in MDG achievement in Africa (see NEPAD, 2011), and some are as follows:

- NEPAD established regional strategies on agriculture that pushed for the allocation of 10 per cent of national budgets to agriculture, which helped some countries achieve MDG 1 on eradicating extreme poverty and hunger;
- It disbursed €20 million through the NEPAD Spanish Fund for African Women's Empowerment to empower women to access knowledge development, education, HIV/AIDS prevention and information and communications technology skills, which helped some countries achieve MDG 3 on promoting gender equality and empowering women and MDG 5 on improving maternal health;
- It allocated US$ 1.5 million to train nurses and midwives to the post-graduate level, which contributed to efforts towards MDG 5;

- It initiated research into herbal remedies to treat HIV/AIDS through the NEPAD African Bioscience Initiative, which contributed to efforts towards MDG 6 on combating HIV/AIDS, malaria and other diseases;
- It established the Action Plan of the NEPAD Environment Initiative and a pan-African policy mechanism for reforms in the fisheries sector, which contributed to efforts towards MDG 7 on achieving environmental sustainability; and
- It initiated a method for African countries to review each other's governance and hold each other to account, indirectly facilitating MDG governance and accountability.

The world's oldest regional organisation established in 1948, the OAS is the main political, juridical and social forum in the Americas that currently brings together 35 independent countries. It has also granted permanent observer status to 69 countries and the European Union (OAS, 2016b). The OAS helped countries reach their MDGs targets through the adoption of regional and national public policies, specifically contributing to efforts towards MDGs 1, 3, 7 and 8 in Latin America and the Caribbean by initiating a number of initiatives, including:

- The Inter-American Social Protection Network helped lower poverty rates in Brazil, Chile and Mexico, thereby contributing to efforts towards MDG 1, by strengthening the institutional capacities of national social development agencies to formulate and implement poverty alleviation policies, particularly conditional cash transfer programmes (Insulza, 2010).
- The Inter-American Network for Labor Administration (RAIL) was established in Mexico in 2005 to boost cooperation among ministries of labour in the Americas to build their human and institutional capacities and improve the employment situation in the region (RIAL, 2016), thereby contributing to efforts towards MDGs 1 and 3.
- The Inter-American Biodiversity Information Network promotes technical collaboration and coordination for the collection, sharing and use of biodiversity information, which is relevant to policy- and decision-making on natural resource conservation and development (OAS, 2016a), thereby contributing to efforts towards MDG 7. The OAS also contributed to efforts on MDG 7 through its Integrated Water Resource Management initiative (Khan, *et al.,* 2012).

- The OAS supported historically marginalised groups, who often operate in the informal sector or engage in trade, through its Economic Empowerment and Trade programme, thereby contributing to efforts towards MDG 8 (Insulza, 2010).

Certain regional efforts are also observed in South Asia, for instance, SAARC Food Bank (SFB), SAARC comprehensive framework on disaster management, etc. While the SFB was established to provide food security to the people in the SAARC countries, a SAARC Comprehensive Framework on Disaster Management was developed for efficient regional disaster management system. The agreement on SFB was signed during the 14th SAARC Summit held in New Delhi on 3-4 April 2007. The Disaster Management Framework was also approved during the same summit. Although the agreement for the SFB was signed in 2007, unfortunately it is not yet effectively operational. Problems have been identified related to transportation systems, border formalities, institutional mechanisms, and price negotiation and withdrawal, etc., (Pant, 2014). On the other, the SAARC Disaster Management Framework was developed in line with the Hyogo Framework for Action (HFA) for the period (2005-2015). The implementation of the framework did not make significant progress due to limited resources, lack of accountability by the member states, scarcity and conservation in sharing data, etc., (SDMC, 2014). However, SAARC Disaster Management Centre (SDMC) organised a number of consultations on post-2015 Disaster Risk Reduction in most of the SAARC member states and a regional consultation workshop was also held during 20-21 February 2014. Specific priority areas and actions were recommended to achieve the proposed goals of HFA-2 in the workshop considering the HFA gaps and challenges faced in the region (SDMC, 2014).

Regional Aspects of the 2030 Agenda: New Opportunities

Regional Issues in the 2030 Agenda
The SDGs are much more holistic than the MDGs. The 2030 Agenda refers to multiple regional aspects (see UN, 2015b), which, among others, include:
- Policy frameworks, based on pro-poor and gender-sensitive development strategies, to support accelerated investment in poverty eradication actions;

- Soundly managed and diversified seed and plant banks for agricultural diversity;
- Quality, reliable, sustainable and resilient infrastructure to support economic development and human well-being;
- Regional development planning to support positive economic, social and environmental links between urban, peri-urban and rural areas; and
- Cooperation on and access to science, technology and innovation.

In the "Means of implementation and the Global Partnership" section of the 2030 Agenda, focussed support to regional organisations in order to sustain achievements and address ongoing challenges and the promotion of regional economic integration and interconnectivity with a focus to provide trade-related capacity building for developing countries are mentioned (UN, 2015b). To summarise, regional perspectives are covered in the areas of poverty, food security, infrastructure, inclusivity, oceans, seas and marine resources, and science, technology and innovation (UN, 2015b). Follow-up and review processes, which build on existing platforms and processes where they exist at the regional level, are also mentioned. There are also areas in which regional perspectives are not covered – health, energy, economic growth and employment, sustainable production and consumption patterns, and global partnership (UN, 2015b). Although the 2030 Agenda acknowledges the need for peaceful societies based on effective rule of law and good governance at all levels, regional perspective or mechanisms are yet to be clarified in this regard.

The MDGs and SDGs in SAARC Summit Documents

SAARC with the objective to promote and improve the quality of life of South Asian people provides them a platform to work together. After the adoption of MDGs, regions and countries started to localise the goals. SAARC, in this regard, also made attempts for South Asia. However, despite its potential – it failed to play a role in advancing a regional approach to the MDGs. The inter-governmental organisation was founded in 1985 to reduce suffering due to perpetual war, poverty and underdevelopment and promote the welfare of the various peoples of South Asia (NTI, 2011). A review of SAARC summit declarations found references to achieving the MDGs in the 13th and 14th summit declarations. In the 13th summit declaration, heads of state and government decided that finance ministers should meet during the first quarter after every summit and on the sidelines of the World Bank and the Asian Development Bank (ADB) annual meetings with regard to the achievement of the 22 SAARC Development Goals, which were adopted at the Summit for a period of five years from 2007 to 2012, since they are "co-related" to the MDGs. They called for effective measures to ensure universal primary education and stated their full support for a comprehensive approach to facilitating the MDGs in a time-bound manner (SAARC, 2005). In the 14th summit declaration, the work of the Independent South Asian Commission on Poverty Alleviation, which reflects the regional determination to attain the MDGs, was appreciated (SAARC, 2007).

Moving forward, SAARC indeed has the potential to advance a regional approach to the SDGs. A review found references to the post-2015 development agenda, which would become the 2030 Agenda, in the 18th SAARC Summit declaration – the latest to be issued. Commitments to poverty alleviation and the initiation of an inter-governmental process to contextualise the SDGs at the regional level were expressed (SAARC, 2014). Notably, no references of the MDGs or SDGs can be found in the 15th, 16th and 17th SAARC Summit declarations. As an inter-governmental organisation that is committed to promoting regional development and integration, SAARC can build on the commitments in the 18th Summit declaration to build momentum and contribute to efforts towards the SDGs.

Benchmarking the SDGs in South Asia for Moving Forward

While they share similar geographical and cultural features, South Asian countries are very diverse in terms of populations, income levels and natural resources. Most countries in the region face problems including poverty, corruption, inter- and intra-state conflicts, political instability and challenges related to climate change (Kumar, 2014). With regard to sustainable development, the statuses of key indicators within the economic, social and environmental dimensions are discussed below for benchmarking the SDGs.

Economic Dimension

South Asia is expected to maintain its lead as the fastest-growing region in the world in upcoming years. The World Bank projected that economic growth would accelerate from 7 per cent in 2015 to 7.4 per cent in 2016, noting that the forecasting is significantly influenced by strong expansion in India (World Bank, 2015a). Trend analysis using data from the World

Bank's World Development Indicators database reveals that annual GDP growth in South Asia has been on the upswing recently and is beating the world average.. However, weaknesses in fiscal space and financial sectors persist (World Bank, 2015b).

South Asia had the second lowest gross national income (GNI) per capita (at purchasing power parity [PPP]) in 2014 at US$ 5,298.53, after Sub-Saharan Africa at US$ 3,396.26 (Table 2). Among the eight countries in the region, the Maldives had the highest GNI per capita (PPP) at US$ 10,920, while Afghanistan had the lowest at US$ 2,000 (World Bank, 2016).

Table 2: GNI Per Capita by Region (at PPP; Current International $)

Region	2010	2011	2012	2013	2014
East Asia and the Pacific	11,576.08	12,390.75	13,273.4	14,043.68	14,891.01
Europe and Central Asia	25,710.31	27,033.73	27,592.34	28,067.42	28,813.10
Latin America and the Caribbean	13,077.12	13,890.61	14,354.71	14,748.14	15,184.35
Middle East and North Africa	16,360.30	16,846.05	17,491.94	17,731.86	n/a
South Asia	4,127.22	4,409.77	4,646.23	4,951.71	5,298.53
Sub-Saharan Africa	2,945.21	3,058.61	3,155.46	3,270.04	3,396.26

Note: 'n/a' stands for 'Not available'.
Source: World Bank (2016).

In mobilising the tax revenue, South Asia is lagging behind. Although South Asian countries have undertaken considerable tax policy reforms, they have been less successful in generating tax revenue to meet their financing needs (Gupta, 2015). South Asia's tax revenue is 10.73 per cent of GDP which is lower compared to that of the world (14.38 per cent) in 2012 (World Bank, 2016). In 2014, exports of goods and services of South Asia was 21.50 per cent of GDP, which is also much lower than that of the World (30.36 per cent of GDP) (World Bank, 2016). Analysis of growth in four key sectors – agriculture, industry, manufacturing and services (value added) – over the period 2000-14 in South Asia reveals that growth in the region has been largely led by services. The industrial and manufacturing sectors have been stagnant, while the agricultural sector has been declining. Sustainability in the agricultural, manufacturing and industrial sectors is an important prerequisite for sustainable development. Notably, South Asia has been experiencing the problems of land degradation and low agricultural productivity. It has also been weak in harnessing renewable energy resources and improving energy efficiency. Share of industry in GDP in South Asia is much lower compared to the East and Southeast Asian regions. This is due to lack of substantial backward and forward linkages (UNESCAP, 2015c).

Moreover, South Asia has not been performing well in terms of productive employment, which has led to some vulnerability. The share of agriculture in total employment has been declining in the region, but the agricultural sector still generates about half of total employment. Although official unemployment figures in South Asia have been low and declining, underemployment has been generally high across the region. Therefore, ensuring productive employment in the region should be on priority.

The mitigation of these problems is possible through the implementation of the 2030 Agenda. SDGs 8 and 9 specifically deal with inclusive and sustainable economic growth, industrialisation and full and productive employment. Fundamental requirements that undergird progress on these goals include health (SDG 3), education (SDG 4), access to water and sanitation (SDG 6), energy (SDG 7) and transport (SDG 11).

Social Dimension

The social dimension generally considers indicators on poverty, income inequality, gender equality, voice and accountability, political stability and absence of violence/terrorism (Bhattacharya, 2015a). Analysis of the share of women in wage employment in the non-agricultural sector in South Asia shows that proportions vary across countries, with a low of 12.6 per cent in Pakistan in 2008 and a high of 40.5 per cent in the Maldives in 2010 (Table 3). Timely data for comparative analysis is evidently largely unavailable for countries in the region, with no data at all available for Nepal.

Table 3: Share of Women in Wage Employment in the Non-agricultural Sector (percentage of total non-agricultural employment) in South Asia

	2005	2006	2007	2008	2009	2010	2011	2012	2013
South Asia	18.41	n/a	n/a	n/a	19.43	19.36	n/a	n/a	n/a
Afghanistan	25.90	18.00	17.60	18.40	n/a	n/a	n/a	n/a	n/a
Bangladesh	20.10	n/a	n/a	n/a	n/a	18.30	n/a	n/a	n/a
Bhutan	n/a	n/a	n/a	n/a	26.80	n/a	27.70	26.30	n/a
India	18.10	n/a	n/a	n/a	19.10	19.30	n/a	n/a	n/a
Maldives	n/a	30.00	n/a	n/a	n/a	40.50	n/a	n/a	n/a
Nepal	n/a	n/a	n/a	n/a	n/a	n/a	n/a	n/a	n/a
Pakistan	13.90	13.40	13.20	12.60	n/a	n/a	n/a	n/a	n/a
Sri Lanka	31.10	34.60	33.10	34.20	33.10	32.70	32.30	32.40	32.40

Note: 'n/a' stands for 'Not available'.
Source: World Bank (2016).

Gender disparity exists in tertiary education and political representation in South Asia. Moreover, female child mortality and child marriage remain higher in South Asia compared to the other regions (UNESCAP, 2015c). Therefore, gender equality and empowerment should be prioritised in each and every sector. SDG 5 deals with achieving gender equality and empowerment in the 2030 Agenda.

Environmental Dimension

While South Asia as a region has improved its forest area coverage, not all countries managed to record improvements over time. Specifically, Afghanistan, Bangladesh, the Maldives and Pakistan continue to lag behind (Table 4).

Table 4: Forest Area Coverage (percentage of land area) in South Asia

	2005	2006	2007	2008	2009	2010	2011	2012	2013
South Asia	16.94	17.02	17.10	17.18	17.26	17.33	17.36	17.39	17.42
Afghanistan	2.07	2.07	2.07	2.07	2.07	2.07	2.07	2.07	2.07
Bangladesh	11.18	11.16	11.14	11.12	11.10	11.08	11.06	11.04	11.02
Bhutan	69.67	69.93	70.19	70.45	70.71	70.97	71.23	71.49	71.75
India	22.77	22.91	23.05	23.19	23.33	23.47	23.53	23.59	23.65
Maldives	3.33	3.33	3.33	3.33	3.33	3.33	3.33	3.33	3.33
Nepal	25.36	25.36	25.36	25.36	25.36	25.36	25.36	25.36	25.36
Pakistan	2.47	2.41	2.36	2.30	2.24	2.19	2.13	2.08	2.02
Sri Lanka	33.77	33.73	33.68	33.63	33.58	33.54	33.43	33.32	33.22

Source: World Bank (2016).

Moreover, South Asia's per capita CO_2 emissions are lower than the world average, but the region is highly vulnerable to climate change. Extreme heat and disruptive changes in seasonal rainfall have been negatively affecting the agricultural sectors of countries in the region, particularly Bangladesh, India and Pakistan.

The poor rural populations of Bangladesh, India and the Maldives will likely bear the most adverse impacts of rising sea levels. Climate change impacts will lead to economic and social disruptions, with environmental refugees pressing already stressed cities (IFAD, 2009). SDGs 13 to 15 deal with climate change and other environmental issues. SDG 12 on sustainable consumption and production patterns specifically addresses the management of waste and control of pollution. Regional cooperation in these is again crucial.

It may be mentioned here that the 21st Conference of Parties (COP) meeting held in Paris (from 30 November to 11 December 2015) came up with two major issues of negotiation, i.e., reduction of CO_2 emissions and finance for adaptation, loss and damage and low carbon growth (for developing countries). South Asian countries (except for Nepal and Pakistan) pledged to reduce emissions as well (Table 5) (Khatun, 2015).

Table 5: CO_2 Emission Reduction Pledge in Intended Nationally Determined Contributions (INDCs) by South Asian Countries

Country	Co_2 Emission Reduction Pledge in INDCs
Afghanistan	13.6% conditional*
Bangladesh	5% unconditional** 15% conditional
Bhutan	Pledge to be carbon neutral, and to make 60% of the country forest
India	33 to 35 % by 2030 compared to 2005 levels; 40% of electricity from non-fossil fuel sources
Maldives	10% unconditional 24% conditional
Pakistan	No measurable target
Sri Lanka	7% unconditional 23% conditional

Notes: *Conditional: with external support;
**Unconditional: without external support. Source: Adapted from Khatun (2015).

In case of climate financing, US$ 3.45 million is approved for South Asia region under the category 'bilateral climate finance' (excluding global projects). Country specific approval under the category 'multilateral climate finance recipients' are provided in the Figure 1.

Figure 1: Funding Approved under the Category 'Multilateral Climate Finance Recipients' (US$ million)

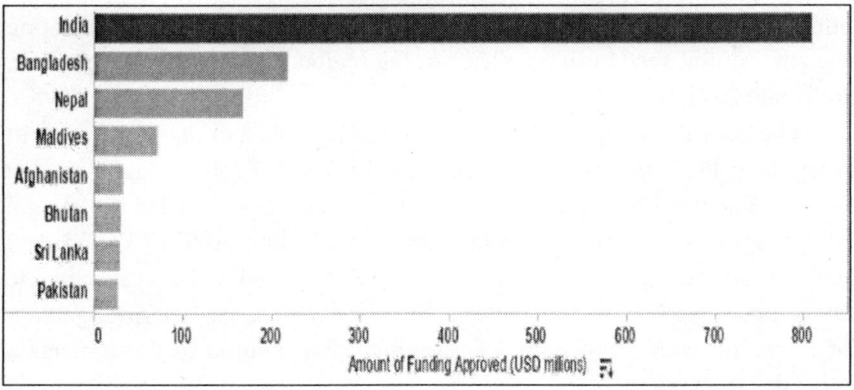

Source: From http://www.climatefundsupdate.org/data (accessed on 16 August 2016).

However, the analysis of the outcome of the Paris COP21 meeting receives both positive and negative feedbacks from different sectors. Although it has been criticised as 'ended up balanced politically but not morally', and for not reflecting 'climate justice' and 'polluter-pay principle', it could be a stepping stone for taking things forward (Khatun, 2015). South Asian countries should concentrate on their commitments in line with the agreement in this regard. However, continuous and ambitious measures from big emitter countries are essential to successfully combat climate change.

Successful implementation of the 2030 Agenda can contribute to long-term sustainable economic growth and development in South Asia and beyond. Many South Asian countries have the potential to accelerate economic growth in the short- to medium-term. Others, such as Bangladesh, Nepal and Sri Lanka, are bracing for sluggish economic activity in the short-term, with the reasons being stagnant productivity growth and capital accumulation in Bangladesh, the earthquakes in Nepal and revisions to national accounts in Sri Lanka (World Bank, 2015b). Moving forward, regionally coordinated strategies for balanced agricultural, industrial, manufacturing and services growth along with productive employment across all South Asian countries are essential. Regional cooperation on gender-responsive policies, regional connectivity and strategies to deal with environmental challenges are of critical importance.

Governance, Peace and Security: An Area of Special Focus for South Asia

The Relationship between Security and Development

The global recognition of the relationship between security and development is not new. Relationships between peace, the environment, development and the economy as matters of security were successively recognised by the Brandt Commission in 1980, Brundtland Commission in 1987, Rio Declaration in 1992, UN Development Programme in 1994, Commission on Global Governance in 1995 and UN Security Council in 2007 (Kumar, 2014). The Millennium Declaration made reference to the correlated relationship between security and development, which was based on the fact that approximately 65 per cent (22 out of 34) of the poor countries farthest from reaching the MDGs were in or emerging from conflict. Moreover, conflict and state fragility created serious obstacles to achieving MDGs (Denney, 2012). The World Bank (2011) stated:

> "People in fragile and conflict-affected states are more than twice as likely to be undernourished as those in other developing countries, more than three times as likely to be unable to send their children to school, twice as likely to see their children die before age five, and more than twice as likely to lack clean water . . . . The average cost of civil war is equivalent to more than 30 years of GDP growth for a medium-size developing country. Trade levels after major episodes of violence take 20 years to recover. In other words, a major episode of violence, unlike natural disasters or economic cycles, can wipe out an entire generation of economic progress."

Notably, the Organisation for Economic Co-operation and Development (OECD) demonstrated that the 50 countries and economies on its "2015 fragile states list" account for 43 per cent of the world's population living in extreme poverty and suggested that even under the best-case scenario 62 per cent of the global poor may be located in fragile states (OECD, 2015).

SDG 16: A Striking Inclusion in the 2030 Agenda

The MDGs were criticised for not properly addressing insecurity, abuses of human rights and weak governance. UN member states recognised the importance of these issues and included a separate goal on governance, peace and security – SDG 16 – in the 2030 Agenda, after which the UN Statistical Commission finalised indicators (Table 6). SDG 16 includes 10 targets and two suggested means of implementation (target 16.a and target 16.b). Targets 16.1, 16.2 and 16.4 concentrate on peace and security, whereas targets 16.3 and 16.5 to 16.10 deal with governance (Fiedler*et al.*, 2015). SDG 16 tackles important omissions of the MDGs by focussing on governance, peace, justice, participation, rights and security. Having the potential to catalyse profound social transformations, the goal has been appreciated by experts on the SDGs as being key to the success of the 2030 Agenda (FDSD, 2016).

Table 6: SDG 16 and Its Targets and Indicators

Goal 16. Promote peaceful and inclusive societies for sustainable development, provide access to justice for all and build effective, accountable and inclusive institutions at all levels	
16.1 Significantly reduce all forms of violence and related death rates everywhere	16.1.1 Number of victims of intentional homicide per 100,000 population, by sex and age 16.1.2 Conflict-related deaths per 100,000 population, by sex, age and cause 16.1.3 Proportion of population subjected to physical, psychological or sexual violence in the previous 12 months 16.1.4 Proportion of population that feel safe walking alone around the area they live
16.2 End abuse, exploitation, trafficking and all forms of violence against and torture of children	16.2.1 Proportion of children aged 1-17 years who experienced any physical punishment and/ or psychological aggression by caregivers in the past month 16.2.2 Number of victims of human trafficking per 100,000 population, by sex, age and form of exploitation 16.2.3 Proportion of young women and men aged 18-29 years who experienced sexual violence by age 18
16.3 Promote the rule of law at the national and international levels and ensure equal access to justice for all	16.3.1 Proportion of victims of violence in the previous 12 months who reported their victimization to competent authorities or other officially recognized conflict resolution mechanisms 16.3.2 Unsentenced detainees as a proportion of overall prison population

16.4 By 2030, significantly reduce illicit financial and arms flows, strengthen the recovery and return of stolen assets and combat all forms of organized crime	16.4.1 Total value of inward and outward illicit financial flows (in current United States dollars) 16.4.2 Proportion of seized small arms and light weapons that are recorded and traced, in accordance with international standards and legal instruments
16.5 Substantially reduce corruption and bribery in all their forms	16.5.1 Proportion of persons who had at least one contact with a public official and who paid a bribe to a public official, or were asked for a bribe by those public officials, during the previous 12 months 16.5.2 Proportion of businesses that had at least one contact with a public official and that paid a bribe to a public official, or were asked for a bribe by those public officials during the previous 12 months
16.6 Develop effective, accountable and transparent institutions at all levels	16.6.1 Primary government expenditures as a proportion of original approved budget, by sector (or by budget codes or similar) 16.6.2 Proportion of the population satisfied with their last experience of public services
16.7 Ensure responsive, inclusive, participatory and representative decision-making at all levels	16.7.1 Proportions of positions (by sex, age, persons with disabilities and population groups) in public institutions (national and local legislatures, public service, and judiciary) compared to national distributions 16.7.2 Proportion of population who believe decision making is inclusive and responsive, by sex, age, disability and population group
16.8 Broaden and strengthen the participation of developing countries in the institutions of global governance	16.8.1 Proportion of members and voting rights of developing countries in international organizations
16.9 By 2030, provide legal identity for all, including birth registration	16.9.1 Proportion of children under 5 years of age whose births have been registered with a civil authority, by age
16.10 Ensure public access to information and protect fundamental freedoms, in accordance with national legislation and international agreements	16.10.1 Number of verified cases of killing, kidnapping, enforced disappearance, arbitrary detention and torture of journalists, associated media personnel, trade unionists and human rights advocates in the previous 12 months 16.10.2 Number of countries that adopt and implement constitutional, statutory and/or policy guarantees for public access to information

16.a Strengthen relevant national institutions, including through international cooperation, for building capacity at all levels, in particular in developing countries, to prevent violence and combat terrorism and crime	16.a.1 Existence of independent national human rights institutions in compliance with the Paris Principles
16.b Promote and enforce non-discriminatory laws and policies for sustainable development	16.b.1 Proportion of population reporting having personally felt discriminated against or harassed in the previous 12 months on the basis of a ground of discrimination prohibited under international human rights law

Source: UN (2016a).

SDG 16 and its targets and indicators should contribute to addressing long-hidden issues like corruption, exclusion, injustice and violence. Still, criticisms regarding the effective implementation of and measuring progress on the goal have been voiced. For instance, effectively tracking progress requires a new and disaggregated set of data, which necessitates significant funding and strengthened capacities of national statistical systems. Thus, governments worldwide must go a lot further than simply introducing SDG 16. Strong national, regional and global commitments to providing funding for data collection and statistical production, capacity building of national statistical systems and relevant research are needed (Lawson-Remer, 2015).

Why does SDG 16 Matter for South Asia?

Security threats have led to crises in South Asia during the 21st century. The security situation in the region is characterised in two ways. One is conventional security threats, such as the territorial and boundary conflicts between India and Pakistan over Kashmir and those between Pakistan and Afghanistan regarding the recognition of the Durand Line. The other is non-conventional security threats, such as ethnic and separatist movements and internal migration and refugee flows in the region due to civil strife and natural disasters (Wagner, 2014).

In the case of governance, South Asia has been lagging behind on all of the World Bank's Worldwide Governance Indicators (Parnini, 2015). The Worldwide Governance Indicators, which cover 215 economies from 1996 to 2014, are considered as refined form of assessment criteria of a country/

regional governance system. They measure governance of a country on the basis of "voice and accountability", "political stability and absence of violence", "government effectiveness", "regulatory quality", "rule of law" and "control of corruption".

Analysis of data from the Worldwide Governance Indicators database shows that in 2014, compared to other countries, Bhutan appeared strongest in South Asia in terms of political stability and absence of violence/terrorism as well as government effectiveness. India received the strongest score on voice and accountability, while Afghanistan remained the weakest, followed by Pakistan. Except in India, regulatory quality across South Asia appeared to be unsatisfactory. Rule of law seemed particularly weak in Pakistan, Bangladesh and Nepal. Still, Afghanistan's scores were the weakest across the board (Table 7).

Along with weak governance, South Asia is home to unstable and relatively fragile states. Afghanistan, Bangladesh, Nepal, Pakistan and Sri Lanka are among the 67 countries and economies that have been on the Organisation for Economic Co-operation and Development's annual fragile states list at least once between 2007 and 2015. Afghanistan is in the group of 23 "chronically fragile countries" that have appeared on every list (OECD, 2015).

South Asia also faces the threats of crimes such as human trafficking, prescription and drug trafficking, smuggling of migrants, economic and cyber-crimes. There is also new form of crime, for example, piracy that has surfaced in the Indian Ocean, affecting especially Bangladesh, India, the Maldives and Sri Lanka (UNODC, 2013).

Apart from human-made security threats and crimes, as mentioned, South Asia is particularly vulnerable to natural disasters and extreme weather events. Afghanistan, Bangladesh and Pakistan are listed as fragile states that have experienced an average of more than three natural disasters each year over the past decade, facing 105, 89 and 83 disasters, respectively (OECD, 2015). Maplecroft's (2014) Climate Change Vulnerability Index identified Bangladesh as the most climate-vulnerable country in the world and suggested that it would feel the economic impacts of climate change most intensely.

Table 7: Worldwide Governance Indicators for South Asian Countries

	Voice and accountability			Political stability and absence of violence/terrorism			Government effectiveness			Regulatory quality			Rule of law		
	2004	2009	2014	2004	2009	2014	2004	2009	2014	2004	2009	2014	2004	2009	2014
Afghanistan	-1.25	-1.46	-1.16	-2.30	-2.70	-2.46	-0.88	-1.50	-1.34	-1.50	-1.67	-1.13	-1.71	-1.91	-1.53
Bangladesh	-0.68	-0.30	-0.47	-1.38	-1.54	-0.88	-0.78	-0.79	-0.77	-1.10	-0.85	-0.94	-1.00	-0.77	-0.72
Bhutan	-0.92	-0.51	-0.14	1.17	0.82	1.00	-0.14	0.48	0.27	-0.81	-1.10	-1.01	0.36	0.18	0.35
India	0.38	0.45	0.42	-1.22	-1.33	-0.96	-0.10	-0.01	-0.20	-0.40	-0.31	-0.45	0.04	0.02	-0.09
Maldives	-1.12	-0.08	-0.33	0.54	-0.22	0.88	-0.11	-0.45	-0.37	-0.10	-0.41	-0.36	0.08	-0.17	-0.49
Nepal	-1.15	-0.47	-0.44	-2.12	-1.62	-0.70	-0.75	-0.94	-0.83	-0.53	-0.70	-0.85	-0.76	-0.90	-0.68
Pakistan	-1.23	-0.90	-0.74	-1.56	-2.63	-2.44	-0.45	-0.78	-0.75	-0.88	-0.55	-0.79	-0.83	-0.84	-0.78
Sri Lanka	-0.19	-0.49	-0.72	-1.06	-1.35	-0.25	-0.40	-0.12	0.09	-0.04	-0.26	-0.08	0.20	-0.07	-0.15

Note: Governance scores range from -2.5 (weak) to 2.5 (strong).
Source: World Bank (2015c).

Evidently, without dealing with the aforementioned challenges of security and governance, ensuring South Asia's inclusive development and prosperity will be impossible. SDG 16 should, therefore, be prioritised across the region. Furthermore, progress on the other SDGs depends on the effective implementation of SDG 16, which calls for good governance among other things. For instance, reducing poverty depends on reducing conflict and building resilient institutions and societies (OECD, 2015).

SAARC: The South Asian Regional Platform for the SDGs?

From the perspective of implementing the 2030 Agenda, many issues require a regional approach. SDGs 1, 2, 9, 11 and 17 include regional aspects, while other goals, targets and means of implementation can be interpreted from a regional perspective. Besides poverty and low human development, South Asian countries suffer from various security threats linked to poor governance, which are captured by SDG 16. A regional platform indeed could help solve problems that are beyond the capabilities of individual countries in the region.

As mentioned, SAARC has the potential to advance a regional approach to the SDGs moving forward. Indeed, the long-established inter-governmental organisation has been identified as a "fundamental and unchallenged building block" in the process of alternative drivers of growth at the regional and sub-regional levels (UNESCAP, 2015b). Successful implementation of the SDGs requires a much more integrated approach than the "silo approach" that focuses on individual sectors. Transforming SAARC into a more effective organisation, that explicitly addresses the SDGs and beyond, could enable it to fulfil its potential. For the SDGs, SAARC should consider an integrated strategy for their implementation and a regional review and follow-up mechanism.

Integrated Strategy for Implementing the SDGs

As a regional platform, SAARC can contribute to SDG implementation by advancing economic integration, improving regional interconnectivity and transportation, boosting trade and business, and creating an enabling environment in South Asia. Besides economic development, regional peace and security has always been an area of focus for SAARC. Integrating national, regional and global strategies to facilitate SDG implementation and prioritising SDG 16 should increase SAARC's effectiveness.

As mentioned, SAARC adopted 22 SAARC Development Goals at the 13th SAARC summit in 2005 for the period 2007-12. These goals, which had associated 67 indicators, were considered to be a "comprehensive roadmap" in line with achieving the MDGs. Unlike the MDGs, the SAARC Development Goals were narrowed down to four major categories, namely livelihood, health, education and environment (Singh and Singh, 2009). The terminal year of the SAARC Development Goals was extended from 2012 to 2015 at the third SAARC Ministerial Meeting on Poverty alleviation in 2013. Since South Asian countries have begun implementing the SDGs, SAARC could realign the SAARC Development Goals to support regional-level implementation of the SDGs.

Regional Review and follow-up Mechanism
The monitoring and review processes for the MDGs were criticised for being fragmented and incoherent. They were characterised by poor delineation of responsibilities and lacking in quality and ownership (Janus *et al.*, 2015). Furthermore, the reporting system of the MDGs was inefficient due to the low capacities of many national statistical systems, especially those of developing countries. Learning from MDG experiences, UN member states identified inter-linkages between levels of governance – national, regional and global – as a major component of the accountability framework for the SDGs (Janus *et al.*, 2015). The 2030 Agenda includes commitments to review and follow-up of the SDGs as well as discussing regional-level peer learning, voluntary reviews, sharing of best practices, and shared targets (UN, 2015b). Regional-level peer learning mechanisms would help countries in the same regions to jointly address shared or similar challenges. The 2030 Agenda provides countries with the opportunity to select suitable regional forums in this regard. Some regions already have forums for "peer review", but the African and Asian UN regional commissions have been criticised for insufficient capacities (Beisheim, 2016). In South Asia, SAARC could establish a regional review and follow-up mechanism to support the SDGs. For instance, a Group of Eminent Persons (GEP) may be established to monitor the progress of SDGs and prepare reports. Other expert groups or sub-groups may be created to address data and other challenges at the country level as well as regional level in tracking the SDG progress. It may also establish a peer review mechanism in the context of the 2030 Agenda by learning lessons from the African Union's African Peer Review

Mechanism (African Peer Review Mechanism, 2016). Besides, independent assessments, review reports, etc., could be prepared by the think tanks, Civil Society Organisations (CSOs), business bodies and the private sectors to feed into the SDG implementation and monitoring status prior to each SAARC Summit (Bhattacharya and Rezbana, 2016).

Towards the Upcoming SAARC Summit

Discussions and decisions on greater regional cooperation and integration to implement as well as review and follow up on the SDGs in South Asia need to be identified as priorities in the agenda for the upcoming 19th SAARC Summit that will be held in Islamabad, Pakistan during 8-10 November 2016. SAARC should consider the following in this regard:

- Effectively countering extremism and terrorism in South Asia by partnering economic connectivity with transparent, accountable and inclusive government was emphasised at the 18th SAARC summit, the theme of which was deeper integration for peace and prosperity. Ensuring good governance and adopting environmentally sustainable growth policies for the region were also highlighted (Biswal, 2014). As promised at the 18th Summit, a follow-up and update on the inter-governmental process to contextualise the SDGs at the regional level are expected at the upcoming summit.

- To deal with the SDG issues, SAARC could establish a Group of Eminent Persons (GEP). It may be mentioned here that SAARC once established a GEP at its ninth summit in 1997 to enhance the inter-governmental effectiveness. This group could set common regional indicators alongside the global indicators, agree on definitions and identify relevant country-specific data sources. Supportive research initiatives may be considered, including peer learning and the sharing of best practices. The group could develop a regional data tracking system along with a detailed plan for a regional follow-up and review mechanism. It could also prepare a detailed action plan framework for the SDGs and may consider publishing an annual detailed progress report to clarify the facts of development progress in the region.

- It could create a regional trust fund for data and statistics to help track progress on the SDGs.

- It could devise sectoral funding mechanisms for regional priorities such as infrastructure, poverty alleviation and climate change.

- It could consider raising the efficacy of SAARC technical committees in different areas such as agriculture, communications, education, environment, health, population and child welfare, drug trafficking and drug abuse, rural development, technology, women in development and transport. The same consideration could be given to commissions, such as the Independent South Asian Commission on Poverty Alleviation, and various projects. Technical committees and commissions should consider work programmes from the perspective of the SDGs.

- Priority should be given to operationalising the SAARC Food Bank and SAARC Seed Bank. Notably, the regional exchange of seeds through the Seed Bank could improve food security and facilitate climate change adaptation in South Asia.

- Regarding SDG 16, SAARC should consider sharing best practices on governance, peace and security in South Asia. It needs to invest in regional institutions for the purpose of skill-building, training and sharing intelligence on capital movements to address money laundering. Addressing human and drug trafficking through research and action in the region is also important. Establishing links with regional research institutions, facilitating peer learning and information exchange, and funding research and development on SDG issues would benefit all South Asian countries.

- Regarding regional economic integration, South Asia has been slow compared to other sub-regions. The full potential of sub-regional cooperation arrangements, such as Economic Revisiting and expediting existing regional and sub-regional cooperation arrangements from the perspective of the SDGs should be considered.

- A number of regional strategies for implementing the SDGs need to be devised. They should cover a renewed approach to poverty eradication, boosting productive capacity, bridging gaps with political goodwill, regional commitments and good leadership, reducing adverse impacts of climate change and ensuring climate-induced migrants' resettlement and rehabilitation, strengthening regional interconnectivity and tracking contributions from all SDG stakeholders.

References

African Peer Review Mechanism. 2016. *African Peer Review Mechanism: Historical Background.* http://aprm-au.org/ about-us (accessed 17 August 2016).

Beisheim, M. (2016). Follow-up and Review: Developing the Institutional Framework for Implementing and Reviewing the Sustainable Development Goals and Partnerships. *SWP Working Paper FG 8, 2016/02.* German Institute for International and Security Affairs (SWP), Berlin.

Bhattacharya, D. (2015a). Regional Integration and the Post-2015 Framework: A South Asian Perspective. *South Asia Economic Journal, 16,* 119S-141S.

Bhattacharya, D. (2015b). Regional Monitoring and Review Mechanism for Effective Implementation of Post-2015 Agenda. An Expert Paper to Facilitate Discussion, *UN ESCAP, Asia-Pacific Forum on Sustainable Development 2015,* Bangkok, 20 May 2015. Retrieved from: http://www.unescap.org/sites/default/files/regional-effective-monitor-paper.pdf (accessed on 22 June 2016).

Bhattacharya, D. and Rezbana, U.S. (2016). *South Asian approach to Sustainable Development Goals.* Trade Insight, (01). Retrieved from http://www.sawtee.org/publications/Trade-Insight34.pdf. Accessed on 17 August 2016

Biswal, N. D. (2014). Statement by the United States of America at the 18th SAARC Summit. Retrieved from http://www.state.gov/p/sca/rls/rmks/2014/234448.htm (accessed on 22 June 2016).

Denney, L. (2012). *Security: The missing bottom of the Millennium Development Goals? Prospects for inclusion in the post-MDG development framework.* Overseas Development Institute (ODI), London.

FDSD. (2016). *UN Sustainable Development Goal (SDG) 16 – Importance of Participatory Institutions and Policymaking.* Foundation for Democracy and Sustainable Developmetn (FDSD), London. Retrieved from: http://www.fdsd.org/ideas/sustainable-development-goal-sdg-16-democratic-institutions (accessed on 1 June 2016).

Fiedler, C., Furness, M., Grävingholt, J. and Leininger, J. (2015). Goal 16: Promote peaceful and inclusive societies for sustainable development, provide access to justice for all and build effective, accountable and inclusive institutions at all levels in M. Loewe and N. Rippin (Eds.), *Translating an Ambitious Vision into Global Transformation: The 2030 Agenda for Sustainable Development* (pp. 95-100). Discussion Paper 7/2015. German Development Institute (DIE), Bonn. Retrieved from: https://www.die-gdi.de/uploads/media/DP_7.2015_NEU2_01.pdf (accessed on 29 May 2016).

Gupta, P. (2015). Generating Larger Tax Revenue in South Asia. *MPRA Paper No. 61443.* Munich Personal RePEc Archive (MPRA). Retrieved from https://mpra.ub.uni-muenchen.de/61443/1/MPRA_paper_61443.pdf (accessed on 18 August 2016).

Heyzer, N. (2008). The MDGs in Asia and the Pacific: Regional Partnerships are Key to Addressing Gaps in Implementation. *UN Chronicle, 45*(1). Retrieved from: http://unchronicle.un.org/article/mdgs-asia-and-pacific-regional-partnerships-are-key-addressing-gaps-implementation (accessed on 22 February 2016).

IFAD. (2009). Climate Change Impacts: South Asia. International Fund for Agricultural Development (IFAD). Retrieved from: https://www.ifad.org/documents/10180/55aca6fe-7127-4c48-b63d-13cfd7766527 (accessed on 1 June 2016).

IISD. (2016). *UN Statistical Commission Agrees on SDG Indicator Framework as Practical Starting Point.* International Institute for Sustainable Development (IISD). Retrieved from: · http://sd.iisd.org/news/un-statistical-commission-agrees-on-sdg-indicator-framework-as-practical-starting-point (accessed on 22 June 2016).

Insulza, J. M. (2010). *Intervention by OAS Secretary General Jose Miguel Insulza at the United Nations High-Level Plenary Meeting on the Millennium Development Goals.* Draft. Organization of American States (OAS), Washington, D.C. Retrieved from: http://www.un.org/en/mdg/summit2010/debate/OAS_en.pdf (accessed on 22 June 2016).

ILO. (2014). *Global Employment Trends 2014: Risk of a Jobless Recovery?* International Labour Organization (ILO).

Janus, H., Keijzer, N. and Weinlich, S. (2015). Follow-up and Review: The Accountability Framework for the 2030 Agenda in M. Loewe and N. Rippin (Eds.), *Translating an Ambitious Vision into Global Transformation: The 2030 Agenda for Sustainable Development* (pp. 11-14). Discussion Paper 7/2015. Bonn: German Development Institute (DIE). Retrieved from: https://www.die-gdi.de/uploads/media/DP_7.2015_NEU2_01.pdf (accessed on 29 May 2016).

Khan, N., Justice, K., Torres-Vasquez, O. and Keller, N. (2012). *Organization of American States: Background guide 2012.* National Collegiate Conference Association, New York. Retrieved from: http://www.nmun.org/ny_archives/ny12_downloads/igos/OAS.pdf (accessed on 22 June 2016).

Khan, T. I. (2013). *Regional Co-operation for Food security in South Asia.* Presentation made at the Sixteenth Sustainable Development Conference of the Sustainable Development Policy Institute (SDPI), Islamabad.

Khatun, F. (2015). *Reflections on COP21: Bangladesh Perspective.* Presentation, Dhaka. Retrieved from http://cpd.org.bd/wp-content/uploads/2015/12/Reflections-on-COP21-Bangladesh-Perspective.pdf (accessed on 17 August 2016).

Kumar, C. (2014). Climate Change in South Asia: A Framework of Sustainable Development and Human Security. *Journal of Environment Pollution and Human Health, 2*(5), 100-109.

Lawson-Remer, T. (2015). *How can we implement Sustainable Development Goal 16 on institutions?* Retrieved from: http://www.brookings.edu/blogs/future-development/posts/2015/10/01-global-goals-institutions-lawson-remer (accessed on 1 June 2016).

Maplecroft. (2014). *Climate Change and Environmental Risk Atlas 2015.* Bath: Maplecroft.

Müller, J. (ed.) (2006). *Reforming the United Nations: The Struggle for Legitimacy and Effectiveness.* Leiden: Martinus Nijhoff.

NEPAD (2011). Ten years on - NEPAD's track record shows successes. *Diplomat Africa,* 86-89. Retrieved from: http://www.nepad.org/resource/ten-years-nepad%E2%80%99s-track-record-shows-successes (accessed on 23 February 2016).

NTI (2011). *South Asian Association for Regional Cooperation (SAARC).* The Nuclear Threat Initiative (NTI, Washington D.C. Retrieved from: http://www.nti.org/learn/treaties-and-regimes/south-asian-association-regional-cooperation-saarc (accessed on 1 June 2016).

OAS. (2016a). *What is IABIN?* Organisation of American States (OAS). Retrieved from: http://www.oas.org/en/sedi/dsd/iabin (accessed on 23 February 2016).

OAS. (2016b). *Who we are.* Organisation of American States (OAS). Retrieved from: http://www.oas.org/en/about/who_we_are.asp (accessed on 23 February 2016).

OECD. (2015). *States of Fragility 2015: Meeting post-2015 ambitions.* Revised edition, June. Organisation for Economic Co-operation and Development (OECD), Paris. Retrieved from: http://dx.doi.org/10.1787/9789264227699-en (accessed 1 June 2016).

P. Collier and D. Rohner. (2008). Democracy, Development and Conflict. *Journal of the European Economic Association,* Vol. 6, No. 2-3, 2008. Cited in Grono, N. 2010. Fragile States and Conflict. Retrieved from: http://www.crisisgroup.org/en/publication-type/speeches/2010/fragile-states-and-conflict.aspx. (accessed on 11 July 2016).

Pant, K. (2014). *Making the SAARC Food Bank Work.* Presentation made at Seminar on Regional cooperation on trade, climate change and food security in South Asia: Some reflections and way forward organised by South Asia Watch on Trade, Economics and Environment (SAWTEE), Oxfam and Swedish Standards Institute (SIS), in Lalitpur, Nepal on 13-14 March.. Retrieved from http://www.sawtee.org/presentations/p7_13%20March%202014.pdf (accessed on 17 August 2016).

Parnini, S. N. (2015). *Poverty and Governance in South Asia.* Abingdon and New York: Routledge.

Planning Commission of Bangladesh. (2015). *Millennium Development Goals: Bangladesh Progress Report 2015.* Dhaka: General Economics Division (GED), Planning Commission, Government of Bangladesh (GoB). Retrieved from: http://www.bd.undp.org/content/bangladesh/en/home/library/mdg/mdg-progress-report-2015.html (accessed 11 May 2016).

Rahman, A. (2004). SAARC: Not yet a community in J. Rolfe (ed.), *The Asia-Pacific: A Region in Transition* (pp. 133-148). Honolulu: Asia-Pacific Center for Security Studies (APCSS). Retrieved from: http://apcss.org/Publications/Edited%20Volumes/RegionalFinal%20 chapters/Chapter9Rahman.pdf (accessed on 1 June 2016).

RIAL (2016). *What is RIAL?* Inter-American Network for Labor Administration (RIAL), Organisation of American States, Washington, D.C. Retrieved from: http://www.rialnetportal. org/index.php?option=com_content&view=article&id=26&Itemid=24&lang=en(accessed on 23 February 2016).

Saferworld. (2016). *Peace and the 2030 Agenda.* Retrieved from: http://www.saferworld.org.uk/ what/post-2015 (accessed on 22 June 2016).

SAARC. (2005). *Dhaka Declaration.* South Asian Association for Regional Cooperation (SAARC), Kathmandu. Retrieved from: http://w HYPERLINK "http://www.saarc-sec.org/SAARC-Summit/7"ww.saarc-sec.org/SAARC-Summit/7 (accessed on 22 June 2016).

SAARC. (2007). *Declaration of the Fourteenth SAARC Summit.* South Asian Association for Regional Cooperation (SAARC), Kathmandu. Retrieved from: http://www.saarc-sec.org/ SAARC-Summit/7 (accessed on 22 June 2016).

SAARC. (2014). *Kathmandu declaration.* South Asian Association for Regional Cooperation (SAARC), Kathmandu. Retrieved from: http://www.saarc-sec.org/SAARC-Summit/7 (accessed on 22 June 2016).

Sanga, D. (2011). The Challenges of Monitoring and Reporting on the Millennium Development Goals in Africa by 2015 and Beyond. *African Statistical Journal,* 12, 104-118.

SDMC (2014). Post-2015 DRR Framework For SAARC Region (HFA2) SDMC. SAARC Disaster Management Centre (SDMC), New Delhi. Retrieved from: http://www.recoveryplatform.org/ assets/HFA2/Post-2015%20Drr%20Framework%20SAARC.pdf (accessed on 17 August 2016).

Singh, A. K. and Singh, R. G. (2009). *SAARC Development Goals: Commitments and Achievements.* South Asian Network for Social and Agricultural Development (SANSAD), New Delhi. Retrieved from: http://sansad.org.in/SAARC_Development_Goals_Report.pdf (accessed on 1 June 2016).

UN. (2015a). *The Millennium Development Goals Report 2015.* United Nations (UN), New York. Retrieved from http://www.un.org/millenniumgoals/2015_MDG_Report/pdf/MDG%20 2015%20rev%20(July%201).pdf (accessed on 22 February 2016).

UN. (2015b). *Transforming our World: The 2030 Agenda for Sustainable Development.* A/ RES/70/1. United Nations (UN), New York. Retrieved from: https://sustainabledevelopment. un.org/post2015/transformingourworld (accessed on 23 February 2016).

UN. (2016a). *Report of the Inter-Agency and Expert Group on Sustainable Development Goal Indicators.* E/CN.3/2016/2/Rev.1. United Nations (UN), New York. Retrieved from: http:// unstats.un.org/unsd/statcom/47th-session/documents/2016-2-IAEG-SDGs-Rev1-E.pdf (accessed on 1 June 2016).

UN. (2016b). *The Sustainable Development Agenda.* Retrieved from: http://www.un.org/ sustainabledevelopment/development-agenda (accessed on 1 June 2016).

UN. (2016c). *UN Statistical Commission agrees on Global Indicator Framework.* Retrieved from: http://www.un.org/sustainabledevelopment/blog/2016/03/un-statistical-commission-endorses-global-indicator-framework (accessed on 1 June 2016).

UNDP. (2015). *Human Development Report 2015: Work for Human Development.* United Nations Development Programme (UNDP), New York. Retrieved from: http://hdr.undp.org/sites/ default/files/2015_human_development_report.pdf (accessed on 22 June 2016).

UNESCAP. (2012). *Regional Cooperation for Inclusive and Sustainable Development: South and South-West Asia Development Report 2012–13.* New Delhi: Routledge.

UNESCAP. (2015a). *Achieving the Sustainable Development Goals in South Asia: Key Policy Priorities and Implementation Challenges.* United Nations Economic and Social Commission for Asia and the Pacific (UN ESCAP), Bangkok. Retrieved from: http://www.unescap.org/ sites/default/files/SDGs%20South%20Asia%20report%202016%20rev%2014%20April%20 2016.pdf (accessed on 1 June 2016).

UNESCAP. (2015b). *Ahead of 19th SAARC Summit, regional seminar explores ways to unlock potential of regional economic integration in South Asia*. Retrieved from: http://www.unescap. org/announcement/ahead-19th-saarc-summit-regional-seminar-explores-ways-unlock-potential-regional (accessed on 1 June 2016).

UNESCAP. (2015c). *South and South-West Asia Development Report 2015-16: Regional Cooperation for Inclusive and Sustainable Development: Executive Summary*. United Nations Economic and Social Commission for Asia and the Pacific (UN ESCAP), Bangkok. Retrieved from: http://www.unescap.org/sites/default/files/Cover_Exec%20Summary_final%20 draft%20for%20upload_20160111.pdf (accessed on 10 May 2016).

UNESCAP. (2015d). *India and the MDGS: Towards a Sustainable Future for All*. United Nations Country Team—India, New Delhi. Retrieved from http://www.unescap.org/resources/india-and-mdgs-towards-sustainable-future-all (accessed on 18 August 2016).

UNESCAP, ADB and UNDP(2015). *Making It Happen: Technology, Finance and Statistics for Sustainable Development in Asia and the Pacific*. Asia-Pacific Regional MDGs Report 2014/2015. United Nations Economic and Social Commission for Asia and the Pacific (UN ESCAP), Asian Development Bank (ADB) and United Nations Development Programme (UNDP), Bangkok. Retrieved from: https://www.adb.org/sites/default/files/publication/159951/asia-pacific-regional-mdg-report-2014-15.pdf (accessed on 11 May 2016).

UNODC. (2013). *Regional Programme for South Asia: Promoting the Rule of Law and Countering Drugs and Crime in South Asia*. United Nations Office on Drugs and Crime (UNODC), Regional Office for South Asia, New Delhi. Retrieved from http://www.unodc.org/documents/southasia//webstories/RP_South_Asia_FINAL.pdf (accessed on 17 August 2016).

Usman, M. (2015). *Multifaceted issues: Govt admits failure to achieve MDGs. The Express Tribune*, 25 December. Retrieved from http://tribune.com.pk/story/1016104/multifaceted-issues-govt-admits-failure-to-achieve-mdgs/ (accessed on 18 August 2016).

Von Grebmer, K., Bernstein, J., de Waal, A., Prasai, N., Yin, S. and Yohannes, Y. (2015). *2015 Global Hunger Index: Armed Conflict and the Challenge of Hunger*. Bonn, Germany; Washington, D.C. and Dublin, Ireland: Welthungerhilfe; International Food Policy Research Institute (IFPRI) and Concern Worldwide. Retrieved from: https://www.ifpri.org/publication/2015-global-hunger-index-armed-conflict-and-challenge-hunger (accessed on 22 June 2016).

Wagner, C. (2014). Security Cooperation in South Asia: Overview, Reasons, Prospects. *SWP Research Paper 6*. German Institute for International and Security Affairs (SWP), Berlin.

World Bank. (2011). *World Development Report 2011: Conflict, Security, and Development*. The World Bank, Washington, D.C. Retrieved from: http://siteresources.worldbank.org/INTWDRS/Resources/WDR2011_Full_Text.pdf (accessed on 22 June 2016).

World Bank. (2015a). *South Asia Economic Focus, spring 2015: Making the Most of Cheap Oil*. The World Bank, Washington, D.C. Retrieved from: https://openknowledge.worldbank.org/handle/10986/21735 (accessed on 22 June 2016).

World Bank. (2015b). *South Asia Grows Strongly but Fiscal, Financial Weaknesses Remain*. The World Bank, Washington, D.C. Retrieved from: http://www.worldbank.org/en/news/press-release/2015/10/04/south-asia-grows-strongly-fiscal-financial-weakness-remain (accessed on 23 February 2016).

World Bank. (2015c). *Worldwide Governance Indicators*. Retrieved from: http://info.worldbank. org/governance/wgi/index.aspx#home (accessed on 1 June 2016).

World Bank. (2016). World DataBank: World Development Indicators. Retrieved from: http://databank.worldbank.org/data/reports.aspx?source=world-development-indicators (accessed on 1 June 2016).

《O》.